C. R. KING

A FRATERNITY OF GUNSLINGERS:
TRUE STORIES OF WILD WEST GUNMEN, VOL. 2

...and eight lady gunslingers

Fraternity Gunslingers: True Stories of Wild West Gunmen, Vol 2

This historical book is published by C. R. King, self-publisher, e-book, Los Angeles, California. Paperback copies are available upon special order.

The right of C. R. King to be identified as the author of this work has been asserted in accordance with the Copyright, Patents and Designs Act of 1988. First draft copyrighted March 8, 2013.

Copies of this book in part or complete and introduced into a retrieval system, or transmitted, in any form, or by any means or any format (electronic, mechanical, photocopying, recording, or otherwise), without the prior written permission of the publisher. Any person who does any unauthorized act in relation to this publication may be liable to criminal prosecution and civil claims for damages.

Book Cover: "Rose of Cimarron" (Rose Dunn) Public domain photograph circa 1890s with background picture, courtesy of Bing photographs, the ghost town of Bannack, Montana.

Copy edited: by J.Jeffers.

All photographs and illustrations are of public domain unless otherwise noted in the content of this digital book.

Copyright © **Charles R. King, 2014**
Los Angeles, California

Vol.2. A Fraternity of Gunslingers

Table of Content

Prologue

1. Moorman Pruiett aka Moman Pruiett

2. Michael "Mike" Meagher

3. Clay Allison

4. William D. "Bill" Fossett

5. Lady Outlaws and Women of The Law

    Rose Dunn

    Cattle Annie and Little Britches

    Pearl Hart

    Belle Star

    Mamie Fossett and Sara Burche. U.S Deputy Marshals

    Florence Miller

6. "Mysterious" Dave Allen Mather

7. Virgil Walter Earp

8. Patrick "Pat" Sughrue

9. The Montana "Vigilance Committee"

10. Henry Plummer

    John X Beidler

11. Johnny Bull

12. Life in a Mining Town

Epilogue

Suggested Readings

Prologue

*T*he western frontier was in full swing from the end of the Civil War, spilling over into the twentieth century. During this period, the ravages of the Civil War were still felt; the resentment between the North and the South was as heartfelt as ever. As this volume progresses, we see that the outlaws born after the war were just as vicious as their earlier counterparts who learned killing as soldiers. In the Twin Territories of Oklahoma, between 1872 and 1896, one hundred and three Deputy United States Marshals were killed in the line of duty. Most of these marshals worked out of Fort Smith, Arkansas, under "hanging judge" Isaac Parker. Between 1872 and 1907, fifty lawmen and town marshals died bringing law to the frontier.

Yesterday's famous gunslingers were not always well-known in their lifetimes, while many that were known are all but forgotten. This book and its predecessor, volume one of the same title, are my attempts to give the reader a mix of the famous, not-so-famous, and forgotten gunmen. It is full of facts and, hopefully, entertaining as well. I am including a chapter on eight lady gunslingers. The lady outlaws, five in total, include Rose of Cimarron, Cattle Annie, Little Britches, Pearl Hart, and Belle Star. There are three lady Deputy U.S. Marshals: Mamie Fossett, Sara Burche, and Florence Miller—true women pioneers in law enforcement. Their careers were short, so I placed them in the same chapter.

We travel from Oklahoma to Colorado, Texas to Kansas, Montana to Idaho, Nebraska to California, and Washington to Nevada. Our time span ranges from 1861 to 1909. In three chapters we overlap with the Montana Vigilance Committee and the hanging of twenty-three men in six weeks. Virgil Earp is in this book. We delve more into his presence of mind, how he thought, his psyche. If you understand one of the Earps, you pretty much understand all of them. The final chapter will give you insight into life in a mining camp. We focus on Austin and Virginia, soon to be named Virginia City, both rip-roaring silver- and gold-mining towns. We learn that not all the towns' citizens were criminals as we get into the types of jobs, pay scales, transportation costs, and living conditions in Nevada Territory of the early 1860s. Enjoy.

C. R. King, July 2015

Moorman Pruiett aka Moman Pruiett (1872-1945)

The *Daily Oklahoman* newspaper once proclaimed Moman (born Moorman) Pruiett "the greatest master of backwoods psychology, actor, hypocrite, fakir, lawyer, showman, and publicity expert the courts of Oklahoma ever will look upon." In his obituary, on December 31, 1945, *Time* magazine proclaimed that Moman was "a menace to the community." Moman's biographer Howard K. Berry's book entitled, *He Made it Safe to Murder: The Life of Moman Pruiett*, tell it all when it came to his professional life.

Some say that Moman was not a criminal even though he started out as such. He was born on the banks of the Ohio River when his parents were en route from Kentucky to Arkansas to start a new life. For so many Confederate soldiers, times were hard. Warren, Moorman's father, had been a prisoner of war, and during his absence, his first wife died. Remarried, a baby on the way, with no work insight for Warren and wanting a fresh start, Warren he moved his family moved to Arkansas seemed like a beacon of light, a place to start over.

Moorman was a rough kid. He relished fighting. He was not interested in school. At sixteen, he had received only ten months of formal education, yet he was bright, very bright. He was fond of hell-raising, in trouble nearly daily, and eager to be known as a tough kid. Moorman knew poverty. His family was never well-to-do. He worked and contributed his income to the family. Among odd jobs, he polished shoes. Sixteen was a milestone; Moorman found himself in prison; his crime, forgery. He was sentenced to two years of hard labor. His stepmother, Betty, started a campaign to have her son released. Six months into his incarceration she convinced the governor to pardon him. Upon his release, the family moved to Paris, Texas. There Moorman secured a position cleaning the offices of attorney Jake Hodges. He was allowed access to law books. Interested, the lad, now eighteen years old, studied the books in his spare time. Having not learned his lesson, Moorman was still managing to get himself into trouble. Once more Moorman Pruiett was arrested, this time for theft. Tried and found guilty, he received five years confinement. Angrily touting his innocence, he looked at the jury and vowed, "You'll all regret this. Ever' damn one of you will. You'll regret it....As sure as I live I'll make you sorry. I'll empty your damned jails, an' I'll turn the murderers and thieves a' loose in your midst. But I will do it in a legal way."

Betty came to Moorman's rescue and, as before, pleaded for her son's release. This time it took two years before she got the governor to pardon her son. It was too late for family members. Moorman's grandmother denounced him for disgracing the family name. To appease his grandmother, he changed his name to Moman, and he added the letter *e* to Pruitt, the original spelling of his last name.

For the next five years Moman studied law. He moved to Indian Territory, where he was officially licensed by U.S. District Judge David Bryant to practice in 1895. His license covered two territories commonly called the Twin Territories—Oklahoma and Indian, often abbreviated as O.T. and I.T. In the early part of the nineteenth century, the federal government moved the Cherokee, Choctaw, Chickasaw, Creek, and Seminole nations—the "Five Civilized Tribes," as they were called,—to what is now Oklahoma.

The term "civilized tribes" came from European settlers during the colonial and early federal periods because the tribes adopted many of the colonists' customs and had generally good relations with their neighbors. The tribes hailed from the southeastern part of the United States. The tribe culture was that of farmers; they grew crops of corn and beans. They were matriarchal societies in which women had central roles of political leadership and established normal (moral) behavior and control of property. Thus, the five tribes were considered to be "civilized."

Since 1890, the term "Twin Territories" refers to the Indian and Oklahoma Territories. Oklahoma was the territory "assigned" to the Indians; the Indian was the "unassigned" lands. The state's name derives from the Choctaw language. *Okla* and *humma* means "red people." On November 16, 1907, Oklahoma was granted statehood.

Early in 1896 Moman established his practice in Pauls Valley, I.T. He was twenty-three years old and about to make good his promise to that jury, "to free the murderers and thieves." His career would span fifty years. Once called the "Queen of the Washita," Pauls Valley was located in the middle of the Chickasaw Nation. Although a newspaper was established in 1887, the township of Pauls Valley was not laid out until 1892. Three years later a U.S. Courthouse was built. The railroad had a large influence on the establishment and naming of this town. Smith Paul, a white man, was the first to settle the area. He founded the town. He lived and married into the Chickasaw Nation. The railway—the Atchison, Topeka and Santa Fe—laid tracks in anticipation of the upcoming land rush of 1898. There was an agreement between the railroad and the people of the area to name the depot Smith Pauls Valley. The name was too large for a depot sign, so the railway reduced the name to Pauls Valley. The name stuck. It was not long before the town started to look like it was there to stay. Brick buildings replaced wood and tent structures. The town quickly grew; it thrived. Like all of the wild west boomtowns, there were problems. Mix drink with guns, saloons, brothels, and dance halls; add gambling to this concoction; and you have the results of nightly gunfire, shootings, thievery, prostitution, and more. Pauls Valley was an ideal place for Moman to put up his shingle, "Moman Pruiett—Lawyer." As a tiger cannot change its stripes, neither could Moman. He was determined to develop a reputation as a bad man. He started fistfights, whipping around a dozen so-called bad men. He gave himself the title "Bad Man of Pauls Valley," but the best was yet to come. Moman found a client— several clients, in fact. They were chicken thieves. Moman went crashing into the courtroom, hyped up. With a blast of his oratory and charm, his clients were freed. His first paycheck was not currency but food produce, with some live chickens thrown into the mix. The locals all heard how Moman handled himself in the courtroom. It was bantered about the town with positive consequences, for Moman earned the reputation of being a lawyer to be reckoned with. It was a short ride for Pruiett. He dropped the chicken thieves, moving straight on to hardened criminals. He specialized in criminal defense in two areas: murder and horse thievery. This is all he wanted and all he would take as a lawyer.

Moman's voice was deep— beautiful, some say— and powerful. He could modulate his voice, raise it to its highest pitch, then lower it, and mesmerize his audience: the judge and jury. Both the judge and jury were entertained; they loved to watch him in action. Moman knew he had a gift, a gift that he cultivated. He could speak equally well to both the uneducated backwoodsmen and the educated. He could make them laugh and cry. His antics, such as chewing tobacco as he spoke and expectorating to hit home a point were wildly successful. When not chewing tobacco, he would smoke cigars—the bigger and smellier, the better. These antics and his props all contributed to a "circus atmosphere" that he carefully crafted. But in the end it was his voice, intelligence, and impressive retentive memory that seduced the courts.

Pruiett's first murder case was that of Henry Gordon, a former slave with four sons who rustled for a living and killed with ease. Uncle Henry, as many called him, was found not guilty. Like the chicken thieves, he paid his lawyer with food: bags of apples, bushels of pecans, and whatever he came up with, including bales of cotton on a periodic basis. After this first successful case, Moman's fees went up. He accepted hard cash or deeds to homes, farms, and cattle. Moman Pruiett was doing well, very well. He had many tricks up his sleeve. It is said that he convinced the attractive sister of a client to seduce and engage a juror in sex. We presume that the juror voted not guilty, for the client was declared such.

One day he received a telegram from a man announcing that he had been charged with murder and had $5,000, cash money, for his defense. Moman, with immediacy, responded that he was on his way with three eyewitnesses! Nothing, when it came to winning a case, was sacred to Moman Pruiett. While defending a man for killing his wife's lover, Moman placed a blacksmith on the stand to testify that he had shod the killer's horse the day prior to the shooting and that, as an expert, he declared the horse had never before been shod. The marshal who captured the killer did so by following the killer's "well shod" horse tracks and knew full well that this horse had been shod many times. The evidence was there against the killer, but Moman had created enough doubt that the killer walked away free. Once again lawyer Moman proved his mastery.

Bulletin 89 from the Department of Commerce and Labor of the Bureau of the Census informs us that in 1907 the population of Oklahoma City was 32,452. Pauls Valley township's population was just under 2,000. Oklahoma City was one of several "stations" established during the Great Land Rush of 1898. The stations of Verbeck, Guthrie, Edmond, Oklahoma, Kingfisher, and Norman were created, with Norman being the oldest. All were built in the latter part of 1886, continuing into 1887. The railroad laid tracks connecting these stations. Oklahoma Station's name soon became Oklahoma City, while Verbeck became Moore. The term "station" was dropped by all. The area was considered "unassigned land." This term, "unassigned land," meant that no Indian tribe was assigned land in this area. It was territory that was owned outright by the United States government; thus, when the Homestead Act of 1862 became law, anyone twenty-one years of age who had never fought against this country could claim up to 160 acres of land. All one had to do was obey the rules of the land rush. One competed in the rush by lining up in a designated, marked area (a long line controlled by the U.S. Cavalry); when the signal was sounded, one rode hard—as hard as one could—to be the first one to make the claim on the section of land one found desirable. Plant one's claim stake and head back to the station to file the claim. Another rule was that one had to live on the land for five years, improve it, and then file for the deed. Once done, that person would become the proud owner of 160 acres. But problems arose. There were "Sooners," people who cheated; they sneaked out to make a claim on the better land, waited for the appropriate time to avoid being caught, and headed back to the station to file the claim for the fee of eighteen dollars. Most Sooners were caught and placed in stockades until after the land rush was completed. A good many tried to declare plots in designated township lots. Some were challenged a few years later, and the land confiscated. There were shootings as well. Another nickname for the people who participated in the land rush was the "Boomers." The Boomers were those who followed the rules, participated, and filed their claims accordingly.

Moman had business in Oklahoma City. It was his first trip. He completed his business and took a good look around. He liked it. It was a large town with brick walkways, with lots of night and day action. Crime was rampant. There were all kinds of people making up the population, from the very good to the very bad, from whites and blacks to Indians. There was an area called Hell's Half Acre. This area was made up primarily of saloons, dance halls, gambling joints, whorehouses, and the city police station and jail. North of Hell's Half Acre was Bunco Alley, bordered by Battle Row, Front Street, and Main Street. The area was more of the same. Bunco Alley would be Moman's playground and his main source of income. He saw dollar signs everywhere. He left Pauls Valley for Oklahoma City and established his law office above a saloon. He traded his string tie, old western hat, and boots for stylish button-down shoes, a proper in-vogue tie, a hat, and nice business suits. Oklahoma City was full of hard-drinking, fist-driving men, his type of customers were every where. Moman fitted in with ease. This town, this city, was in need of his skills, and the criminal element was in abundance. Since the turn of the century, a syndicate controlled all the biggest and most lucrative gambling concerns. The "Big Four," as they were called, consisted of Jake Barnes, Clint Stout, Cecil Proctor, and William Monnahan. They had their fingers in both city politics and law enforcement.

Oklahoma was in a quandary; it had been from its conception. The good people wanted a dry state to rid Oklahoma Territory of all alcohol and, hopefully, vice. Prohibition is what they wanted, but that would not be until January 2, 1919, when the Eighteenth Amendment came to Oklahoma; quickly ratified, the manufacturing of liquor was outlawed in the entire United States. Before Prohibition, the Oklahoma City police looked away. By then Moman was the most famous criminal defense attorney in the west.

Moman was nearing the end of a big murder case. He was defending James Stevenson for the murder of Deputy Marshal R. W. Cathey when Jim Miller and his business associate Berry Burrell approached Pruiett. Miller was a professional assassin working out of Fort Worth, Texas, who openly advertised his profession. He had been hired to kill Gus Bobbitt, a Deputy United States Marshal turned farmer who had created enemies while enforcing the law. Leaving law enforcement, Gus married and settled near the township of Ada, Oklahoma. He was very well liked by the townsfolk. Jesse West, rancher, and Joe Allen, farmer, were business partners with a grudge against Bobbitt for having accused them of cattle rustling. They wanted the man dead. It took them nearly ten years, but finally they sought out Miller in Fort Worth and paid him well to do the deed. Burrell was Miller's right-hand man. His job was to trail the victim, learn his habits, and then report the victim to trail to Miller. Together they would explore the area and plot the best place to ambush. For Gus Bobbitt it would be at the gateway to his ranch as he was bringing home a wagonload of supplies. Miller's weapon of choice was always an 8-gauge shotgun. (This gauge is currently illegal and has been for over fifty years). For the first time ever in Miller's career there were hard evidence and eyewitnesses that led the town of Ada to the doorsteps of Allen and Burrell. Based on various newspaper articles from the *Ada Weekly, Fort Worth Record,* and the *Resister,* wire cutters were found that had been used to cut wire fences at the site of the killing and led back to Burrell, who purchased them in town. A distinctively marked horse that Miller had borrowed from his nephew had been seen by Bobbitt's foreman, who was a distance behind his employer the day of the shooting, in a wagon filled with supplies. Allen left behind an oilcloth that was used to wrap his shotgun. The oilcloth was identified by two citizens who had seen Miller's shotgun and cloth as he left the hotel with them in hand. This evidence led directly to the killers of Gus Bobbitt. There was no doubt the assassins were Miller and his helper, Berry Burrell. Miller's nephew was questioned, and he confessed that his uncle had borrowed the farm horse the day of the shooting. His nephew had no knowledge of the assassination nor his intent. Another man who supplied Burrell and Allen with some information about Bobbitt's habits was also arrested and questioned. With all this information, warrants were issued. Burrell was the first to be arrested in Fort Worth. He took the arrest with ease and laughed it off. Miller was hiding out. He sent word that he would give himself up if he could post bond. Captain Tom Ross of the Texas Rangers refused the request. It did not take the lawmen long to find Miller's hideout. He was arrested and brought back to Fort Worth. Burrell was already in Ada, awaiting trial. There were two or three Oklahoma lawmen in the posse. After Miller was jailed, these men transported Miller by train to Ada. West and Allen were sent a telegram they believed to be from Jim Miller, asking them to meet him and Burrell in Ada to provide bail and necessary funds for their defense. On their way to

Ada, West and Allen stopped off at Oklahoma City and hired Pruiett to represent them. Pruiett gladly accepted. He advised the men to go on ahead. He would follow within a day, two at the most; the James Stevenson verdict was due in. As the men left Moman's office, heading for the depot, they were arrested by police officers. Soon they were in the city jail in Ada.

The case Moman was working headed as he said it would. The killer of Deputy U.S. Marshal R. W. Cathey, James Stevenson, was found not guilty. Pruiett wrapped things up as quickly as he could, then headed out by train to Ada. The Stevenson case was big news. It hit the papers throughout the state. The town of Ada read the news. They were upset. They knew of Moman's reputation and feared that the killers of their friend would be freed as well. Who, what, or how it came about, no one knows, for no one ever told. A decision was made. With Pruiett as their lawyer, this professional assassin and his cohorts getting off was a given. Around 3:00 a.m. on April 19, 1909, a large gathering of men stormed the jail. It is believed thirty to forty men were involved. The mob took the four men to a barn located nearby behind the jail. One by one they lynched the four. They remained hanging until seven that morning. In this case Moman Pruiett's reputation for getting killers off scot-free backfired. The men were dead before Pruiett arrived.

*****

Among the 1914 graduating class of the University of Oklahoma College of Law was Orban Chester Patterson. Moman Pruiett took this young man on as his junior partner. Patterson was to handle all the misdemeanor police-court cases while Pruiett handled the most lucrative felonies. Moman had an ability to create headlines. He loved his name in the papers; the bigger the trial, the better he liked it. Bootlegging, corrupt politicians, and vice in general were rampant. Patterson soon learned that bonding out minor criminals was lucrative. A hard worker, Patterson was soon known as the "attorney's bondsman" of the underworld.

Three years into his partnership with Pruiett, Patterson needed the services of his partner. There was an ongoing feud between Orban's father and Samuel L. Williams, a banker and farmer from the town of Purcell. Old man Patterson was shot down and killed on the streets of Oklahoma City by the son of S. L. Williams. Williams had been involved in a number of lawsuits, one of which may have triggered the bad feelings and eventual shooting. Regardless, the feud escalated, and a man was murdered. Old man Patterson was dead, and Williams was acquitted. Within a year, Orban's sister, despondent over her father's death, committed suicide. Orban ran into S. L. Williams numerous times when Williams came to Oklahoma City on business. Each time they ran into one another there was a confrontation. The confrontations kept getting uglier. Finally Williams threatened to kill Orban on sight the next time they met. They crossed paths on September 17, 1917. Williams reached in his back pocket while Patterson pulled his revolver from his waistband. Five shots rang out, four hitting their mark—S.L. Williams. Orban was arrested for murder; to his rescue came Moman, who made short order of the charges. Orban was acquitted on the grounds of self-defense.

Patterson started a new billing concept. He would openly charge his customers what he happily called "protection money." Today, it's called a retainer," a monthly fee for a lawyer's services. In short order he became known to the Oklahoma underworld as their "fixer." *Oklahoma Justice,* the book written by Ron Owens, describes Patterson's life further in detail.

With all of his political connections his influence was so great that he could end the career of Police Commanders and City Managers....His second office was located at the police station....and for the next two decades he would hold undisputed claim to the title of "King of the Underworld."

Orban lived until 1944, dying at the age of fifty-two from complications while in surgery.

*****

In 1906 Moman was invited to be a member of the Democratic State Committee and to take part in the State Constitution Convention. At his usual best, he drew a lot of attention to himself during the convention. He befriended Charles Haskell and Lee Cruce, who were political heavyweights in the Twin Territories. It was figured that Lee Cruce would become the first governor of Oklahoma. Moman was highly regarded as an important voice during the convention, so much so that a county was named after him— Moman County. He was on fire with his loud, captivating voice and his charm. He wholeheartedly threw his weight behind Cruce, and Cruce would be forever grateful. It was a great plan to further Moman's political ambitions. Charles Haskell, a master politician, was heavily backed by the religious community, the Women's Temperance Union, and the Anti-Saloon League; thus, he was a man "with whom to be reckoned." As the convention progressed and backroom deals were sealed, Charles Haskell made his move. At odds with his choice, Moman decided to remain in the Cruce camp. Drawing attention to oneself can backfire, but Moman, the lawyer, had always won. He worked on his new friend, Mr. Haskell, to draw him into the Cruce political circle. Haskell resented Moman's efforts to do so; the result was the loss of their friendship. In short order, the two became bitter enemies. Before the convention had ended, Haskell and his followers challenged and successfully changed the proposed Moman County to Creek County, as it is today. Years rolled into decades as Pruiett tried to get Creek County changed back to Moman County, but failed. Charles Haskell became the first elected governor of

Oklahoma. On November 16, 1907, Oklahoma officially became the forty-sixth state. Moman ran for state office in various counties, the Haskell machine blocking his every move. Pruiett had fallen out of political favor. His political ambition was never to be, so he went back to doing what he did best—being a criminal lawyer.

In 1908 Big Anne, a well-known madam, the owner of Big Anne's Place 444, was on trial for murder. One of her former prostitutes testified against her. She testified that Anne had conspired to murder and rob a "customer." It cost Big Anne $75,000 to escape the hangman; like a champ, Pruiett won an acquittal. In today's money Big Anne had paid Pruiett $1.88 million. Anne Wynn, after having been a fixture in the city for eighteen years, had enough. No longer welcomed or trusted, she closed up shop and moved to Los Angeles.

On April 30, 1918, Moman and William Maben of Shawnee, a former judge of the tenth judicial district, were arrested and charged with "lugging liquor." They were aboard a train headed to Oklahoma from Texas. Upon entering Oklahoma, federal revenue agents stopped the train and boarded it. They searched the handbags of all passengers and found six quarts of liquor in Maben's luggage and twelve quarts in Pruiett's; the two men and thirteen others were arrested. A trial was held in federal court. Moman did something unusual. Defending himself, he stood up to enter his plea—guilty as charged. Pruiett accepted responsibility and full ownership of the whiskey, including the whiskey found in Judge Maben's handbags. With a big grin, Maben was dismissed. Pruiett received a stiff fine and a rebuke from the federal judge. He paid the fine and walked out of court, free and defiant.

In 1935 the Oklahoma Bar rendered Pruiett a one-year suspension for attempting to blackmail a businessman. The man was having an affair. Moman wanted a good sum of money to keep quiet, or he would expose the affair. This blackmail attempt backfired. Not allowed to earn his keep, a chronic alcoholic with an out-of-control gambling habit, Moman was broke and desperate. He was reinstated in 1936 but was hard up for cases. His mind was not as sharp as it once had been.

Books on Trial: Red Scare in the Heartland by Shirley and Wayne Wiegand describes Moman's attempt to defend the owners of the Progressive Book Store in 1940 for selling political literature. This was in violation of Oklahoma's criminal syndicalism laws. (Syndicalism is defined as an economic system that would replace capitalism and be an alternative to state socialism). Moman took the case. The prosecutors objected to his involvement. Pruiett had not paid his bar association dues; therefore, he was no longer a member, could not represent himself as an attorney, and thus could not have clients. The newspapers crucified Pruiett over the case. Pruiett, for the first time in his life, was relieved from a case. He managed to pay his association dues and thus was able to work a few more cases. His last case, a criminal one, was in 1942; he defended a murderer. The win or lose of this case does not matter, his record, as noted below, speaks volumes.

Pruiett's violent side included the following, as reported by the Oklahoma Historical Society: "In 1899 he pistol-whipped attorney Leonidos C. Andrews, in 1902 he shot drifter Charley Wiseman, in 1903 he shot Dr. Waller Threldkeld, in 1909 Fred Carwell, counselor for Haskell, charged him with assault, in 1921 he shot and killed bootlegger Joe Patterson, and in 1922 Frank Eckerly accused him of assault with a gun."

In the end, in 1945, Moman was residing in a "flophouse" on Northwest Second Street in downtown Oklahoma City, above a cleaning shop. The flophouse was referred to as the "Bat Cave." The rent was fifty cents a night. He was sixty-eight years old, destitute and desperate. The alcohol had eaten away his mind, and his constitution as prone to illness. On December 12, 1945, Moman died of pneumonia.

In his fifty-year career as a criminal-defense lawyer, Moman defended 343 persons accused of murder. Of these, he obtained 303 acquittals. No man accused of murder that Moman Pruiett had defended was ever executed. There are those legal scholars who consider Moman Pruiett the "lawyer of the century." He may very well have defended more murderers and thieves successfully than any other lawyer in history. Very few can argue against his quick wit, his masterful oratory, his flamboyancy, or his courtroom charm. Legal scholars and those of his time say that he was an abuser of the law and a man who had no respect for it, yet they cannot argue his success.

Michael "Mike" Meagher (1843-1881) John Meagher (1845-1930)

This chapter is dedicated mainly to Michael Meagher, but to speak of Mike, one has to mention John. For so many years they were attached, working side by side.

Mike and his brother, John, were born in County Cavar, Ireland. Like so many Irishmen during the Great Potato Famine of 1845 to 1852, their father, Timothy, moved his family to the United States when the brothers were five and three. Nearly all historians state that the brothers were twins, but the 1880 census states otherwise. Mike was thirty-seven years old; John, thirty-five. A close look at the photograph above shows that the brothers, although very much alike, were not identical twins but fraternal. Could the historians be correct and the censes be incorrect? Yes. The importance of the men being fraternal or not lies in historical correctness. This author is trying to lay out the facts, not half truths or legends.

The family settled in Illinois. The Civil War broke out, and the boys joined up. John and Michael fought for the Union as sailors. Stationed out of Cairo, Illinois, they helped man a gunboat on the Mississippi River as part of a blockade that prevented supplies from reaching the southern ports while preventing the Confederates most important crop, cotton, from being shipped out to places as far away as England. The negative impact on commerce helped facilitate the fall of the Confederate States of America. The cities and townships of Mississippi—including Corinth, Greenville, Jackson, Natchez, and Vicksburg, the Confederate capital—were the most important to protect. Vicksburg was bombarded by naval vessels, including gunboats, in the Union's attempt to conquer the South by taking out their leadership. The brothers were together on the Mississippi during at the time. They survived the war with no known wounds or problems.

They yearned for adventure; the frontier called to them. The boys ventured to Salina, Kansas, securing positions as stage drivers in 1867. A year later the brothers were hired as freighters to deliver a load of lumber for the Munger House in Wichita (now the oldest standing building) and remained in Wichita; it had more "snap." Mike had a bent for law enforcement. Well liked, Mike managed to get himself appointed as city marshal of Wichita on April 13, 1871. John was appointed assistant marshal, until the fall of 1871 when he ran for and was elected the Sedgwick County Sheriff. John was the second man to be elected as such. Reappointed as Mike's assistant city marshal, John continued to draw two paychecks. It was a common practice to serve both the county and the townships. He served as sheriff until 1873.

*****

The cow town of Wichita is named after the Wichita Indian tribe that had long before settled on the banks of the Arkansas River at the present site of the modern city. During the Civil War two men settled the area and founded a trading post next to the tribe: Jesse Chisholm, who established the now famous Chisholm Trail, and his partner James R. Mead, who ran the Mead Trading Post. Chisholm was part Cherokee. The tribe was forced to relocate to the Oklahoma Territory in 1867; the post remained. Chisholm was caught in a severe rainstorm while returning from a "trading expedition" in the Southwest. His wagon wheels carved deep grooves in the soft prairie soil, thus marking what would soon become known as the Chisholm Trail. Chisholm promoted the trail by going to Texas to personally encourage the cattlemen to follow his well-marked path to the railways to sell and ship their herds. This was the first trail that created the long drives of cattle to market, that helped build Texas and the lives of the former southern soldiers who herded.

For years this trail was utilized by the cattle drovers to reach their destinations, and is perhaps the most famous trail of the Old West. The Mead Trading Post became a center of commerce and a stopping point for the Texas cattlemen driving their steers to Abilene, which was established in 1867. The post put in a "watering hole" for the cattle drovers, naming it the First and Last Saloon, a big hit with the drovers coming and going both ways.

The settlement of Wichita was laid out in 1870 and incorporated in 1871. Then in 1872 the railroad came to town. Wichita became known as the "cow capital," for that first year 350,000 head of cattle were driven to market via Wichita. As with Ellsworth, Hays City, Abilene, Ellsworth, and later Dodge City, Wichita was banking big money. With the cattle drovers came the saloons, dance halls, gambling dens, and houses of ill repute. Wichita went from a mild-mannered new town to a rough a very rough place during the cattle season.

Mike Meagher was not the first man to be appointed city marshal of Wichita. Two others came before him, but he was the first man to win an election to the marshal's position. When first formed, the village was run by a board of trustees. Town marshals were appointed. By early 1871 the village was upgraded to a level-three-status town. Level three made it mandatory that a mayor and town council be elected. With the election completed and the city fathers in place, they immediately appointed Meagher to the city marshal position. This occurred on April 13, 1871. A calaboose (jail) was commissioned to be built. Then, with the council's blessing, signs were posted that read, in part, "no firearms allowed in the City," and that declared all guns had to be checked in. A year later Wichita was declared a city of the second class, resulting in special elections for the marshal and school board positions. Mike ran for office and won without much effort.

In the towns mentioned before, shootings, killings, and thievery were daily occurrences. Wichita was no different. The Meagher boys needed good help. Among those hired was a young Wyatt Earp. Earp was officially hired on April 21, 1875, but many historians argue that he was a private policeman prior to this date. October 1874 the *Wichita City Eagle* mentioned him working on behalf of M. R. Moser, collecting money. Earp and fellow deputy John Behrens were hired at the same time. The hiring of Wyatt turned out to be a good thing, for the *Wichita City Eagle* had declared him to be an "effective policeman."

December 31, 1876, Mike was on duty; Sylvester Powell (a stage driver who was a daily bus driver) and his partner started celebrating early on that day. On January 4, 1876, the *Wichita City Eagle* reported that Sylvester Powell was arrested for public intoxication and assault. The assault was on a man who caught Powell and his cohort Al Singleton taking over his horse. As Singleton stepped up to Powell to inform him that he was the owner of the horse, Powell grabbed a nearby neck yoke, swung wildly, striking the man and breaking his arm, and then proceeded to threaten him if he complained. The victim went ahead and filed a complaint with Marshal Mike Meagher. The marshal arrested Powell and locked him up in jail. Later that night W. A. Brown, a stagecoach official, paid bail to have Powell released after Powell promised to not drink anymore. Sylvester Powell wanted revenge; he armed himself with a revolver. Having done this, he went looking for the marshal, loudly proclaiming that this was Meagher's last day on earth. Past midnight, officially January 1, 1876, Powell located the marshal behind Hope's Saloon; he was using the outhouse. Powell hid behind a coal bin and waited for Meagher to exit. When Mike exited, Powell shot twice. The first bullet creased Meagher's knee. The second bullet went through the upper part of Mike's coat. The men were but a few feet apart. Meagher reached out his hand while lunging to grab the barrel of the gun. A third shot went off. This time the bullet grazed the marshal's hand, wounding him slightly. Powell turned and ran from his location, heading up the alley toward the main street. He shot a fourth time over his shoulder as he ran. Meagher returned fire, missing Powell. Meagher ran in an opposite direction to try to head Powell off. Successfully doing so, Meagher confronted Powell in front of Hill's Drug Store. Without hesitation, the marshal raised his gun and shot once. The bullet found its mark —Sylvester Powell was shot in the heart. He was dead before he hit the ground. This was Mike Meagher's one and only killing, a self-defense act which would come back to haunt him.

The cattle boom of Wichita lasted until 1880. The cattle were being replaced by homesteaders, who blocked parts of the Chisholm Trail with barbed-wire fences to protect their crops from the massive herds. The railroad had extended to Dodge City, which had become the new destination for drovers. Saloon owners, gamblers, prostitutes, and merchants who where directly involved in making a living from the cowboys moved their operations to Dodge City.

The boom could have been shorter, said Eric Cale, director of the Wichita-Sedgwick County Historical Museum: "Park City residents tried to lure cowboys off the dusty Chisholm Trail, telling them the waters in Chisholm Creek through Wichita were poisonous and that if they went by Park City it would be a straighter route to Abilene. Wichita leaders N. A. English, Mike Meagher, J. R. Mead and J. M. Steele lure cowboys off the dusty Chisholm Trail, telling them the waters in Chisholm Creek through Wichita were poisonous and that one" Cale went on to say, "Those four men put us on the map."

Fort Reno, I. T. 1891

With the end of Wichita's heyday, Mike Meagher, the five-term marshal, left for good. He worked in Indian Territory for a short time as a Deputy U.S. Marshal working out of Fort Reno, which was established as a permanent post in July 1875 in present-day Oklahoma. The fort's main purpose was to support the army after the Cheyenne uprising in 1874. Mike was near his brother, John, who had moved into Oklahoma Territory before him. Mike had the duty to patrol the Chisholm Trail between the fort and Caldwell, Kansas. His position as a Deputy U.S. Marshal was short-lived. Mike moved with his wife, Jenny, whom he married in August 1875. As business in Wichita began to decline, the cattlemen started switching to the ever-growing Dodge City, in part to avoid the barbed wire fencing of the squatters. The Cowley, Sumner & Fort Smith Railroad came to Caldwell in the spring of 1880, and in April of that year, so did Mike and John. With the railroad in Caldwell, the Chisholm Trail forked to serve both cities. One part went westward to Dodge City; the other, northeast toward Caldwell. Caldwell would soon be known as the "Border Queen."

Mike sensed that Caldwell was the place to be. He and Jenny set up shop. There, with a partner by the name of Shea, he opened up the Arcade Saloon. This was on Main Street, halfway between Fifth and Sixth Streets. It was an ideal location in the heart of the city. On April 5, 1880, Mike Meagher was elected mayor, the third man to be such. This was a few weeks prior to the railroad. Caldwell was not Wichita. Giving a stern look or an evil eye was pretty much all that had to be done by this large-framed man to tame the cowboys. Deputies, the likes of Wyatt Earp and John Behrens, were quick to "buffalo" (smack one across the side of the head with a gun) and cart off to jail those who defied Wichita's laws. Meagher also manhandled those in need of learning a lesson. But Caldwell was more troublesome and violent than Wichita.

Mike's first official act as mayor was to replace the police department. He first fired the current city marshal George Flatt and his deputies and then appointed a new police force with the city council's approval. William Horseman was the new marshal, Dan Jones was assistant marshal, and James Johnson was named policeman. Frank Hunt was later included in the hiring as a policeman, while Dan Jones was identified as a constable. The *Caldwell Post* as most newspapers do get things mixed up. The titles, other than city marshal, mattered not; they were simply deputies.

*****

George Flatt and William Horseman were partners in a saloon that they had recently opened in May or June of 1879. Both would become Caldwell town marshals. Their saloon was located "one door from city hall" as mentioned in the *Caldwell Post* newspaper of July 24, 1879. In July of that year Caldwell, located near the southern border of Kansas, had no police force. On July 7, as reported in the *Post* three days later, some men—cow drovers—came into town and proceeded to get drunk. That evening there was trouble. While being egged on by a local ruffian, they thought they could take over the town. They left the Occidental Saloon and went out onto the streets, shooting their guns "promiscuously" and endangering the citizens. Back into the saloon they went for more rotgut; they continued their bad behavior by intimidating saloon patrons. Constable W. C. Kelly and his deputy John Wilson asked for help; they needed a posse to enter the saloon to arrest the three men. George Flatt stepped forward. Wilson entered the saloon, heading toward the center and back of it. Flatt came in next and stopped at the bar near the men. The drovers recognized that they could be in trouble so they pulled their guns out of the holsters, cocked them but kept the weapons pointed downward at their sides. The two most vocal started to back out of the saloon. Flatt, with his two revolvers hidden behind his body, started backing out as well in an attempt to block the men from leaving. One drover, closest to the exit, raised his gun and shot at Flatt. Almost simultaneously Flatt produced his two revolvers from their hiding place and commenced shooting at the two adversaries. The first man closest to the exit open fire first. He shot at Flatt but missed, then turned his attention to Wilson. Flatt fired at the second cowboy striking him twice. The man's trigger finger was shot off, then the second bullet entered his body, passing through both lungs and out his back. The impact knocked him out the saloon doorway, where he rolled off the walkway and onto the street, dead. The cow-drover who shot at Flatt before turning his attention on Wilson, was hit twice. The first bullet entered the cowboy's right hand; the second entered below the ribcage and went into his abdomen. Wilson's wrist was grazed and was also struck and in the hip—nothing serious. The two cow drovers were dead. On August 21, 1879, a month after the posse's impressive handling of the drunken cowboys, the city fathers officially appointed George Flatt as the town's first-ever marshal.

Flatt was a true gunman, as fast as any on the draw and deadly accurate with either hand. He was also a bragger, a bully, and a drunk. It did not take the city residents long to tire of George, so upon the election of Mike Meagher as mayor on April 5th, 1880, Flatt found himself out of a job. Flatt was not happy; he let it be known. He continued his old ways, loud and drunk, bullying those near him. He confronted the town's marshal and deputies, doing his best to draw them into a fight. Then one night, June 19, 1880, it all came to an end. Up to his old drunken tricks, having started a series of loud arguments with policeman Frank Hunt and "others," a couple of Flatt's friends talked him into going to bed to sleep it off. Flatt wanted something to eat first; at 1:00 a.m. they headed to Louis Segerman's restaurant for "lunch" before heading to the I. X. L. Saloon, where Flatt often slept in a back room. On the way to Segerman's, on the south side of Main Street in front of Bailey's Harness Shop, Flatt was flanked by friends C. L. Spear and Samuel H. Rogers, a current member of the city police force. Rogers was on the outside, closest to the street, a pace behind Flatt. Spear, a few feet in front, was on the inside of the walkway, closest to the storefronts. Flatt was in the middle. A little past 1:00 a.m. shots rang out. Six to twelve individuals said they witnessed the shooting. Flatt was hit in the base of his skull; his spinal cord was severed—George Flatt died instantly. It was later determined that a No.1 or No.2 pellet from a shotgun inflicted the kill shot. (In other words, a 12- or 20-gauge shotgun was used to bring Flatt down). Oddly, the two flanking him were never hit. The local newspaper and the county sheriff believed that there was a conspiracy. Sheriff Joseph Thralls and deputies from Wellington showed up on June 25 and arrested the following: Mayor Michael Meagher; City Marshal William Horseman; policemen Frank Hunt, James Johnson, and Dan Jones; George W. McFarland; and R. H. Collins—in short, the Caldwell city government. Along with a host of witnesses, the men were taken by train to Wellington, the Sumner County seat. No evidence was brought forward. The newspaper declared that Wellington was creating a sham. The only man to be placed on trial was William Horseman, who was acquitted a year later. Mike Meagher knew that his time as a public servant was over; he finished out his mayorship and refused to ever run for office again. Four days after Flatt was murdered, his wife gave birth to his child.

December, 17, 1881, a quiet Saturday, Caldwell was in for another incident. "Run you little one's Hell is in session, hide out little ones," was voiced by James Daniel Sherman aka Jim Talbot as he stood in the middle of the street at the northwest corner of 5th and Main. A gun in each hand, Talbot knew who he wanted to kill and by god he was going to have his way. He took aim at an imposing man down the street on the walkway in front of the Danford building. He shot and miss his mark, Mike Meagher. Talbot shot at those in his way as he warned innocent bystanders and children to hide. Within moments three of his Gang backed his play. They stood on each side of their leader, in the middle of the street, all commence firing as they moved slowly up Main

Street towards their target, Mike Meagher. Prior to this triangular show of force, Talbot had pulled his guns while confronting Marshal John Wilson, firing two shots in the air. The crowd ran for cover as Talbot turned and bolted south on Main. But he soon stopped, turn towards the Danford building, also known as the Opera House where he fired those two shots. Next to Meagher was Marshal Wilson. Talbot first one of the shots at him. With his Winchester rifle in hand (one of his men must of fetched it), Talbot then turned looking south, further down the street and fired at a figure near the Arcade Saloon. It was William "Bill" D. Fossett, the new Assistant Town Marshal—indeed, Hell was in session. Talbot was at full strength for all six of his Gang members had joined in. The battle between Jim Talbot's gang and the City of Caldwell went on for hours! It would soon be the last day on earth for two men. As the *Caldwell Post* wrote on December 22, in their article:

WAR ON THE BORDER
Two Men Killed and One Wounded
A Desperate Fight with Outlaws

"...One Jim Talbot who had been around the city for about a month, gambling, drinking, bullying, and attempting to bulldoze every one, was the leader of the party. He has a wife and little boy and girl living on Chisholm Street in this city, and came up on the trail with Millett's herd this fall". "...With Talbot on the drinking spree during the night were Jim Martin, Bob Bigtree, Tom Love, Bob Munson, Dick Eddleman and George Speers". "Speers... [was] in the act of saddling one of Talbot's horses when he was shot". "After the fighting in the city and Mike Meagher and George Speer were killed, the five outlaws....rode off to the east. A party of citizens organized, mounted horse and started in pursuit... ."

Eight men armed men did their best to capture the city of Caldwell by force, why? After the violent death of his father, followed by his mother's passing away, Jim Talbot (James Sherman) was taking in by his Aunt. He grew up and became close to his cousin, Sylvester Powell, the one and only man that Meagher had ever killed. From the movement that Talbot arrived in town he had a dislike for Meagher, a taste in his mouth for revenge. The Millets Ranch located in Texas had a custom of hiring only harden cowboys, many were outlaws. Young JimTalbot fitted right in. He started his outlawing at an early age. Meagher had always had the feeling that the shooting of Powell would come back to haunt him, he even mentioned it once half out-loud, half to himself, within a day of the killing. It was over heard and noted.

Talbot was five feet, ten inches tall, lean, solid as a rock and strong as an ox. He had no fixed or full time job; he earned an income by racing his horse. He rented a house from Dan Jones, then a policeman (constable). What type of man was Talbot, had he morals? According to Historian Rod Cook in an article he wrote, *The Talbot Raid*, in November, 1881, John Danford, president and owner of the Merchants and Drovers

Bank of Caldwell skipped town by stage. When the citizens learned of that their deposits were missing, Talbot, new in town, saddled his race horse and went after the stage. He caught up with it, turn it around by gun point and headed it back to town. Back in Caldwell, the stage coach and Danford was surrounded by disgruntled citizens. One man spoke up "I would pay twenty-five dollars if someone would shoot you". Talbot re-drew his Colt, cocked it then said, "let me see the money" or words to that effect. The man had a change of heart so Talbot offered to shoot him for twenty dollars. There were no takers. Talbot holstered his revolver. John Danford survived the day.

Talbot and his friends were constantly pushing the envelope. They challenged the police force, threatening lawmen who dared intervene or asked them to quiet down, or fired their weapons at random ("hurrahing"). The Talbot Gang kept the police and citizens in a constant flux.

Using eye witness testimony from the coroner's report, and the *Caldwell Post* article of December 22, told the public that the night prior to the shoot out, Friday, December 16, Talbot and friends had started a drinking spree. Belligerent as usual, they went to see the play Uncle Tom's Cabin, showing at the Opera House. They entered during the play, with prostitutes on each arm, loudly, and crudely disrupting the play until twenty-two year old "Comanche Bill" Mankin sat down facing the group with his gun across his lap. After the play, they went to the Arcade Saloon where Mike Meagher was engaged in a high stakes poker game and preceded to disrupted and disrespect Meagher all night long. At one point, during the course of the night, Tom Love decided to shoot Meagher, luckily, "Comanche Bill," was there to disarm him. He was friendly with the Gang but never apart of it. He and Talbot lived next door to one another. Bill, was one of two town marshals hired by the railroad for Hunnewell, Kansas. Hunnewell was located less that seventeen miles east of Caldwell. At a trial after the shootout, "Comanche Bill" testified that he disarmed Tom Love and others prior to shootout. In the early morning of December 17, the day of the shootout, the Gang started their drinking at the Arcade Saloon then moved over to the Robinson's Saloon. They continued to drink while loudly vocalizing their displeasure of Mike Meagher and making threats. Mike was in the very saloon playing cards. Having too much drink himself, Meagher, knowing that he was at a disadvantage, went to Marshal John Wilson early that morning asking for help. Wilson had served under Meagher as a deputy in Wichita. Meanwhile, for the fun of it, Tom Love shot out a window at the Moores Brothers' Saloon. Marshal Wilson with the aid of Assistant Marshal Bill Fossett arrested Tom Love. While taking him to the jail, two of Talbot's Gang members, Jim Martin and Bob Munson, armed, came at the two lawmen. This was around eight o'clock that morning. The ruckus they caused allowed Love to escape, temporarily. Mike Meagher came to the aid of his friends. Guns were pulled, Martin and Munson aimed at the un-armed Meagher threatening to kill him. Meagher pushed their guns aside, but they re-pointed them. Meagher moved up the stairway of the Police Court, located on the second floor of the Danford building, as Marshal

Wilson, with both guns now un-holstered, move in front of the steps. He stood between Meagher and the two Gang members. "Comanche Bill" appears on the scene, he steps in and brokered a truce. Munson and Martin would be allowed to take their weapons to Talbot's house and leave them there, then go to lunch, when done come back to the court to received their fines for interfering with the law and brandishing weapons; Tom Love was back in custody.

Later that day, around one o'clock, Jim Martin, who was still armed, was arrested and brought before Judge Kelly at the Police Court. Fined a sum of money, the two lawmen were taking Martin to retrieve his money in order to pay. As they exited on to the Main Street, Martin, was loudly objecting to the price of his fine. A large crowd gathered; Talbot showed up well armed. He, Talbot, told Love he did not have to pay the fine. Two of the Gang members strong armed the lawmen, then grabbed Martin and blended into the crowd to escaped. To help the escape, Talbot shot twice in the air, turned and bolted south before turning to shoot twice at Wilson, as he stood in the middle of the street. He then turned facing the Arcade Saloon, then shot at the man in front of it—the battle was on. This battle has been since referred to as "The Talbot Raid," Talbot proclaimed that "hell was in session," was on. Unarmed residents, ran to the two general stores, The York Parker and Draper Mercantile and The Hardesty Brothers who freely handed out weapons and ammunition. The shootout was "fluid," the outlaws were ever changing their location as were the police, the citizens hid behind walls, buildings, where ever they could shield themselves. Talbot and a few of his men ran down an passage way on the south side of the Pulaski Building to get to Talbot's home, a short distant, from the shortcut just taken, to fetch their stash of guns then back to Main and Fifth Street. The shooting was general. People on both sides of the law were using the sides of the building for shields as they fired at others. Almost every building on the block was hit, chips of brick flying with the striking of each bullet--all the buildings were scared. The new assistant marshal, Bill Fossett must have been a great shot and a dangerous man to reckon with for he was under fire, continually, by at least two of the outlaws and for a while three, Talbot himself, joined the barrage aimed at Fossett.

The Talbot Raid was raging, George Speer, was saddling up a horse for Talbot's escape; they knew they could not stand off the town much longer. One well place shot though his heart ended Mr. Speer, the horse was not saddled. Several of the outlaw gang were on horseback waiting for George.
Prior to this, Talbot had position himself behind a shed, across an alley, behind Main Street, just south of Fifth Street. He spotted Mike Meagher; they exchanged gunfire. Mike moved to another position near the rear of the Pulaski building. This brick building was next to a passage way that lead to Main Street and the same passage that Talbot had taken to retrieve the stash of arms at his house. From here, Jim Talbot had a clear shot of Meager. A marksman, in the first order, Talbot took quick aim with his

Winchester rifle, fired once, striking Meager. The bullet went though the fleshly part of his right arm, entered his upper torso and passed though both lungs. Mike dropped. Alive, Meagher knew he was doomed. Marshal Wilson and a citizen, Edward Rathbun, ran a freight line and was involved in the fight, helped Meagher up, setting him on a box, then re-joined the fighting. At a loll in the shooting, the two men took Mike to Sherer's Barber Shop, shortly thereafter, on a old, discarded, door, he was carried him home. It was here that Mike Meagher, age 38, died. He had lived between twenty-five to thirty minutes after having been shot.

Main Street looking South, Caldwell, Kansas, 1800s. Photo from the White Collection, courtesy of the Caldwell Museum and Historical Society.

Jim Talbot had revenged the death of his cousin, Sylvester Powell. Meagher was buried at the Wichita cemetery, in his family's plot.

The shooting was intense, the Talbot Gang was out numbered and out gunned. It was only a matter of time before the town would take control. Four of the men made a break across Main toward Talbot's home on Chisholm, slightly north of Fifth. Talbot seeing this decided to give the fight up as well. He ran to join the others. What happen next is incredible. From the book *The Chisholm Trail (*see suggested readings, chapter 2):

"...Dozens of men were shooting at him with all kinds of firearms. His course was over open ground, a distance of about one hundred and fifty yards down a gradually sloping hill, and in covering this distance he would zigzag, run, fall down and roll over. He accomplished this escape successfully, ...and reached the point where their horses had been left."

The outlaws played hell getting away but they did. They were five men on four horses with a posse hot on their trail. Over the course of the chase two horses were wounded and one was killed. Bob Johnson, also known as Doug Hill, was wounded in the heel of his foot. When they could they would commandeer fresh horses. It was difficult to do for the posse was near enough to fire, yet they did. Bullets were flying all-about, the outlaws were able to mount fresh horses and hit the road hard. Once more, horses were shot, and the men were back to having only three horses for the five. Once more, they were able to commandeer two horses. Finally, they were boxed in a canyon but the posse could not reach them safely. The posse positioned themselves about the rim of the canyon while they continued to fire at the concealed outlaws. One outlaw had a commanding view from an outcrop and could get the drop on any posse member who dared get too close. One tried. With holes in his clothing and hat, he ran back to safety. It was night fall, some of the posse members settled down while others went back to town. Additional help would be on its way by morning. With not enough men to completely circle the rim of the canyon, the outlaws, slipped away during the night. County Sheriff Thralls was called in to chase down the cowboys. The outlaws that escaped were Jim Talbot, Doug Hill (Bob Johnson), Bob Bigtree, Jim Martin and Bob Munson. Doug Hill was captured the following year, receiving a four month prison sentence. Fellow gang member Dick Eddleman, got himself in hot water when he escaped from the county jail, but was recaptured and was looking at seven years. We have no ideal what he received as a sentence, that paper work has yet to be found. It was not until 1895, fourteen years later, that Jim Talbot was located, in Ukiah, California and brought back to justice. He stood trial, his friends, testified on his behalf countering the prosecution's main witness. Some of the potential wittiness had died or moved away— Talbot was set free. A citizen noted and told others, that John Meagher had followed Talbot, as he left the courthouse. A year later on August 11, 1896, as he approached the gate of his ranch, in Ukiah, Talbot was shotgunned to death.

Talbot lived by the gun and died by the gun. Two possible suspects were John Meagher and, some claim, the lover of Talbot's wife. Since no name of this lover ever came to light.

Clay Allison (1841-1887)

Clay Allison was born in 1841 and raised in Wayne County, Tennessee. During the Civil War he joined the Ninth Tennessee Regiment, Company F, serving under Generals Nathan Bradford Forrest and Benjamin McCulloch for two years as a scout. After that he roamed the frontier from Mexico to Texas and Kansas before settling in the Texas Panhandle in Hemphill County. He was tall and dark and walked with grace. He was six feet two inches in height, one hundred eighty pounds, and handsome. He had broad shoulders and was agile, with slender hands and feet and black wavy hair; he was vain and downright mean. The *Kinsley Graphic* Newspaper reported: "His manners were gentlemanly and courteous and stood tall as an arrow...."

General Forrest was considered the most formidable cavalry commander of the Civil War. His style was to fight guerrilla-like, and he was notoriously bloodthirsty and vengeful, as the *New York Times* reported in an article on October 30, 1877. General McCulloch rose to the level of brigadier general serving under Forrest and had an interesting life before and after the Civil War. His family members were neighbors to both Sam Huston and Davy Crockett. He was one of the "Tennessee Boys" that followed Crockett to the Alamo. Fortunately McCulloch came down with the measles while en route to San Antonio. He remained behind to recover. McCulloch reached the Alamo after the battle had ended; thus, he was the only one of the "Tennessee Boys" left alive. McCulloch immediately joined the Texas Army under Sam Huston's command, where he served with distinction in the Battle of San Jacinto. For his efforts and service McCulloch was granted a total of 960 acres of land. He became a lieutenant in the Texas Rangers in 1838, rising to the rank of captain before he ran for and was elected to the Republic of Texas House of Representatives. When Texas became a state in 1845, McCulloch was elected to the first Texas House of Representatives. Seven years later he was appointed as Deputy United States Marshal for the territory of the district court for the eastern district of Texas. When war broke out between the states, McCulloch was given a colonelcy in the Confederacy by Jefferson Davis. Within a month he made the rank of brigadier general. He died when he was shot off his horse by a sniper. This was during the Battle of Pea Ridge in 1862. Benjamin McCulloch was brilliant, dedicated, and fearless.

Clay Allison served under these two generals. His ability with weapons was honed during the Civil War, as were the abilities of so many other gunmen. He participated in ruthlessness. The sum of his experiences—including the influences of those about him, such as Generals Forrester and McCulloch—made him the man that he was. He was a loner, one who did not like to take orders. The book *Robert Clay Allison* by James S. Peters claims that Clay faked mental illness three months into his service. It was his attempt to be discharged from the army. It worked. He hated the infantry; being a foot solider was not his "cup of tea." He saw the army as a "bunch of crap." When Clay arrived back home, his father did not take his medical discharge kindly. Nine months later, with his father on his back, Clay rejoined the army, but this time it was the cavalry. General Forrester became Clay's hero. Clay grew a vandyke (a pointed goatee) similar to the general's. Forrester once said, "War means fightin', and fightin' means killin'." Clay found that he liked fighting and killing; he had a talent for it. He mostly enjoyed killing with his bowie knife, watching the life drain from his adversary. By war's end Allison was a prisoner of war and was released as such in May of 1865. It was ironic that Clay Allison would be a surviving prisoner of war, for he had a policy of not taking prisoners —alive.

The year 1866 found Clay working for Charles Goodnight and Oliver Loving as a cattle herder. It was Goodnight and Loving that blazed the famous cattle trail affectionately called the Goodnight-Loving Trail. This trail started in Young County (located in southwest Texas), crossed over the Pecos River, then went up through the eastern section of New Mexico and into Colorado, ending in Cheyenne, Wyoming. Allison was one of eighteen men who worked the cattle and helped forge the new trail. Four years later Allison left the Goodnight-Loving Ranch for good. He had married and decided to start his own ranch. He struck a deal for three hundred head of cattle—his payment for herding another rancher's cattle—and moved near Cimarron, New Mexico. Later, around 1880, Clay would move his ranch operation to the Texas Panhandle. Allison was born and raised on a working ranch. This knowledge, along with his herding years for the Goodnight-Loving Ranch, enabled him to build a successful operation of his own.

Due to a series of shootings, he became a widely known and feared gunslinger. A gunman and outlaw by the name of Chuck Colbert had a score to settle with Allison. It seemed that Colbert's uncle, Zachary, had tried to overcharge Allison's family as they crossed the Brazos River. Zachary ran a ferry-crossing business. He was severely beaten by Clay for his attempt to cheat. Some time later Colbert and Allison collided on January 7, 1884. Friendly but not trusting of each other, one of the men suggested a horse race. Who won is unknown today, but after the race Colbert invited Allison to have lunch with him. Clay happily accepted. The men entered the Clifton House in Colfax County, New

Mexico, and ordered up a fine meal. They had a lively and cordial conversation throughout the lunch. Toward the end of the meal Colbert reached for a drink with one hand. As he raised his glass, his other hand was under the table, holding a revolver, and he began to raise the gun hand at the same time. The gun butt hit the table accidentally, causing his shot to go wide. Allison pulled his gun and shot more deliberately. Shot in the face just above his right eye, Chuck Colbert was killed instantly. Colbert, who boasted of having killed seven men (most of which cannot be verified), was buried behind the inn in an unmarked grave. Someone asked Allison why he accepted the offer to dine with his would-be assassin. His reply was, "Because I didn't want to send a man to hell on an empty stomach."

In another incident a man by the name of Kennedy was accused by his wife of mass murder and the killing of their infant child. She went to Clay for help. In searching the Kennedy ranch, a bunch of bones were discovered. Kennedy was arrested and placed in jail for safekeeping. The marshal and deputies were gathering the bones to determine if they were human or not. Clay, having formed his own conclusion, led a group of men to the jail, overtook the jailer, and lynched Kennedy. Clay was not done. He cut off the dead man's head, impaled it on a tall stick, and then rode some twenty-six miles to one of his favorite watering holes. His words, combined with deeds like these, helped to create his reputation and legend.

In 1872 Cimarron became the county seat. The town was the headquarters of the Maxwell Land Grant. This land grant was the largest private landholding in the entire history of the United States. The grant, contiguous in scope, encompassed the towns of Cimarron, Colfax, Dawson, Elizabethtown, French, Lynn, Maxwell, Miami, Raton, Rayado, Springer, Ute Park, and Vermejo Park. Its size was 1,714,764.93 acres, as reported by the New Mexico Historical Organization.

The original grant, smaller in size, was given by Mexican Governor Manuel Armijo in 1841. He was the last governor of New Mexico under Mexican rule. Partners Charles Beaubien and Guadalupe Miranda were proud owners of the grant. Beaubien was a wealthy early pioneer. Miranda was the personal secretary to Governor Armijo, and the driving force requesting the grant. It took only three days after the formal request for the partners to receive their grant, which became known as the Beaubien-Miranda Grant.

Now partners the two immediately gave a one-fourth interest to Governor Armijo and a one-fourth interest to trader Charles Bent. Bent had to colonize the grant to earn his interest. Lucien Maxwell moved to Cimarron, establishing a store. He married one of Beaubien's daughters. Together they did well, for in 1857 Maxwell was wealthy enough to purchase a good part of Miranda's section of the grant. Miranda wanted to return to Mexico. Somewhere along the line Governor Armijo had sold his shares to his partners. When Charles Beaubien died in 1864, Maxwell approached and purchased the balance of the grant from the heirs. Maxwell then approached Bent's heirs with the same success and became the sole owner. In doing so, the grant title would forever be known as the Maxwell Land Grant. By 1869 Lucien Maxwell was sole owner. The grant had grown to almost two million acres, making Maxwell the largest landowner in the entire continent.

Maxwell's store and farms were lucrative. His two largest customers were the nearby army post and the Cimarron Indian Agency. A generous man, Maxwell allowed the Jicarillas and Ute Indians to hunt on his land. Settlers would rent farmland. In the late 1860s miners were allowed to lease claims—1,280 were filed. So much land and so many issues and problems to deal with made Maxwell stressed and aged before his time. These factors contributed to Maxwell selling all of the grant, except for a small portion around his home and a few mining interests. New owners formed the Maxwell Land Grand and Railroad Company, who sold out within the year to a Dutch interest. By April 1870 the Dutch sold their interest to a confederation of English investors with Dutch financiers backing them. They needed to get the grant legally approved by the United States. The federal government, using Mexican land grants to guide them, ruled that the grant could only be ninety-seven thousand acres. The Mexican land grant law allowed not more than ninety-two thousand acres per single grant; the United States government granted Maxwell an extra five thousand acres. This ruling, coupled with the lack of appreciable income, caused the British owners to default on their taxes. The Dutch backers raised enough money to pay the back taxes to regain control and ownership of the grant. They then resold the grant to a group of New Mexico investors headed by Thomas Catron of the notorious Santa Fe Ring. The land, no longer legally a part of the grant, was now open for settlement. The small farmers who had settled on the grant land were forced off. This forceful eviction became know as the Colfax County War. The farmers were well within their rights. Their land was officially deemed open, yet the Maxwell Land Grant and Railroad Company continued to sell land not belonging to them as they forced the small farmers off.

Thomas Catron was the head of the Santa Fe Ring. He was a lawyer by trade who quickly rose to become New Mexico's attorney general in 1869. Catron used his position as a stepping-stone to control New Mexico, then a territory—he was a powerful man. Catron fought the U.S. court system to reinstate the full Maxwell Grant. It took years, but eventually he was successful. The Santa Fe Ring was a group comprised of powerful attorneys and land speculators, all of whom amassed fortunes via political corruption and fraudulent land deals. Catron cooperated closely with the Murphy-Dolan faction, which was perceived as part of the notorious ring. Competition arose, and the Murphy-Dolan Gang pushed back hard with the results of the now very infamous Lincoln County War. This is where Billy the Kid came to fame. He played a prominent role as he fought and killed those associated with the Murphy-Dolan Gang, who murdered his employer, John Tunstall. Tunstall was the only competition to the Murphy-Dolan mercantile store and cattle ranch. Tunstall was an Englishman who owned a cattle ranch. He partnered with his friend Alexander McSween, a lawyer, and opened a mercantile store and bank. Unfortunately for Tunstall they were successful. The Murphy-Dolan store had been a monopoly, but the competition was hurting it. Thomas Catron owned the Murphy-Dolan mortgage, so he had a vested interest in the store. Hired guns were brought in to kill off the competition, resulting in the deaths of both Tunstall and McSween. The Kid and his pals started to seek revenge on the Murphy-Dolan faction for the murder of Tunstall. In total, Billy the Kid has been credited with killing between fifteen and twenty-one men. He was eighteen years old when the "war" in 1878; it ended with the death of McSween in July 1879, but not for Billy.

The ring encompassed almost every Republican politician; all were in Santa Fe, the territorial capital. Billy was promised a full pardon after he testified in a trial and told all in regards to the "war." He did as agreed, but Thomas Catron, as attorney general of New Mexico, refused to honor the pardon. Billy was imprisoned. He escaped and remained a fugitive until his death a year and a half later. Catron would later become a U.S. State Senator.

There is a clear path between the Colfax County War and the Lincoln County War—the Santa Fe Ring. The Reverend F. J. Tolby, a Methodist minister, spoke loudly and openly against the Maxwell Land Grant Company's (controlled by Catron) ruthless behavior against the farmers. The ring hired assassins to kill the Reverend. Vigilante groups sprung up with a series of retaliatory killings, and in the process the Reverend Oscar P. McMains became the new leader for the settlers. Over the next twenty years he fought for their rights.

Governor Samuel Axtell, who had an interest in the Maxwell Land Grant Company, contacted the army at Fort Union, ordering them to go to Cimarron and arrest Clay Allison. Clay had become one of the leaders opposing the Maxwell Land Grant Company. It was voiced more than once by historians that the governor sent the army to kill off the opposition. Clay, now known far and wide as a ruthless man-killer, was very much a leader in the vigilante activities. Governor Axtell was once described as having committed more fraud, corruption, and murder in his tenure as governor than any other governor in the history of the United States. He would be removed from office, only to be appointed a few years later (after things had simmered down) as Chief Justice of the Territorial Supreme Court in 1882. The Colfax County War continued until 1887, when the Supreme Court of the United States upheld the survey legitimizing the entire land grant. The farmers, for the most part, gave up.

In 1880 Clay sold off his portion of his ranch to his brother, John. He moved his operations to the Texas Panhandle—in his own words, "on the Washita in Hemphill County, Texas." There were many claims made of Clay's involvement in various shootings; some he denied. He wrote a letter to a newspaper, challenging anyone who thought different to come meet him face-to-face. His address, vaguely given, was printed in the *Dodge City Globe* on February 26, 1880. No one took up the challenge. The odd part is that Clay was a cattleman in Hays City at this time. His Hemphill County address was not valid before 1883. Allison may have already owned land in Hemphill County and may not have really wanted people to challenge him, thus the deceit.

Cimarron, New Mexico, 1870s. Public domain photograph

After the Reverend Tolby was murdered by the ring in September, the following month, on October 30, 1875, a mob led by Clay lynched Cruz Vega. Vega was suspected of murdering the reverend. Vega's body was hanged from a telegraph pole near Cimarron. Two days later, Vega's family began making threats—revenge had raised its ugly head. The family leader was Vega's uncle, Francisco Griego. At the Lambert Inn Clay was confronted by Griego for his part in the lynching. Griego reached for his revolver. Clay did as well. Two shots rang out, both hit their mark, and Francisco Griego lay dead; he never got a shot off. On November 10 Clay was charged with the murder of Griego. The shooting was ruled self-defense, and the charge was dropped. Revenge can take a twist as it did here; now two family members lay dead. As a side note, the Lambert Inn still stands under the banner of the Saint James Hotel.

December 21, 1876, Clay and his brother, John, were in Las Animas, Colorado, having a drink at a local saloon. County Constable Charles Faber entered the Olympic Dance Hall Saloon, where he noticed the brothers were armed and disturbing the peace. He approached the two brothers, requesting that they remove their firearms. The brothers refused. The constable left the saloon. He came back with two deputized men. When the three men entered the saloon, Faber was armed with a shotgun. As they walked in, a voice rang out, "Look out!" A gunfight immediately broke out. Clay's brother, John, was hit three times. He suffered a wound to his leg, arm, and chest from Faber's shotgun blast. Clay was able to get off four shots that resulted in Constable Faber's instant death. His two deputies fled the saloon. Clay chased after them, but they escaped, avoiding death. The brothers were arrested and charged with Sheriff Faber's death. The shooting was ruled self-defense when it was learned that the law had opened fire first. There is a report stating that no witness came forward or would testify, which helped free the brothers. A great number of historians believe that this one gunfight raised Clay Allison to legendary status. It may be true, but another incident has been a major force in keeping Clay Allison's reputation and place in western folklore alive. It is the Wyatt Earp-Clay Allison confrontation that still swirls with controversy.

In March 1877 Clay moved his family to Sedalia, Missouri, after having sold his share of the ranch in Texas. Sedalia was his wife's hometown and the county seat. They did not remain long, for they moved to Hays City, Kansas, where Clay set up shop as a cattle broker. Hays City is 105 miles north of Dodge. With Dodge City being the newest and largest cow town, Clay naturally had business there and visited often. Wyatt Earp was a deputy marshal of Dodge and the go-to man for the sheriff's office. Along with Wyatt were some of the biggest frontier lawmen in history: Bat, Ed, and Jim Masterson; Bill Tilghman; Charlie Bassett; Neal Brown; "Ham" Bell; and Morgan Earp. Clay's reputation as a gunfighter of the first order was well-known. Wyatt Earp was not famous as he is today; still, as a deputy marshal of Dodge City the cattle drovers were very well aware of him. Needless to say, he was not well liked. Bat Masterson, on the other hand, was a legend in his own time. Wyatt was heavy-handed in performing his duties but was not a man-killer. It would not be until 1931, when the biography *Wyatt Earp, Frontier Marshal* was published, that his fame and legend took off.

On July 26, 1878, a drover, George Hoyt (sometimes spelled Hoy), attempted to assassinate Deputy Marshal Earp. Hoyt was on horseback, strolling at leisurely pace down the street. He passed Wyatt outside the Comique, which featured vaudeville shows in addition to being a saloon and gambling den. Hoyt, for whatever reason, suddenly turned his horse, spurring it to action. He shot three times as he approached Earp, barely missing. He kept on riding, hard and fast, attempting to make it out of Dodge. Wyatt and Deputy Marshal Jim Masterson had a different idea. They ran into the street, firing at least two shots at the fleeing would-be assassin. At the edge of town, on the bridge that spanned the Arkansas River, Hoyt fell from his mount, wounded; his arm was broken by the fall. Which lawman shot Hoyt no one really knows, but Wyatt always took the credit for it. If so, this was his first-ever recorded shooting of a man. Just shy of a month later the *Dodge City Globe* reported that on August 27, 1878, George Hoyt died from gangrene.

Hoyt was a friend of Clay Allison. Clay came to town to seek revenge. In his official biography, *The Frontier Marshal*, Wyatt said that he and Clay ran into each other in front of a saloon. They talked; then they both backed away. Bat Masterson was across the street, armed and ready to use his rife if need be. Clay, the book reports, basically apologized and rode off. Nearly all historians state that this never happened. Two men intervened. Chalk Beeson (the owner of the Long Branch Saloon) and Dick McNulty (a prominent cattleman). It was they who convinced Clay and his Texas pals—who were ready to aid Clay, just as Masterson was prepared to help Wyatt—to give up their guns and go their own way peacefully. The researchers all say that Wyatt was nowhere to be seen and that Masterson was out of town. An eyewitness who later became a well-known Pinkerton detective, Charlie Siringo, agreed that Wyatt was no where to be found in a written statement years later after he read the August 16, 1896, article in the *San Francisco Examiner* telling Wyatt's version of this clash.

*****

The *Fayetteville Observer* reported on February 5, 1880, that Clay Allison joined a group of investors to build the Nashville, Fayetteville & Huntsville Railroad Company. The original petition can be found in the 1869 volume of the *Acts of the State of Tennessee Passed at the General Assembly, Volume 35* on page 347. It looks like the rail system lasted until 1900, when the Nashville, Chattanooga & St. Louis Railway purchased it, as indicated by the United States Interstate Commerce Commission's article entitled *Louisville & Nashville Railroad Company*. Clay was a hard-drinking man with a world-class temper to boot. He was also business savvy and successful in his endeavors. Clay's investment was strictly that, nothing else.

Dora McCullough and Clay married in Mobeetie, Texas, in 1881. Dora gave birth to two children, both daughters. This did not stop Allison's ruthless and crazy behavior. Among other antics, he once rode nude through the town of Mobeetie. He was involved in a knife fight in which the men dug out a burial plot beforehand, with the promise to bury the one who did not survive.

He was a full-time rancher. His ranch was located on the Texas-New Mexico border, northwest of Pecos. Clay even became involved in area politics. He was slowing down, but not enough, for on September 11, 1886, the *Opelousas Courier*, a Louisiana newspaper, reported a run-in that Allison had with a dentist. The article was echoed by the *New York Commercial*.

A Cowboy's Revenge:

"In Cheyenne he sold his stock, rejoiced and went looking for a dentist. The dentist wanted to make more money so he drilled an whole in a 'sound' tooth but broke it off. Clay left—went to another dentist. That dentist told him that he was the victim of a quack...."

Clay was enraged. He went back to the first dentist, forced him into a chair, and pulled a tooth. He then started to pull another with part of the dentist's lip attached, but the yelling and screams from the dentist brought lots of help that hindered Allison from fulfilling his task.

July 3, 1887, while Clay was on his way to the ranch with a wagonload of supplies, the load shifted. It was reported that a bag of seeds fell off the wagon and that Allison reached for it. Instead of catching the burlap or canvas bag, he fell. He landed under the wagon's rear wheel, which ran over his neck, breaking it. Clay Allison died on the spot; he was forty-six years old. The following day Clay was buried in the Pecos Cemetery. Eight-eight years later he was reinterred in Pecos, Texas, near the Pecos Museum.

William D. "Bill" Fossett (1851?-1940)

W. D. FOSSETT.

The first time that Mr. Fossett popped up in western history, to the best of my knowledge, was in Caldwell, Kansas, on December 17, 1881. This was the day that "hell was in session"—the shootout between the Jim Talbot Gang and the citizens of Caldwell, the town known as the "Border Queen." Bill Fossett was a deputy marshal in Caldwell. He worked at the pleasure of City Marshal John Wilson and the mayor. Chapter two of this book goes into details of the Talbot Raid, as most historians refer to it. Bill's role in the shootout is discussed. During Fossett's fifty-year career in law enforcement, he worked most of those years as a policeman. He is one of the very few frontier marshals who survived those wild west days.

There is an assumption on my part concerning Fossett and the Caldwell shootout of 1881. Bill must have been well-known by the outlaws and general hell-raisers. He did have a reputation as an excellent marksman. In time he would be considered one of the greatest shooters. During the raid three of the seven outlaws were concentrating on Fossett. Bill fought back. In the end the shootout was a standstill. Fossett survived unharmed, but the criminals got away.

Bill's father was born in Dublin, Ireland; his mother, Susan Corrigan (may be spelled Carrigan), in Glasgow, Scotland. Soon after their marriage they headed to America, landing there in 1833. His father died at the age of seventy-nine in Caldwell. The family had a history of long lives, especially for those days.

Bill was twenty-one, married, and the father of a baby boy when they arrived in Caldwell in 1873. He worked for various ranches during the next eight to nine years before taking on the job of deputy city marshal.

During the Civil War Texas was a mess with men fighting the war. There were few able bodies left to take care of the ranches, so cattle roamed and multiplied. Pork was once the meat of choice, but by the war's end the demand for beef was so high that it took over the position of number one. The ranchers were contacted and invited to gather up their Texas longhorns, combine herds, and drive them to the nearest rail station for shipment back east. The nearest destination was Kansas. Its grasslands were perfect for cattle grazing as they waited their turn for boarding the railcars. Cattle brokers were at hand, offering top dollar. Massive corrals were built to handle the large numbers. Abilene was the first destination set up for the cattle business. As the rail system extended, other cities in Kansas would become more accessible. By 1879 it was Caldwell, with its location three miles north of the Oklahoma border, that made the town desirable for the cattlemen. Being located on the Jesse Chisholm Trail made it even easier for the drovers. Fossett participated in many cattle drives, becoming familiar with the trail. He also partook in herding horses up from Mexico for his then employer W. R. Colcord, father of Charles R. Colcord, who became Oklahoma City's first chief of police in 1890. Although only nineteen years old, Charles was the range boss. Texas cattle were known to carry tick-borne disease. It became a major problem, so much so that Kansas outlawed Texas longhorns from parts of the state. They feared that the tick-borne disease would infest other herds (Kansas bred) and wipe them out. To get around this problem, Colcord and his business partners built large holding pens outside Caldwell, just inside the Indian Territory. The loading point for the railway and cattle was technically not in Kansas. By doing so, they skirted the law, and the cattle came in droves. Taking a break from ranching, Bill tried his luck gold prospecting; he was soon back to ranching.

Bill and five other men were assigned the task of bringing up a herd of horses from Mexico. Outside and south of Laredo, Texas, the men were ambushed by bandits. Taken by surprise, four of the men were killed almost instantly; the last two, Fossett and co-worker Bud Milnee, had the good fortune to dive off their horses and sought cover quickly. Well armed, the two fought a gallant battle. Bill claimed five kills; he later said his partner "got his share" as well. At any rate, the two, as expert shots, chased away the remaining bandits. They collected all but two horses and buried their dead companions before heading back to the ranch. This was not the first time Bill dealt with death. On one of his early cattle drives, while Bill and the crew slept, a handful of men snuck in and stole horses and mules, then headed toward Kansas to sell off their loot. The drovers caught up with the bandits, retrieved their property, and left those men swinging in the cotton trees. Charles Colcord recalled another incident in later years:

"I had roped a big mare, put on the hackamore, and then turned the rope over to [Jesse] McCartney to take her out of the corral. He got outside of the gate, and the boys ran the mare through....The mare came out with such a terrible rush that it jerked him off his feet, and he fell flat, face down in the dust, with the mare and the rope gone. Of course, everybody was laughing. When he got up he was the angriest man you ever saw. He grabbed a broken bar from the gate four or five feet long and rushed at me. I saw he was enraged! I waited until he got almost up to me, then drew my six-shooter and fired, but as I leveled my gun, Bill Fossett ran between us and knocked my gun up and took the bullet in his hand....Fossett has the mark of that bullet on his hand today."

By late 1881, when "hell was in session," Bill Fossett was known as a quiet, respectful man who was extremely handy with both rifle and revolver. Although his friends spoke of him as being kind and helpful, a man with a big heart, Bill would become known as "Wild Bill" Fossett. After the Talbot Raid Bill moved to Kingman, Kansas, where he stood tall as the town marshal and remained as marshal until 1887. Kingman's location was not far from Dodge City, southeast of it. It was never a cow town. In Tennessee author Jim Fulbright, in his book, said that W. D. "Bill" Fossett was "legendary among his peers in the Old West." Although Bill may not have achieved legendary status, he ran with those who did—men such as the Three Guardsmen of Oklahoma (Heck Thomas, Bill Tilghman, and Chris Madsen), as well as Jim Masterson, C. R. Colcord, Sam Bartell, Frank Canton, John Hubatka, and Jack Love, to name a few; all were great lawmen in their time.

April 22, 1889, Bill Fossett was among the thousands lined up for the largest land rush in this country's history. In Oklahoma Territory, just west of Kingfisher Station, Bill lined up, ready for the starter revolver to fire and set off the start of the land rush. This was the first land rush into the "Unassigned Lands," which includes today's counties of Cleveland, Canadian, Kingfisher, Logan, Oklahoma, and Payne. Fifty thousand people were lined up that historical day. Bill's claim was a section of land that would soon be located within the township of Kingfisher, a town that sprung up overnight with an instant population of fifteen thousand souls!

Oklahoma Land Rush, April 21, 1898 some where near Kingfisher. Public domain photograph.

Bill's claim was the first claim filed in Kingfisher. As he put it, as reported in the Jim Fulbright biography *W. D. reported in the Jim Fulbright biography's*, "I had been so familiar with all the Oklahoma country and the trails that I made the run for the hundred and sixty acres that the land office was located on at Kingfisher...I beat them all...."

The location of Bill's claim was the northwest corner of section fifteen, which was situated 250 yards west of the land office. The town itself would be built on the south half of this section. It caused a stir. Although he had filed his claim properly, there were those who wanted that section of land and were extremely vocal. They claimed he jumped the gun (not that he was a "Sooner") the day of the land rush. The truth of it—from the files (file 10) at the Indian Archives located within the Oklahoma Archives, Oklahoma City—was that Fossett, after a day and a half of a hard ride, made it to the starting point just "minutes" before the land rush started. It was recorded that he was legally registered and lined up in a position just west of Kingfisher Station. His horse was considered one of the fastest in the territory. With the firing of the guns, the race was on. Bill's horse outdistanced them all.

The people felt, if anything, that section fifteen should have been offered as town lots, not as a 160-acre claim. Bill, fed up, drew a line in the dirt. Holding his rifle, he announced to the crowd that he would shoot anyone who stepped over that line. The crowd was over one hundred strong; Bill had no chance, but he stood there facing them, not moving an inch. Friend and eyewitness Joe Grimes, who later served as a Deputy U.S. Marshal, said, "Bill Fossett was the coolest headed man I ever saw...." Bill stood there while the people yelled, screamed, and threatened him. His friend went on to say that Bill was "white as a ghost," but Fossett never batted an eye or flinched. The land office manager intervened. He persuaded Bill to go with him to the office. He did so, and the crowd dispersed.

Fossett was the first to stake a claim and the first in the territory to file a lawsuit in defense of a claim. It took time, but he won his case. When the land office closed down, a U.S. Post Office was built in its place. One can only assume that Bill Fossett made an excellent return on those acres. Meanwhile, Bill built a livery stable on Main Street and ran a hog farm nearby.

He had a relationship with the Rock Island Railroad, having first worked as a laborer after he resigned his marshal position at Kingman, a railroad town not far from Caldwell. He worked as town marshal from 1883 to 1887. He remained with the railroad part-time. After he staked his claim, Bill renewed his affiliation with the railroad, resuming his part-time detective work.

*****

Fall 1889, the Rock Island Railroad extended from Caldwell south to Kingfisher. Bill started working full-time as a special agent for the railroad. His area of responsibility was from the Missouri River west. An article from the *Kingfisher Times* of October 17, 1929, told this story as recalled by Bill Fossett. On April 9 Bill was on the Night Express Train No.1, heading south from Caldwell with a friend, Lew Humprheys (could be a misspelling of Humphrey). They were headed home from an evening together in Caldwell, having taken the train there for a nice dinner at the Harvey House. (There were no good dinner houses in the territory). Leaving Caldwell, they entered Oklahoma. Their first stop was approximately twenty-five miles into the territory, at Pond Creek Station. The train took on water and a couple of passengers. Fossett and Humprheys were in the smoker car, enjoying themselves, and were joined by the conductor, Joe Reed. They rolled past the townsite of Round Pond three miles farther south. Sometime near 9:30 p.m. the train abruptly braked. Two shots were fired outside the train on the west side. A porter in the smoker ran out onto the front platform, more shots were fired, and the porter never reentered the car. Fossett realized a train holdup was unfolding. He was not carrying his gun. He turned to Reed, asking if he carried one; the man replied by handing Bill a small revolver, perhaps a pocket pistol. Taking Reed's gun, Bill went outside to investigate. A fire was burning on the tracks, actually within the train tracks. The train had stopped and blocked the trail that crossed over. Two men had boarded the train at Pond Creek Station. They were Bob Hughes and Jim Borland. At the sight of the fire, a signal, the men entered the engine cab, holding the operators, the engineer, and the fireman at bay with drawn guns. Bill was on the move during all of this. He was able to secure a shotgun from a train guard; meanwhile, shooting continued. On the west side one of the bandits was firing into the windows to discourage the passengers from interfering. Yet a passenger took aim and fired back at the gunman. He dropped and died on the spot. He fell on his back, his gun in hand, his arm extended. With the killing of the outlaw and with Bill and a train guard holding their own, the rest of the gang of outlaws hurried off the train. They could see the townspeople and local law enforcement coming down the tracks from of Round Pond. A running gunfight then prevailed as the outlaws quickly mounted their horses and flee. The dead man was Bob Hughes.

There was a man on board by the name of Hill who caught Bill's eye. A few days later in town Bill instructed one of his men to follow Mr. Hill. Two days or so later Bill took over trailing Hill. He followed him to a remote dugout in a big ravine. He headed back to town for help. The only trusted man he could find was his fifteen-year-old son. They secured guns and loads of ammo; father and son headed back to that ravine, but the outlaw was not to be found. Bill's son, Lew, stood guard as his father entered the dugout. Bill found enough evidence, including a letter, to link Hill with the outlaws and the killings that occurred on the Night Express Train No.1. As the legendary deputy marshals known as the Three Guardsmen were looking for the Dalton Gang, based on false information, Fossett and his former deputy from Caldwell, Bedford Woods, remained in El Reno. They spotted Hill and a few other men. Three men were quickly arrested. The first two men arrested were delivered to the jail by Deputy Woods. Good timing prevailed. Woods returned, in the nick of time, to take the third arrestee, Nate Silvey (often spelled Silva), off Bill's hands, for Bill had just spotted Hill. Woods hurried Silvey to jail; Bill went after Hill. Hill fired several shots at Fossett as he ran to his horse. Bill, running after, shot and killed Hill's horse. Citizens were running for cover. Having shot Hill's horse Fossett once more took aim. One shot rang out; Hill was wounded. The battle was over. Hill, in custody along with his three companions, was taken to Pond Creek Station to stand trial. It turns out that Felix Young was Hill's actual name. Both he and Nate Silvey were known outlaws and extremely dangerous. Of the four outlaw leaders only Jim Borland escaped. He changed his ways somewhat and became a deputy marshal. Bitter over the botched train robbery, Borland did his best to get even with Fossett. In 1901 Borland faced off against Fossett. Another man, a citizen whom Borland was using to get at Fossett, actually shot Jim. Needless to say, Borland died in the street that day.

Why was Bill Fossett never hired as a Deputy United States Marshal? The railroads paid better and allowed him to answer to few. Fossett was well-known within the marshal ranks, his handling of the train robbery and its outcome put him on the map as a major lawman. In time the Marshals Service would come knocking.

The following year Fossett led a posse that flushed out the persistent Zip Wyatt and his partner, Ike Black. Wyatt's other alias was Dick Yeager; his real name was Nathaniel Ellsworth Wyatt. These two daredevils robbed and killed and were often blamed for others' misdeeds. It was said that they joined the Dalton-Doolittle Gang, but they did not. The reward on Wyatt was up to $5,000. More than once the two were surrounded, wounded, and even captured, yet managed to escape and slither away. Wyatt had been wounded multiple times, but he healed quickly. But there comes the day when luck runs out. Bill and his posse tracked them down and flushed the pair into open ground. During an exchange Ike Black was shot in the head, dying on the spot. Wyatt escaped, but Bill knew where he was headed. Fossett led his posse to the home of Zip's lady friend. Other posses were about as well; they were closing in from all sides, hiding and waiting. Fossett's men found Zip asleep in a cornfield near the homestead. Two sheriff's deputies, members of the posses, aimed their rifles at Wyatt. Awakened by the deputies, Wyatt reached for his gun. The two deputies cut loose with theirs. Wyatt was hit twice, one shot from each deputy, in the stomach area. Wounded he was taken to Enid, there the doctors believed that Zip Wyatt had but a few days to live. He lived another month in great pain, but on September 6, 1895, Zip Wyatt succumbed to death due to lead poisoning. For his efforts and contribution to the capture of Wyatt and Black, Bill Fossett was promoted to chief special agent of all the lines of the Rock Island Railroad west of the Missouri River.

Baggage theft was out of control on the Rock Island. Bill rigged an alarm system that stopped a clock when a bag was opened and its contents stolen. He would check the clock and use the time that it stopped to determine which of the employees would have been working in that area of the train. The thieving stopped as the employees responsible were arrested.

*****

November 8, 1897, William D. "Bill" Fossett was appointed Chief Deputy United States Marshal for the Oklahoma Territory. His newly appointed boss was Marshal Canada Thompson. Thompson held that position from October 25, 1897, until January 13, 1902, when he retired due to ill health. Marshal Thompson was a master politician with strong connections to the Rock Island Railroad. It was no surprise that Bill Fossett would step in as his chief deputy; Bill was well respected by the deputies.

Deputies had learned of the general location of "Little Dick" West, the last member of Bill Doolin's gang. This was April 7, 1898. Deputy Marshal Heck Thomas, one of the Three Guardsmen of Oklahoma, informed his boss, Fossett. Bill organized a posse comprised of himself, Heck Thomas and son Albert, Bill Tilghman, Frank Rinehart, and Ben Miller. The following day the posse approached a farmhouse not far from Guthrie. It was early morning, still dark but turning light quickly. Fossett and Rinehart were together, the other men most likely taking positions around the farmhouse, concealing themselves. Standing by a shed attached to the barn was Dick West. The men spotted each other at about the same time. West fired two shots at Fossett and Rinehart, then took off running. The shots barely missed the two marshals. They returned fire, also missing their target. West stopped and spun, taking aim and firing once more. He missed. Running for his horse and attempting to reload at the same time, he stumbled and fell, then attempted to get up. Bill had him in his sights. Fossett did not miss; the bullet struck West on his left side, exiting below the right shoulder blade. Meanwhile, Rinehart, using a shotgun, shot but missed; the distance was too great. Cautiously they approached West. By the time the two deputies reached him, he was dead. They found Dick's horse; it was a beauty, pure white. Bill was able to acquire the horse as a present for his daughter, Mamie.

Bill served as chief deputy marshal until the retirement of Canada Thompson. In

March 1902 Fossett was appointed marshal of the Oklahoma Territory by President Teddy Roosevelt and served in that position until his term ran out in February of 1906. With the appointment of the new marshal Bill went back to his old position as chief deputy marshal. He had also worked as the town marshal for Kingfisher. In 1921 Bill became a special plainclothesman for Oklahoma City. This same year, he was appointed deputy marshal for the western district. It was March 21, 1940, when Bill Fossett died. He had fallen ill a few weeks earlier. He lived a good part of his life in Kingfisher and was buried in the Kingfisher Cemetery.

*****

From, in part, an article posted in the *Kingfisher Free Press* on March 18, 1940. In Bill's own words, published three days prior to his death:

W. D. "BILL" FOSSETT'S OWN STORY

"I have been asked why, in a terrain like that of Oklahoma notorious criminals roamed at liberty for years without apprehension. Of course, portions of the state, notable in the west, are rough and broken: there are large areas of dense black jack pines, or deep cedar bend canyons. Settlers sheltered the bandits, fearing reprisals if they should give information to the officers. But the main reason for the criminals' immunity lay in the fact that the deputy marshals did not desire to lose those lucrative fees. All the outlaws understood this condition thoroughly, and felt fairly safe so long as they did not flaunt their lawlessness needlessly under the very eyes of the marshals.

Scores of ex-cowboys and criminals took advantage of the situation to secure appointments, in which they could rob the government by padding accounts. It would be unjust and untrue to brand all early deputies with this stigma. There were many conscientious deputies who made every effort to apprehend the law violators. Nevertheless, I challenge anyone with knowledge of early Oklahoma history to name half a dozen of the earlier outlaws who had not previously been cowboys or deputy marshals of the United States of early [times who] felt fairly safe so long as they did not flaunt their lawlessness was more profitable—if not quite so safe."

These deputies could work both sides of the road without danger of violating a statute of the United States or of losing reputation, except amen the better-informed citizenry.

Many Settlers Abused

"One of the most frequent, most lucrative and most dastardly abuses practiced by them was made possible by a federal law that forbade the cutting of green timber on government land. In those days, the southwestern portion of Oklahoma was covered with dense areas of mesquite. Small cedars filled the deep canyons. For the benefit of those who have not seen mesquite, it is liken it to a discarded, deserted peach orchard, scrubby and useless. Most of the wood is underground. It makes good firewood, but that is about all. Some of the cedars were large enough for the manufacture of fence posts.

The poor settlers, reduced to extremity by the severity of unplowed wilderness, would cut and haul a load of posts a hundred miles, perhaps to earn the wherewithal to buy a few meager grocery supplies and thus feed their starving families. It became a favorite means of graft among these "brave" deputy marshals of that undesirable type I have described to swoop down upon some miserable homesteader, hauling a load of ill-shaped fence posts or firewood to market, arrest him, take him before a United States commissioner and have him bound over to the next term of court.

The nearest commissioner was in Wichita, from 300 to 400 miles distant; while the federal court, presided over by the famous hanging jurist—Judge Parker—was at Fort Smith, Ark. Each mile that the homesteader traveled to commissioner or court—often driving his own skinny team—and paying his own subsistence—added to the deputy's fee."

Charges Mounted Fast

"The commissioner would charge his fees to the government; the deputy would charge his arrest fee, his mileage fee, transportation for himself and prisoners, subsistence and sometimes the routine fees for guards to keep the "outlaw farmer" from escaping. There have been well-authenticated instances when a deputy had run his account to $700 or $800 in a few days' time by gathering 40 or 50 homesteaders —and with very little legitimate expense.

When I was appointed United States Marshal for Oklahoma, I explained to the department of Justice that mesquite was detrimental to the land and thus won leniency in the attitude of the department. I cut the marshal's force from 150 men to 15 and found that I had plenty of officers to conduct the legitimate business of the territory. Never during my nine years as chief deputy and United States marshal did I permit the arrest of a homesteader for cutting green timber. I did not feel that the government should penalize pioneer heroism, regardless of any statute."

Bill Fossett was under attack by the newspapers when he was first appointed Chief Deputy U.S. Marshal for the above graft by the deputies and unfair prosecution of poor homesteaders, yet he had never served in the Marshals Service until he was appointed chief deputy in 1897. Bill had always gone after, as he put it, the "big fish." He cut out the graft when he became the marshal of Oklahoma Territory in 1902. He reduced the force of deputies from 150 men to 15, all handpicked—a job well-done, by anyone's standard. In the end the folks of Kingfisher called him "Uncle Bill" as an elder, ruthless to the outlaws and kind to all others. Bill led a dangerous but fulfilling life. When he passed away in 1940, he was nearly eighty-eight years old.

Vol.2. A Fraternity of Gunslingers

Lady Outlaws and Women of The Law

Information on the various women outlaws and law-women is lean. This chapter will encompass seven—five criminals and two Deputy U.S. Marshals. We start first with the Rose of Cimarron.

Lady Outlaws and Women of the Law

Rose Dunn (1879-1955)

Rose Dunn (1879–1955)

    The Rose of Cimarron, whose real name was Rose Dunn, was a teenager when she entered the world of outlawing. She was born near Ingalls, Oklahoma, in 1879; the actual date of her birth is in question. Rose was pretty, with a calm, quieting demeanor, and was formally educated at a convent in Wichita, Kansas, although her family was dirt poor. There is no evidence as to how the family scraped the money together for her education. She may have had a benefactor; more likely, her parents were determined to provide Rose a head start in life. Besides her parents, she had two brothers. The family was close-knit. By the time she was twelve, her brothers had become "minor" outlaws. It was due to her brothers' influence that she took to the other side of the law; they were her mentors. She was an accomplished rider, roped well, and was handy with guns.

One day the brothers introduced her to George Newcomb, better known as "Bittercreek" Newcomb, a member of the outlaw gang known as the Dalton Gang. She was now fourteen years old and hopelessly in love with twenty-eight-year-old Bittercreek.

The gang participated in the Adair, Oklahoma train robbery of July 1892. It was a botched robbery. Two guards and two citizens, both doctors, were wounded, one fatally. Historians claim that over two hundred rounds were fired between the train guards and the gang. The two doctors were hit by stray bullets; one passed away the following morning. After the shooting, three men were relieved of the gang affiliation. Newcomb was told that he was too wild for the Dalton brothers' taste. The other two were Bill Doolin and Charlie Pierce, who were too quick to use their weapons. The Daltons broke away; the Doolin Gang was formed with Pierce and Newcomb as charter members. Doolin, Pierce, and Newcomb would rise to the highest ranks of outlawing; their gang would soon be known as the Wild Bunch. Three months later, on October 5, the Daltons attempted to rob two banks at once in Coffeyville, Kansas. All but one, Emmett Dalton, were shot down in the street; the Dalton Gang no longer existed. Emmett was shot twenty-three times, but survived. After fourteen years in prison he moved to Hollywood, worked as an actor, and wrote two books. He died in California in 1937 at the age of sixty-six. Brother Bill did not participate in the Coffeyville raid. He would join the Doolin Gang as co-leader to Bill Doolin. There were initially two names for this gang: the Doolin Dalton Gang, and the Oklahombres; as mentioned, they became better known as the Wild Bunch.

When Doolin started up the Wild Bunch, it seemed appropriate to use "wild" in honor of Bittercreek. The town of Ingalls, Oklahoma, was their headquarters—a little town off the beaten path. The relationship between Rose and Bittercreek remained strong. Her brothers took a turn in their lives. They realized that outlawing was not the way to go, but bounty hunting was. They called themselves the Dunn Brothers while pursuing wanted criminals.

After each robbery the newly formed gang disappeared, leaving the law at odds in trying to locate them. Their hideout was discovered. The people of Ingalls knew that this group of men were outlaws, but they always protected them by remaining silent. Loaded with lots of money, the gang would spend it. The merchants, the saloon keeps, the hotels and restaurants—all benefitted. For their loyalty and silence the gang was respectful of Ingalls's citizens. September 1, 1893, deputy marshals and other posse members attempted to enter Ingalls, under canvas covers in two wagon beds. It did not work. Gang member Tom "Arkansas" Jones happened to be looking out of his hotel room when he noticed suspicious activity. As the two wagonloads of men rode in, he opened fire—and the battle began. (For details on the Battle of Ingalls, see the chapter on James "Jim" Masterson in volume one.)

The Rose of Cimarron legend started at this battle. Her lover, "Bittercreek" Newcomb, wounded in the shootout, lay in the middle of the street. She grabbed two ammunition belts and a Winchester and proceeded to run through a rain of gunfire, from the Pierce Hotel to her man. Although badly wounded, Newcomb reloaded his revolvers while Rose held off the marshals with the Winchester. In the chaos, due to her efforts, Bittercreek escaped. From this time on, songs were written of her. She became romanticized by legend. The reality is that Newcomb was slightly wounded. The deputies reported that at most Newcomb was able to get off two shots before fleeing with fellow Wild Bunch member Charley Pierce. Pierce was also wounded, or believed to have been so, by the law officials. Once the gang got away, they headed to another hideout near Norman, Oklahoma. Rose was never arrested for taking part in the shootout, for she did not. She made it to the hideout, where she nursed the wounded men back to health. Three lawmen died during the shootout, three outlaws were wounded, and one—Tom "Arkansas" Jones—was captured by Deputy Jim Masterson.

Newcomb had a bounty on his head of $5,000. Rose aided her man by traveling with him. She would interface with the towns to purchase supplies in addition to cooking for and servicing Newcomb. She was well liked and respected by the gang members; like big brothers, they were protective of Rose. Rose was at the family farm on May 2, 1895; Newcomb and his buddy Charlie Pierce went to visit her. The two men rode up and dismounted in front of the home. As they did so, Rose's brothers, the two bounty hunters, were lurking inside the house. As the two outlaws dismounted, the bounty hunters surprised them, immediately opening fire. In a hail of bullets Newcomb and Pierce were dead. The next day, the bodies were loaded in the back of a wagon and brought to town. The boys wanted the bounty. Newcomb, thought dead, was not. As the wagon headed to town, he moaned, requesting water. One of the brothers turned and shot the man one more time—now he was dead. Not aware of her brothers' intentions prior to the killings, Rose was, nonetheless, accused of aiding her brothers. Though she always denied this and her brothers backed her claim, this denial did not help; the suspicion never went away. Her life with the Wild Bunch became legendary. Songs were sung and stories were told, even though that lifestyle was short. Later she married a local politician, Charles Albert Noble, and lived out her life in respectability. Rose Dunn, the Rose of Cimarron, was a living legend. She died at the age of seventy-six in the little town of Salkum, Washington, in 1955.

*****

 Cattle Annie (1879-1978) and Little Britches (1879-?)

Cattle Annie and Little Britches

I write of these two young women in the same subchapter because they worked as a pair; these two were connected to the Wild Bunch. Anna McDoulet, who would later be known as Cattle Annie, was born in 1879 to James C. and Rebekah McDoulet of Lawrence County, Kansas. The third child of eight and one of two sisters, Annie helped the family by working as a dishwasher and, on occasion, did domestic work. Annie's education was limited. When she was twelve, the family moved to the Cherokee Nation. Her formal education was at the mission school. She was schooled during the day and worked at night. Restless, the family made another move, this time to the Otoe Reservation near Skiatook, now a suburb of Tulsa. Annie's life would soon take a turn toward life as an outlaw.

Little Britches, whose real name was Jennie Stevenson, was also born in 1879. Her parents were Daniel and Lucy Stevenson of Barton County, Missouri. They were farmers—hard-working, honest people. When Jennie was eight, in 1887, the family moved west to Seneca, near the Missouri border; a few years later they moved to the Creek Nation. Fifteen years old, she longed for the stories of the Doolin Gang. She was impressed by their daring deeds as outlaws. Jennie began to dress in men's clothing. How romantic it would be to be an outlaw and tie up with the Doolin Gang. She left her family and rode off in search of the gang. The first night out she lost her horse. She managed to get to a neighbor's farmhouse and was returned to her parents. Some say members of the gang found her and took her to the neighbor's homestead. The truth be told, her parents were not please. Jennie's friends made fun of her. Humiliated, Jennie ran off with a horse dealer,

Benjamin Midkiff, a deaf-mute. They married and established a home in Perry. She must have taken a liking to men, for when her husband was away, she "entertained." Catching her in the act, her husband promptly returned her to her parents. At sixteen she remarried. Her husband was Robert Stephens. He left the marriage within six months. Free and on her own, Jennie returned to her quest to be an outlaw. She met Anna McDoulet at a dance, and they quickly became close friends. At another dance Anna was introduced to George "Red Buck" Waightman. When she found out that he was a member of the Wild Bunch, it sent her into a tizzy; she immediately fell in love and dropped her current boyfriend. She and Jennie Stevens were introduced to the gang, who welcomed them with open arms. The ladies loved to listen to the stories of the gang. They absorbed every detail. They became known as Cattle Annie and Little Britches. After several months with the gang the two women armed themselves with Colt .45s. They held jobs in town during the day, but at night they dressed as men to work their other trade as petty criminals. Their notoriety was well publicized. They stole horses and sold whiskey to the Indians. Supplying whiskey was a big deal. The federal government considered selling whiskey to the natives a major offense; the marshals were proactive when it came to hunting down these criminals. Horse stealing was equally frowned upon. The two ladies worked together most of the time. They were cagey, with a bent for escaping the law. Because the women used aliases and dressed as men, their true identities were unknown. This allowed them to come and go as they pleased. It also gave an edge to the Wild Bunch; the ladies could get privileged information and warn the gang of any posse about.

    August 1895, Sheriff Frank Lake in Pawnee, Oklahoma, finally arrested one of the girls, Little Britches. A kind man, he took her to dinner instead of keeping her locked in a cell. They were about done eating when Jennie jumped up and ran out the back door. By the time Sheriff Lake reacted, she had stolen a horse, vanishing into the night. Unfortunately for her the horse she stole belonged to a legendary lawman, Deputy U.S. Marshal Frank Canton. A posse of two deputy marshals, Bill Tilghman and Steve Burke, were assigned to track Little Britches. Not far from Pawnee they located both women inside a house. As the men approached the home, shots rang out. The women decided a shootout was in order for their escape. They fired several shots toward the lawmen, then made a quick run to the back of the house. Their impromptu plan was to go out a back window. Little Britches was the first one out. She jumped on Marshal Canton's horse, whipping it to a full gallop. Cattle Annie was half out when Marshal Burke grabbed her from behind and quickly arrested her. Jennie, on the other hand, was a different story. She did her best to escape, but Marshal Tilghman, a horse fancier, was riding one of the fastest in the territory. He caught up, was within sight, and was gaining on her when Little Britches, using her rifle, shot at Tilghman over her shoulder. She fired several times, missing her mark. Not a fool, Bill Tilghman decided to bring her down. Tilghman shot the horse from underneath her. She crashed to the ground. Bill dismounted, ran up to the petite gal, and had to wrestle her to submission. She tried to clear her pistol from its holster but failed to do so. Her last effort was to physically attack the marshal. This maneuver failed as well.

The capture of these two famous female outlaws is part legend. The newspapers credit three men with the capture, Deputy Marshals Frank Canton and Steve Burke and Sheriff Frank Lake. This seems a more likely posse. Sheriff Lake allowed Little Britches to escape, and Frank Canton wanted his horse back. Although they may have been friends with the Wild Bunch, the ladies were never part of the gang. They knew them, they were lookouts and alerted the gang when the law was about, but they were never members by any stretch of the imagination. Regardless of their affiliation status, the two women's days of outlawing were over. In court Jennie was demure; she said little. Anna spoke with defiance; she confessed to have been rightly raised, yet declared she was past redemption and would, when released, resume her outlawing. Jennie received a two-year sentence in a reformatory prison in Sherborn, Massachusetts. She was released in October 1896 after serving one year; she returned to her family. Eventually she married, settled down in Tulsa, and raised a family. Anna was sentenced to a reform school in South Framingham, Massachusetts, and was released on April 18, 1898. She did not return to her home but stayed in Massachusetts, working for Mrs. Mary Daniels of Sherborn as a domestic. Eventually Anna returned to Oklahoma. She married in March 1901, had two children, was divorced by October 1909, and then joined the Miller Brothers 101 Wild West Show. She eventually remarried and lived a quiet life in Oklahoma City. She passed away on November 7, 1978.

Were these two dangerous criminals? No. Petty thieves would be a better description. Dangerous, yes—they could shoot as well as any man. Did they drink, swear, and have sex with members of the Wild Bunch? Most likely, in regards to the swearing and drinking. The sex? For sure, but nothing was recorded, nor would they have gone about bragging of having done so.

*****

Pearl Hart (1871- 1955?)

Both Pearl's age and date of birth are in question. She was born on November 13, 1876 and died in December 1955 as stated on her tombstone, yet 1871 as a birthdate is a better fit. Many historians say she died as early as 1951, while others claim she lived until 1960. Regardless, this lady robbed stagecoaches.

Pearl was born Pearl Taylor in Ontario, Canada. She was petite. Fully grown, she stood five feet. Her parents were religious and well-to-do; her father was a civil engineer. They left Canada for Toledo, Ohio, in 1878. By sixteen she was attending a boarding school. At seventeen she met and married Frank Hart. She gave birth to two children, a boy and a girl. Tired of her life with an abuser of a husband, she left him and headed west to Trinidad, Colorado. She was un-happy, depressed and attempted to commit suicide. She would also try to reconnect with her husband several times over the ensuing years. At twenty-two she met a new man, Dan Bandman, a dance hall piano player. They became a common-law couple living together in Phoenix, Arizona Territory. The Spanish-American War broke out in 1889; Dan enlisted. It was about this time that Pearl sent her children to live with their grandparents. In 1899 Pearl moved to Globe, Arizona, and met a new man, Joe Boot. Joe was a drifter, not working much, and not interested in doing so. Pearl worked as a singer and cook. There were reports that she also ran a tent brothel, comprised of herself and one other woman. Continually short of money, the couple decided to rob a stagecoach. Pearl was dressed up in men's clothing when she and Joe stopped a coach. Hart was armed with a .38, while Boot had a Colt .45. It was May 30, 1899, at a watering point near Cane Springs Canyon, about thirty miles southeast of Globe. The stage was headed in the direction of Florence, located northeast of Globe. The two towns are fifty-four miles apart. It was wide open country, and would be easy "pickens," they reckoned. The robbery was successful. They took over $400 and three guns, in addition to one passenger's pocket watch, then made their escape. Before doing so, Pearl had some compassion for the passengers; she gave each a dollar so they could eat when they reached Florence. After the two rode off, the stage driver unhitched one of the horses and made it back to Globe to alert the sheriff. The couple did their best to confuse any posse coming their way. Their route was zigzagged and circuitous in nature. A posse was hot on their trail. Finally, six days after the robbery, the posse caught up with the pair. Joe Boot remained in Florence, Arizona, to await trial. Pearl was moved to Tucson due to a lack of proper facilities to house female prisoners. Women criminals were a rarity; no woman had ever robbed a coach. Local and national newspapers created a frenzy.

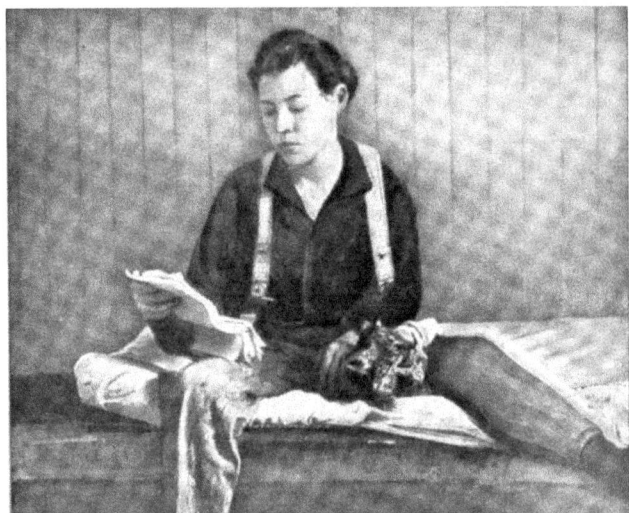

Prisoner No.1559, Hart at Yuma Territorial Prison, 1871

While behind bars, awaiting trial, she was interviewed and photographed continually by the press. Pearl Hart, the outlaw, developed a nickname—the Bandit Queen.

Pearl was able to break through the lath-and-plaster jail-cell wall, creating an eighteen-inch opening through which she escaped. She made it to Deming, New Mexico, before she was captured. She had two weeks of freedom. Her day in court arrived. Pearl pleaded with the jury to let her go free; she only robbed to get money to aid her sickly mother, she said. The jury fell for it; both she and Joe were found not guilty. The couple was rearrested before they could leave the courtroom. This time they were charged with tampering with the United States mail and were found guilty. Pearl received a five-year sentence, while Joe Boot received a whopping thirty years. Off they went to Yuma Territorial Prison. The temperatures in the area are extreme, especially during the summer months. Its first prisoner arrived on July 1, 1876, and its last left the prison in 1909. Of the 3,069 prisoners housed there, only 29 were women. Pearl Hart was one, an oddity. Boot served a little less than two years before he escaped, never to be seen or heard of again. He had become a trustee and was driving a wagon for the prison to bring supplies to the chain gangs when he executed his escape. Pearl was the only female incarcerated. The warden provided her with a mountainside cell that included a small yard. The cell was considered oversized, eight feet by ten. He allowed reporters and others to visit her. One can only imagine the attention she received back then. Pearl used her womanly powers to better benefit her position by playing the guards and trustees against each other. In December 1902 the governor pardoned Hart. The reason is unclear. It is said that she became pregnant, but there is no real evidence to prove such, no record of a child, which would have been her third. Her incarceration lasted almost two and half years. Upon her release she moved to Kansas City, Missouri. Pearl worked for a short time for Buffalo Bill's Wild West Show, under an alias. She continued to live her life under assumed names. It's difficult to pinpoint her death and its location. There are different claims as to where she is buried. Whether she lived to be eighty-four or eighty-nine, Pearl Hart's life as an outlaw was short, her fame was great, and her life was difficult, yet exciting at times. She used sex to get her way and to make money from time to time. The men she picked as mates were not the best influence. Like the other lady gunslingers, once caught and imprisoned, she seemed to avoid her past and lived a normal life.

Belle Starr (1848-1889)

The outlaw Belle Starr's actual name was Myra Maybelle Shirley. She answered to May. She was born on February 5, 1848, in Carthage, Missouri, and died two days shy of her forty-first birthday, on February 3, 1889.

An interesting side note—her mother, Eliza, is a Hatfield, of the famed Hatfield-McCoy feud. Although smoldering as early as 1865, this feud did not flare up until 1882. By then Eliza, her husband, and May were long gone from the West Virgina-Kentucky area.

Early in the Civil War Carthage was attacked by the Confederacy. May and her family moved to Sycene, Texas, just prior to the burning of Carthage. One brother was killed during the Carthage ordeal.

May married Jim Reed, a childhood sweetheart, in 1866 and gave birth to her first child, Rosie Lee (nicknamed Pearl), two years later. Members of her family thought that the father of her first child was Cole Younger, a man she also knew during her childhood. In fact, she was friends with all the Younger brothers and through them met Frank and Jesse James. May and Jim's second child was born in 1871; this time, for certain, the father was Jim Reed. The child was born in California.

Reed tried his hand at farming but was no farmer. He and May became friends of the Starr family. The Starrs were Cherokees, well-known for their horse abilities, whiskey, thievery, and cattle rustling. Back in Texas—it was now 1874—a warrant was issued for the arrest of Reed for stagecoach robbery. Before he was located, Belle's husband was shot and killed in Paris, Texas, by a member of his own gang over some petty argument. On her own, she left Texas for Indian Territory. There she met and moved in with Sam Starr. Sam, much like Jim Reed, thought being a criminal was more profitable than gainful employment. It was around this time that Maybelle became known as Belle Starr. For the next nine years the Starrs avoided arrest. Belle gained a reputation and the nickname Bandit Queen.

Belle had a strong sense of style, which contributed greatly to her legend. Like other frontier women mentioned in this book, she was a crack shot. She dressed in black velvet riding clothes and rode sidesaddle. In 1883 the law arrested her and her common-law husband, Sam, for horse theft. Both were sentenced to five months in the Detroit federal prison. When their term was up, the couple headed back to a life of crime. In the meantime, Belle and Sam's home was open for friends to use as their headquarters. Frank and Jesse James hid out there; the Youngers were no strangers. Belle participated in cattle and horse thievery in the Dallas, Texas area. Her reputation was cemented; her lifestyle would never change. In 1886 her man was involved in a gunfight with an "old enemy" and was killed.

Belle wasted no time in finding a third companion—a Creek Indian named Jim July, an outlaw who was fifteen years her junior. In 1889 July was arrested for robbery and summoned to Fort Smith, Arkansas, to face charges. Belle accompanied Jim partway, deciding that it would be in her best interest to not venture to Fort Smith. On her way home someone in hiding shot Belle in the back with a shotgun. As she lay on the ground, the shooter walked up and shot Belle in the face. She lay dead with half of her face gone. Her lover, Jim July, believed the murderer was a neighbor, Edger A. Watson, whom Belle had threatened to turn in to the authorities for a murder he had committed in Florida. A grand jury was convened in Fort Smith. There was no evidence to prove Edger's guilt; the man was released. Mr. Watson left the area posthaste and for good.

In an 1889 article, the editor of the *Fort Smith Elevator* wrote:

> "…from Eufala [sic], Indian Territory, that Belle Starr was killed there Sunday night. Belle was the wife of Cole Younger. Belle Starr was the most desperate woman that ever figured on the borders. She married Cole Younger directly after the war, but left him and joined a band of outlaws that operated in the Indian Territory. She had been arrested for murder and robbery a score of times, but always managed to escape."

Newspapers all over the country picked up the story and reprinted it, including the *New York Times*. Dime novels, misinformation, and movies have glorified this lady, the Bandit Queen. In reality she was not much of a bandit. She did some horse thievery (for which she served five months in jail) and allowed real gangsters to use her home as a hideout. Knowing the Younger Gang and James Gang as intimately as she did was her claim to fame. Belle was never married to Cole; this is part of her legend. Belle Starr went down in western folklore more for whom she knew than for what she did.

Mamie Fossett—United States Deputy Marshal (1879-1926?) and
Deputy U.S. Marshal Sara Burche

It is difficult to locate much information on female deputy marshals.

There is little information on the lady marshals. Mamie and her partner, Sara M. Burche, worked as field agents, for a short period of time. Their contribution to frontier law is enormous, and a credit to their gender. These ladies faced the unruly, and harsh conditions in the early ninetieth century. Florence M. Miller was the first woman to be appointed a deputy marshal. It is odd that so little about these remarkable law enforcement officers exists today in comparison to the amount of information available about the female criminals.

Mamie was the daughter of Bill Fossett, from Bill's from Bill's first wife. She and her dad were inseparable. From the beginning, Bill, a great horseman, taught his daughter how to ride. He also instructed Mamie in the fine art of gunmanship. She rode like a man and became an excellent "markswoman," equally confident with both rifle and handgun.

Her parents divorced when she was seven. At fourteen Mamie's mother passed away. From that point on, she and her father were never far from one another. Bill began teaching her the skills mentioned. In addition, her father often brought Mamie to work with him. She learned detective skills and observed firsthand her father's ways of handling unruly travelers, card sharks, and other situations. Mamie may have been a tomboy, but she was all woman. An 1898 Chicago newspaper article entitled "Female Officers of the Law" was provided to me by fellow historian Fred R. Egloff. This article reinforces that Mamie and Sara M. Burche were two young women working as field officers for the United States Marshals Service out of Guthrie, Oklahoma. Mamie's father had been appointed Chief Deputy United States Marshal in 1897, a year prior to Mamie's appointment by Territorial Marshal C. H. Thompson. It is said that her father had little to nothing to do with her appointment but she was not the normal woman of the times. She was a well-trained law officer; her appointment seemed to be a natural step. Both women were described as young, fairly good-looking, well educated, fearless, and independent.

Sara Burche, on the other hand, was hired as a stenographer before taking on the duties of a field officer. Her tenure as a field deputy also started in 1898, ending a year later in 1899. There is nothing about her life, professional or otherwise, mentioned after this.

Fieldwork was dangerous; hundreds of deputies died in the line of duty. It had to be scary for these two women, yet they proved themselves to be very capable. They were teamed up as partners and worked closely together. There was one other woman working as a field deputy, Florence Miller. We will speak of Deputy Miller shortly.

Mamie's great-granddaughter, Deb Durr, had more to say concerning her ancestor. She noted that Mamie was a clerk within the Marshals Service headquartered out of Guthrie, as was Sara Burche. She and Sara were deputized occasionally for special assignments (fieldwork).

Jim Fulbright, author and historian, sent me an email concerning Mamie. It is as follows:

"…her husband, Richard Miller, died suddenly in 1907. Their daughter, Madeline was taken to Kingman, Kansas and raised by the Miller family. Mamie, disliked by the Miller family, essentially disappears from her daughter's life and in general becomes a recluse, probably with mental and alcoholic problems."

Bill's great-great-granddaughter, granddaughter to Madeline, noted the following (also found in the Fulbright article):

"Mother, Elizabeth married a man after having divorced her first husband and [she] remarried. Now known as Elizabeth Salsberry, she and her new husband moved to Kingfisher after Bill Fossett had settled in. She died in 1892. Mamie married a man who's [sic] last name is Miller. There is some speculation that he was related to Florence Miller but we have no evidence one way or another, just something to ponder. Personally, I doubt unless the lady marshals crossed paths but considering that they worked out of different areas, I doubt that they did. Mamie and her husband had one child, a girl. After ten years of marriage Mamie was widowed."

David Turk, historian for the United States Marshals Service, said, "Mamie became a hard drinker and alcoholic." Great-great-granddaughter Deborah talked of Mamie's life as having been "sad ." After her husband's death, for whatever reason, Mamie lost custody of her child to her husband's family. From this time on, she saw very little of her daughter. The last mention of Mamie was a post card she sent to her daughter in 1926 from Oklahoma City, where she then lived. Her death and place of burial is unknown to her family. In time she will be found; there is so much more of her story, as well as Sara's and Florence's, to be told.

The 1898 article "Female Officers of the Law" tells us that the ladies were chosen to serve in the worst part of the Indian Territory. This area claimed more lives (federal lawmen) in one year than in all the Union as a total.

The first job of note was a murder case. Unlike today, the victim's family and friends, as well as the "slayers," were able and ready to take matters into their own hands; the net result is that few witnesses were willing to step forward. So into the country of the Sacs and Foxes the two law-women ventured to locate and bring back the "unruly" witnesses; it was dangerous land and dangerous work. These two tribes were always closely allied, spoke similar languages, and were suspicious of all others. The article goes on to say:

They had writs with the names and addresses of the men wanted. They are brave as any man and expert with rifle or pistol. They travel together and can put up a good fight if it comes to that. Few men would undertake to disturb them. None wold [would] make much of a success. They are splendid riders, inured to fatigue and exposure to climatic conditions, prefer active outdoor life to that usually supposed to attract the feminine intellect. So, when told to go get those Indians, they packed their kits, loaded their rifle magazines, mounted, and got their man....

*****

Sara's image is below; both line drawings are from the same news article. There is no image of Florence except in one's mind. These ladies, all pioneers in law enforcement, succeeded so well.

Deputy U.S. Marshal Sara Burche, 1889.

Line Drawing and article provided by Historian Fred R. Egloff

Florence Miller (birth and death dates unknown)

An article from an 1891 issue of the *Muskogee Weekly Phoenix* spoke of Deputy U.S. Marshal Florence M. Miller working the Indian Territory. Florence was commissioned in Paris, Texas, in 1891 in the eastern district. By November she was working with Deputy U.S. Marshal Cantrell. There were three deputy marshals named Cantrell; only one stands out as her potential partner in the Marshals Service ranks—Ben C. Cantrell, who was commissioned on July 4, 1887. Cantrell worked the western district out of Fort Smith, Arkansas, under Marshal Jacob Yoes. Cantrell arrested various criminals who committed the high crime of murder. Among those were four Choctaw Indians who killed a man and robbed and burned his body in a shallow ravine. Then there was the highway robbery committed by Walter Hamilton and his wife. They robbed a man, Daniel Martell, taking his horses, wagon, and personal property; then they shot him multiple times, leaving him for dead. Deputy Marshal Cantrell was assigned the duty to track them down. He did his task well. He arrested the couple and brought them back to Fort Smith to stand trial. I speak of Cantrell because Florence Miller was his partner and could have been part of a number of his adventures. The November 19, 1891 article spoke of Florence Miller having a reputation of being a fearless and efficient officer of the law who locked up more than a few offenders.

She was a young woman of prepossessing appearance, wears a cowboy hat and is always adorned with a pistol belt full of cartridges and a dangerous looking Colt pistol which she knows hot [how] to us [use].

The paper reported that she and Deputy Marshal Cantrell had been in Muskogee for a short time, that she had been assisting in the transportation of prisoners from Talahina to the Muskogee federal jail. On November 6, 1891, the *Fort Smith Elevator* printed an article that stated:

A Paris, Texas, correspondent says that Ben Campbell [Cantrell], a deputy marshal for the federal court at South McAlester, has for his guard a Mrs. Miller, who is said to be a dashing brunette of charming manners. She goes with him on all his trips and wears a Mexican sombrero. The woman carries a pistol buckled around her and has a Winchester strapped to her saddle. She is an expert shot and a superb horsewoman, and brave to the verge of recklessness. It is said that she aspires to win a name equal to that of Belle Starr, differing from her by exerting herself to run down criminals and in the enforcement of the law.

Vol.2. A Fraternity of Gunslingers

"Mysterious" Dave Allen Mather (August 1851—May 1886?)

"Mysterious Dave" Allen Mather was tall (six foot two) with long, lanky arms and legs. He walked, always, with his head down, and seldom looked a man in the eye, thus the handle "mysterious." His family came from Connecticut. His father, Ulysses, was a sea captain who was killed, as reported by his Chinese cook, while in port in Shanghai in 1864.

Dave was the first of three sons born to the Mathers. His brother Josiah "Sy" Wright Mather was born October 11, 1854, three years after Dave. A year later another brother was born; he died in infancy.
Ulysses abandoned his family after the death of his youngest son in 1856; nonetheless, his presence, although short, influenced his sons.

Dave and Josiah were teenagers when their mother passed away. The boys decided a life at sea was their destiny; they signed on and became merchant mariners. This romantic life lasted less than a year before the boys decided this was not what they wanted and jumped ship in New Orleans. After a short stay the boys made their way to northern Arkansas and then to southern Missouri before heading south to Texas. Arkansas is where they met, befriended, and worked with Dave Rudabaugh and Milton J. Yarberry. Their work was comprised of rustling and robberies—the Mather brothers' introduction to outlawing. In 1873 they became embroiled in the murder of a prominent rancher; the men quickly left for Decatur, Texas, where they parted, heading off in different directions. The brothers headed west to Dodge City, Kansas.

Mather's partners in crime, Rudabaugh and Yarberry, were as bad as they came. Rudabaugh went on to become a train robber. In Kansas he was captured after having robbed a train, and he identified his companions for immunity. Upon their capture Rudabaugh was freed. It has been reported that he was mixed up with the Clanton Gang in Tombstone. There was an article published in which Wyatt Earp was interviewed while in Colorado right after the infamous Vendetta Ride, where he and his posse went after the killers of his brother Morgan. Wyatt and Doc Holliday were hiding out from the Arizona posse that was comprised of Cochise Sheriff Johnny Behan, Ike Clanton's brother whom Behan deputized, Johnny Ringo, and about twenty other Arizona ranchers and cowboys. They had warrants to serve on Wyatt, Holliday, and Wyatt's posse members, who were considered Federal due to Earps status as a U.S. Deputy Marshal. The warrants were in regards to the death of Frank Stillwell in Tucson. Wyatt's location was no secret, but one had to approach, arrest, and then get extradition papers to take Wyatt back to Tucson for trial. This would never happen. During the interview Wyatt mentioned that Dave Rudabaugh was at Cotton Wood Springs when he killed "Curly Bill" Broucius. However, there is no other mention of Rudabaugh in Tombstone, and the official list of the men participating in the Cotton Wood Springs shootout does not include Rudabaugh. Kenny Vail—friend, fellow historian, and researcher from Texas—confirmed this and added that Rudabaugh was on the run, wanted for murder in Las Vegas, New Mexico. Rudabaugh would have avoided Tombstone for the likes of men such as Frank Leslie or Morgan Earp, reputed bounty hunters.

*****

Dave Mather was a member in good standing in the Dodge City Gang. The gang, now located in Las Vegas, New Mexico, was comprised of former deputy sheriffs, town marshals, and friends from Dodge. With the help of friend John Allen, Dave attempted to break his friend J. J. Webb—former Dodge City Marshal, current Las Vegas Marshal—out of jail. Webb was incarcerated for the murder of Mike Kelliher, a freighter, and had been sentenced to hang. Mather's attempt failed; Webb remained incarcerated.

Mather killed jailer Antonio Lino Valdez in his efforts to free his friend. Dave managed to escape to Fort Sumner, where he joined up with Billy the Kid. On December 23, 1880, Rudabaugh, Billy, and a few of his gang were surrounded at Stinking Springs by Pat Garrett and posse. Unable to escape, they surrendered. While Billy was sentenced to hang, Dave received a ninety-nine-year prison term. He joined his buddy J. J. Web in jail, and the two hatched a plan to escape. This time they succeeded; the men went separate ways.

There is no doubt that Dave Rudabaugh was a mean and evil man; his time would be up soon. He avoided arrest and went south to Mexico. In one Mexican village Mather rubbed the peasants the wrong way. His mean, demanding, and threatening ways caught up with him. On February 18, 1886, Rudabaugh was involved in a cantina card game in Parral, Chihuahua. Chaos occurred with the accusations of cheating. Rudabaugh quickly reached for his gun, killing two local men over the game. He left the cantina to ride off but was unable to find his horse. Rudabaugh returned to the cantina, which was now in total darkness. As he reentered, a peasant—at the side of the door, up against the wall—with a shovel in hand swung that shovel hard, hitting drunken Rudabaugh in the neck. Dave hit the ground, bleeding, and the peasant continued to hit Dave in the neck with the edge of the shovel until he was beheaded. The head was impaled on a post and displayed outdoors as a reminder for others to take heed. Rudabaugh was thirty-one when he died.

Mather partners in crime, Rudabaugh and Yarberry, were as bad as they came. Rudabaugh, went on to become a train robber. In Kansas he was captured, after having robbed a train and identified his companions for immunity. Upon their captured, Rudabaugh was freed. It has been reported that he was mixed up with the Clanton Gang in Tombstone. There was an article published in which Wyatt Earp was interview, while Colorado right after the "Vendetta Ride." Wyatt and Doc Holiday were hiding out from the Arizona posse that comprised of Cochise Sheriff
Johnny Behan who deputized Ike Clanton's brother Phineas, Johnny Ringo and about twenty other Arizona ranchers
and Cowboys. They had warrants to serve on Wyatt and Holiday for the death of Frank Stillwell in Tucson. Wyatt's posse members would in all likely hood be arrested for their involvement in the other killings. Wyatt's posse included the following men: Warren Earp, Sherman McMaster, Jack Johnson, Doc Holliday, Texas Jack Dan Tipton and Charlie Smith and of course Wyatt. Wyatt was a deputy U.S. Marshal, his posse was Federal. The next man to die was "Indian Charlie" Cruz followed by Curly Bill Broucius. Wyatt's location was no secret but then one had to approach, arrest, then get extradition papers to take Wyatt back to Tucson for trial. This would never happen. During an interview Wyatt mentions that Dave Rudabaugh was at Cotton Wood Springs when, he, killed Curly Bill Broucius. However, there is no other mention of Rudabaugh being in Tombstone, and the official list that I have seen of the men participating in the shoot-out does not include Rudabaugh. My friend and fellow historian/researcher, Kenny Vail, of Texas, confirms this and added that Rudabaugh was on the run, wanted for murder in Las Vegas, New Mexico. Rudabaugh would have avoided Tombstone for the likes of men such as Frank Leslie or Morgan Earp, reputed bounty hunters.

Often called "Dirty Dave" Rudabaugh. Public domain photograph, courtesy of Wikipedia

Dave was a member in good standing with the "Dodge City Gang." The Gang, headquartered in Las Vegas, New Mexico, it was comprised of former deputy sheriffs, town marshals and friends from Dodge. Dave, with the help of a friend, John Allen, attempted to break out of jail, his friend, former Dodge City Marshal and current Las Vegas Marshal, J.J. Webb. Webb was incarcerated for the murder of Mike Kelliher, a freighter and had been sentenced to hang. The attempt failed, Webb remained incarcerated; Mathers killed jailer Antonio Lino Valdez in his efforts to free his friend found himself behind bars as well.

Dave managed to escaped to Fort Sumner where he joined up with "Billy the Kid." On December 23, 1880, Rudabaugh, with "The Kid" and a few of his gang were surrounded at Stinking Springs by Pat Garrett and posse. Unable to escape, they surrounded. While Billy was sentenced to hang, Dave received a ninety-nine year prison term. Once more, he found himself in jail with his buddy J.J. Web; the two hatch a plan to escape. This time they succeeded; the men went separate ways.

There is no doubt that Dave Rudabaugh was a mean and evil man; his time would be up soon. He avoid arrest he crossed over the boarder to old Mexico. He was hanging out in Parral, Chihuahua when he rubbed the peasants, the wrong way. His mean, demanding and threatening ways caught up with him. On February 18, 1886, Rudabaugh was involved in a cantina card game in. Chaos occurred with the accusations of cheating. Rudabaugh quickly reach for his gun shootings, killing two local men over the game. He left the cantina to ride off but was unable to find his horse. Rudabaugh returned to the cantina, which was now in total darkness. As he re-entered, a peasant, at the side of the door, up against the wall, with shovel in hand, swung that shovel as hard as he could hitting the drunken Rudabaugh in the neck. Dave hit the ground, bleeding and the peasant, continued to hit Dave's neck with the edge of the shovel until he was beheaded. The head was impaled on a post and displayed outdoors as a reminder for others to take heed. Rudabaugh was thirty-one when he died. He was often referred to as Dirty Dave Rudabaugh.

*****

Milton Yarberry had a thing about killing men. He would kill, then quickly move on. The next town saw him kill again and move on to another locale, always repeating the pattern—this was his method of operation (MOD). His main source of income was robbing and rustling. The shooting—well, that was something different. One could say he was hot-tempered or outspoken, or one could say he was in the wrong place at the wrong time and, due to his God-given abilities, came out on top in shootouts. Eventually Milton wound up in Albuquerque, New Mexico, where he befriended Bernalillo County Sheriff Perfecto Armijo. Through this friendship Yarberry became the town's marshal in 1880. What was remembered and said of him was that he was not a great marshal, but was very, very handy with that pistol of his. Yarberry killed two men in a short period. The first was his common-law wife's lover (a self-proclaimed gunslinger), Harry A. Brown.

Yarberry and partner, Tony Preston, were in the saloon business in Dodge City. They sold out and moved to San Marciel, New Mexico. Sadie Preston (Tony's wife) and Yarberry began an affair. When Milton left for Albuquerque, Sadie and her four-year-old daughter went with him. On the night of March 27, 1881, Henry Brown took Sadie to dinner; the little girl stayed at home with Yarberry. Milton was not aware that Sadie was having an affair.

That night, with the little girl in hand, Yarberry walked to the restaurant and took the child inside, handing her off to Sadie. How or why he figured things out is a mystery. Most likely someone clued him in. Prior to the handoff, as Yarberry headed toward the restaurant, Brown was informed that Milton was nearby. He left the restaurant, determined that this would be Yarberry's last day on earth. Yarberry brushed past him with the girl and walked into the restaurant, where he handed the daughter to her mother. He turned and went outside to talk to Brown. An argument proceeded. Brown hit Yarberry in the mouth, pulled his gun, and took a shot, hitting Yarberry's hand—more of a graze. For Brown, instant death was two bullets in the chest. Yarberry was arrested, placed on trial, and found not guilty; the jury determined that he acted in self-defense. A month later Yarberry claimed self-defense in the shooting of Charles D. Campbell. His friend Sheriff Armijo, as before, arrested Yarberry, who stood trial. He was found not guilty, then rearrested, and retried. This was a political move by the wealthy. They were afraid that he liked to kill too much and that this would hurt Albuquerque's reputation, scaring away trade.

This time he was found guilty of murder because there was a bullet in Campbell's back and two in the front of his body. Yarberry appealed, lost, escaped, and was recaptured. The day of his execution arrived, February 9, 1883. Guarded by the New Mexico militia called the Governor's Rifles, at three o'clock Milton Yarberry was hanged until dead. Part of the Sheriff's job was to function as executioner. Yarberry and Sheriff Perfecto Armijo were close friends. The sheriff did not want to do the task; he tried to get others to execute his friend. The sheriff of Colfax County, Mason Bowman, was asked to take the job on, but refused. Sheriff Armijo had no choice; he hanged his friend. The sheriff never wavered in his support and loudly proclaimed Yarberry's innocence, before and after the execution. Milton J. Yarberry was a man-killer, outlaw, frontier lawman, and saloon and brothel owner. In the end, he shot and killed one man too many men and paid the price. As Sheriff Armijo pulled the lever, Yarberry proclaimed, "Gentlemen, you are hanging an innocent man." The photograph supplied by Cody Yarberry was taken prior to Milton's death when he was thirty-five.

The photograph supplied by Cody Yarberry, was taken prior to his death at the age of thirty-five.

The Mather brothers worked as buffalo hunters in 1874. While doing so, they became friends with fellow buffalo hunters Bill Tilghman, Bat Masterson, and Wyatt Earp. When the Colorado Railroad Wars of 1879 to 1880 broke out between two railroads—the Atchison, Topeka and Santa Fe and the Denver and Rio Grand—the likes of Mel Yarberry and "Mysterious Dave" Mather were hired as gunslingers by Bat Masterson. In all, there were approximately seventy gunmen working for the Atchison, Topeka and Santa Fe, with Masterson its chief gunman. Control over the Royal Gorge was the prize. The discovery of silver in Leadville was the root cause. In court the judge ruled in favor of the Denver and Rio Grand. With that ruling, the Denver and Rio Grand Railroad hired its own crew of gunmen that joined forces with law enforcement. Armed confrontations brought on heavy fighting. The Atchison, Topeka and Santa Fe Railroad garrisons in Colorado Springs and Denver fell. Masterson's headquarters in Pueblo held out the longest. Surrounded, they realized that the fight was hopeless; they gave up. Mysterious Dave, who had been nicknamed long before this event, was running with the best and the worst of gunmen—he had "arrived." It become obvious that he was accepted by the likes of Bat Masterson, then a living legend.

When the railroad wars ended, Mather headed to Las Vegas, New Mexico, soon becoming a member of the Dodge City Gang. He joined up with J. J. (John Joshua) Webb, Dave Rudabaugh, and Joe Carson; all welcomed him into their notorious group. Its leader, Hyman G. Neil, was commonly known as Hoodoo Brown. Hoodoo had managed to put himself in power in the "anglo" section of Las Vegas called New Town. He was not only a judge (justice of the peace), but also mayor and temporary coroner. Joe Carson was appointed town marshal; Dave Mather, assistant marshal; and Dave Rudabaugh, policeman. Together the Dodge City Gang capitalized on gambling and prostitution, skimming money off the top. With legal power and the ability to control the town, Hoodoo Brown's group were pretty much free to do as they pleased.

In July 1879 the Santa Fe Railroad rail line was completed and the first locomotive rolled into town. With it came the unsavory group of "desperadoes," then known as "sporting men ." Between the two groups (the law and the gamblers), there were problems—lots of problems—including robbery, bunko, and killings. Las Vegas was in the hands of hardened criminals. A month later U.S. Marshal John E. Sherman Jr. deputized Dave Mather. His first choice was a man named James H. Dunagan—a brave man, they say—who was disqualified when he robbed a stagecoach. October rolled around, with eleven Deputy U.S. Marshals posted in Las Vegas. Their job was to capture the train robbers. Mather had a dual reputation as a heavy-handed thug and an experienced lawman. Historians speculate that these two items influenced the marshal's decision to deputize Mather. Mather would often lead posses. These posses were comprised of postal inspectors and railroad detectives. The postal inspectors were there due to stolen mail. According to the U.S. Marshals Service, employing a concentrated number of federal lawmen paid off. Together they arrested at least a dozen train robbers, including policeman Dave Rudabaugh.

The Dodge City Gang had been busy. They robbed at least two stagecoaches and one train (possibly two), all under the watchful eye of Hoodoo Brown. January 22, 1880,

Tom Henry's gang was in town, four men in all: Tom Henry (his real name was Thomas Jefferson House), James West, John Dorsey, and William Randall. The four were at the Close and Patterson Variety Hall. They were rowdy. It seemed that if anyone was looking for trouble, they would provide it—all were armed. Marshal Joe Carson entered the saloon with his assistant, Dave Mather. Carson told the men to check their guns with the bartender. The gang instead shot the marshal eight times, killing him on the spot. Even thought it was too late to save his friend, Mysterious Dave drew his revolvers and commenced firing. Of the four, Randall was killed on the spot, West was dropped, seriously wounded, and Dorsey was wounded but managed to escape with Tom Henry. Dave was not harmed. A posse of seven men was formed with J. J. Webb and Dave Rudabaugh as members. Webb would soon be appointed as a policeman and Mather as town marshal.

Two weeks later Dorsey and Henry were found; the men were holed up at the home of Juan Antonio Dominguez in Buena Vista, a town thirty miles north of Las Vegas. Surrounded, the outlaws surrendered. They were returned to Las Vegas and placed in the town jail to await trial. Vigilantes decided not to wait. They overpowered the jailers and took the men to the plaza in the center of town where a windmill stood. While the outlaws were being fitted for the hangman's noose, Mrs. Joe Carson, still grieving for her husband, grabbed a handgun from one of the nearby vigilantes and immediately opened fire on the two murders. The men were dead. The vigilantes strung them up anyways, leaving them there as a message. Nothing came of Mrs. Carson's revenge; she remained free.

Four days later, on January 26, 1880, the *Las Vegas Daily Optic* reported another killing. The long article on the coroner's report notes that as a constable "Mysterious" Dave, during the discharge of his duty as an officer of the law, was justified, as the coroner's inquest stated, in shooting and killing Joe Castello (or Castillo). Castello was in charge of a group of men who came to town to work on the railroad extension. That evening between 10:00 p.m. and 11:00 p.m. two of his men, having had far too much drink, got into a squabble with each other. A crowd gathered around the men, in front of McKay's restaurant. Joe drew his gun to keep others at bay. Another gun was drawn, "in the hand of one of his men." Mather stepped forward, commanding Castello to drop his weapon. Castello turned, pointing his Colt at Mather and verbally threatening to shoot if Mather took one step farther. Dave did advance and "in the twinkling of the eye…fired one shot." The other man must have dropped his gun, but Joe Castello lay in the middle of the street, dying. He was taken to Hoodoo Brown's office, where Doctor Russell Bayly was summoned. The good doctor remained with Castello until he passed away at six the following morning. Castello had not drunk that night; he was sober. Maybe he was afraid for both his own safety and that of his men. After all, this was Las Vegas, New Mexico, with a reputation as one of the worst and potentially most lawless townships in the territory. Regardless, Joe Castello was dead at the age of twenty-two.

Another killing accrued on March 2, 1880. It was reported in the *Ford County Globe* on March 9, 1880, and also appeared in the *Las Vegas Daily Optic*.

The *Ford County Globe* stated:

"About four o'clock this morning, Michael Kelliher, in company with William Brickley and another man, entered Goodlet & Roberts' Saloon and called for drinks. Michael Kelliher appeared to be the leader of the party and he, in violation of the law, had a pistol on his person. This was noticed by the officers, who came through a rear door, and they requested that Kelliher lay aside his revolver. But he refused to do so, remarking, "I won't be disarmed—everything goes," immediately placing his hand on his pistol, no doubt intending to shoot. But Officer Webb was too quick for him. The man was shot before he had time to use his weapon. He was shot three times—once in each breast and once in the head. . . .Kelliher had $1,090 [$1,900] on his person when killed."

Webb was arrested for murder. The people suspected that Hoodoo Brown, knowing that Kelliher was loaded with cash, ordered Webb to retrieve it. There would be several attempts to free Webb. Dave Rudabaugh attempted to do so, but would be captured. Together, Rudabaugh and Webb would succeed in breaking out. They headed in different directions, where both would meet their fates.

The people of Las Vegas were fed up with all the crime and shootings; they were not fooled by the so-called legal system. On April 8, 1880, a notice penned by was posted, penned by a "party of vigilantes" was posted in the *Las Vegas Optic:*

To Murderers, Confidence Men, Thieves:

"The citizens of Las Vegas have tired of robbery, murder, and other crimes that have made this town a byword in every civilized community. They have resolved to put a stop to crime, if in attaining that end they have to forget the law and resort to a speedier justice than it will afford. All such characters are therefore, hereby notified, that they must either leave this town or conform themselves to the requirements of law, or they will be summarily dealt with. The flow of blood must and shall be stopped in this community, and the good citizens of both the old and new towns have determined to stop it, if they have to HANG by the strong arm of FORCE every violator of the law in this country.

Vigilantes"

Leaving J. J. Webb on his own in jail on murder charges, Hoodoo Brown left Las Vegas in the middle of the night with Kelliher's money and whatever else he had cash wise in his office safe. Hoodoo never returned, nor was he heard from again. With the rise of an active vigilante group, the Dodge City Gang left town —quickly. "Mysterious" Dave went first to Texas, visiting several cities before heading back to Dodge City.

*****

Now living in Fort Worth, Texas, Dave found himself in trouble, having been arrested for theft. In his possession was a gold chain that a "madam" claimed he took from her. The two were an item. It was hard for people to believe who was lying, so the chain was returned and the matter dropped.

Mather had been working in law enforcement for the city, as reported in the *Democrat-Advance* on January 27, 1882. The article mentioned that Dave had worked for Marshal Farmer; thus, he was well-known by some of the policemen. It appears that that he worked when needed since he only knew "some" of the officers.

Dave remained in Texas until March 1883, or maybe longer; the next mention of him was June 5 when the *Ford County Globe* reported that Mather was appointed assistant marshal of Dodge City. His monthly pay was $125. In addition, Sheriff Pat Sughrue hired Mather as a deputy. Dave conducted his duties well. There was a train robbery, with the engineer and fireman killed, in October 1882. Mather was, in a round about way, accused of letting the lead robber, William Byrd, get away. Dave was assigned to go to Texas and bring Byrd back. Seven months later, in January 1884, the *Dodge City Times* reported that Dave "had thwarted a break from the county jail." The Byrd issue in Texas had blown over.

All seemed well, but on April 7, 1884, a new mayor was elected. He appointed Bill Tilghman as town marshal over then marshal Jack Bridge. Bill appointed Tom Nixon as his assistant. Dave was out of a job, but he was part owner of the Opera House Saloon —a fancy name for a saloon and gambling establishment. Dave wanted to add a dance hall section to his saloon. Mather and Tom Nixon were enemies. It was for political reasons that Mather and Nixon disliked each. It all went back to April 3, 1883, when Larry Deger won the mayorship. Although the newspapers declared the election a "fraud," then mayor Bill Harris was out. Bill Harris was part owner of the Long Branch Saloon.

The first order of business for Deger was the passing of two ordinances. The first ordinance, number seventy, called the "Suppression of Vice and Immorality," was aimed at stopping the music, and the girls working in the saloons. At the time, a five-piece band, the Dodge City Band, played at the Long Branch nightly. The second ordinance, number seventy-one, was titled "Define and Punish Vagrancy." According to this ordinance, "keepers of brothels, gambling houses, and those engaged in any unlawful calling whatever" were subject to prosecution. The ordinance was a catchall, as any saloon owner, gambler, or whore, or anyone engaged in any business deemed immoral, could be considered a "vagrant." Obviously no women, bar maids, or prostitutes were allowed in the bars and cathouses. The ordinances had an exception— Abe Webster's Alamo Saloon. Mayor Deger, in short order, made another special deal with Nixon's Lady Gay Saloon. The Nixon and Webster saloons were immune to the ordinances. This grab of power and what followed is now referred to as the Dodge City War. All saloons except for two were pretty much curtailed. Luke Short, part owner of the Long Branch, was escorted to the train depot by armed guards and told to get out of town and never return, with punishment of death if he should.

Luke had friends, and they came to his rescue in June 1883. Bat Masterson organized and brought in a group of top gunmen. This group has been tagged ever since as the Dodge City Peace Commission. The first to enter the city was Wyatt Earp, with his pals Charlie Bassett, "Shotgun" Collins, Frank McLain, and current sheriff of Ford County, Bill Tilghman. The Ford County Historical Society has the original photograph with all copyrights. The third version, with Bill Tilghman standing next to Bat Masterson, can be viewed online. A day or so later followed Jack Vermillion, Dan Tipton, Johnny Millsap, Johnny Green, and Neal Brown—all considered top gunslingers. Both Bat and Short were told to never show their faces in Dodge City, with the implied penalty of death, so the two held back at a local ranch. Make no mistake—these two men master minded the take-over of Dodge City. With the city "under fire," with no help coming to aid them, Mayor Deger wanted to settle the dispute; he gave in to their demands. Masterson and Short rode into town like conquering Romans. The bottom line—there was never a shot fired during this "war." The governor stayed out of it and had ordered the militia to do the same. This problem was between Dodge City's current group of power-hungry, money-grabbing politicians and Luke Short.

The ordinances went by the wayside, Luke Short and his partner, Harris, retained their ownership of the Long Branch, and all the saloons and brothels were reopened. With order restored, the top gunslingers of Kansas left town peacefully, promising to return if need be.

When Mather wanted to add a dance hall section to the Opera House, the city fathers said no. This was due to its prominent downtown location. Another ordinance was passed banning all dance halls, yet the Lady Gay was not included in this restrictive ordinance. Resentment set in again. The two men, Mather and Nixon did their best to put the other out of business; their distrust and dislike for each other continued to grow. Nixon, as assistant marshal, helped collect license fees from the gamblers and prostitutes, which paid the police salaries; he had power and influence. The only dance hall in town was Nixon's; he was making good money.

July 18, 1884, as Dave stood on the steps that led upstairs to his saloon, Nixon took a shot at him. He missed. Mather suffered from powder burns on his face and took some flying splinters in this left hand; otherwise he was fine. Dave did not return fire, nor did he press charges. Three days later, on the evening of July 21, Nixon was on duty, standing on the corner of First Avenue and Front Street. It was 10:00 p.m. He was looking into the Opera House, most likely checking on Mather. From behind him there came a voice. It called out softly, "Tom." Tom turned to face a .45-caliber revolver pointed at him. He had enough time to recognize Mather before being shot. Four bullets entered his body, one piercing his heart. Nixon's gun was in its holster; its master, dead. Bat Masterson was one of the first to arrive, followed by Marshal Sughrue, who arrested Mysterious Dave.

A change of venue was granted for the trial; Mysterious Dave was found not guilty and let loose. The history books all say that not a shot was fired during the Dodge City War, technically a true statement. This shooting of Tom Nixon was a direct result of the foolish ordinances that benefited a few at the expense of all others.

Dave was free to go, so back to Dodge he went, where all remained quiet until May 10, 1885, when Dave and his brother, Sy, killed a man over a card game in the Junction Saloon. During the ruckus, Dave was slightly wounded—a bullet grazed his forehead—but with Sy's help, his attacker lay dead. The man was David Barnes; the game was the game was "seven up," at fifty cents a game. Barnes lost the first hand, but won the second and claimed the pot. Mather picked up the winnings and headed to the bar. The *Dodge City Democrat* reported on May 16, 1885, that they had played three hands. On May 12 the *Globe Live Stock Journal*, the first to report the shooting, stated that they had only played two hands. Two witnesses were wounded in the shootout—one was hit in the calf, while the other was shot through both legs. Barnes's brother, John, was there as well. They were not gunmen, but were in town to "prove up some land." John tried to come to his brother's aid, drawing his weapon, but Sheriff Sughrue had just entered the saloon when the fighting broke out. He grabbed John's arm; someone grabbed his other arm. John could not break loose. He stopped struggling when the sheriff identified himself. It was too late for David. An inquest was held, and it found that David Barnes died by gunshot "by the hands of Dave and Josiah Mather by means of revolver and that…said shooting was feloniously done."

Town Marshal Bill Tilghman had enough of Dave Mather. He ordered Dave to leave town or else. Mather did a wise thing—he left town, as did his business partner, Dave Black, a Texan. They went to New Kiowa, Kansas. Founded in 1872, the town was an important shipping point that handled thousands of cattle from the Cherokee outlet, New Mexico, and Texas. With the coming of the railroad, New Kiowa was booming. The men opened another saloon. It wasn't long before trouble arrived; during the course of a brawl, Dave Black killed a soldier. He was arrested for murder. Mather went about collecting donations to help pay for Black's defense. This angered other soldiers. The soldiers let it be known that they were coming to lynch both men. Quickly gathering the funds, Dave left Kansas for Dallas, Texas, leaving his partner high and dry. Mysterious Dave dropped out of sight; all was quiet.

In May 1886 it was reported in the local newspapers that a tall, dark-haired man was found along the Texas Central Railroad's tracks, shot in the head. No one knew or could identify him. The dead man fit Dave Mather's physical description. A bond of

$3,000 was still held by the bondsman in the Junction Saloon shooting, but the description was enough for the bondsman to release his responsibilities "due to the death of the defendant." It is a controversy among historians as to whether this was indeed the demise of Dave Mather. Yet Dave was never seen or heard of again. His brother, Sy, years later let it be known that he had not seen or heard from Dave ever again. Dave had one enemy too many and met his fate in May 1886 at the age of thirty-five.

   Dave's life was full but short. Like so many others in the Old West, he bounced between outlaw and lawman.

Virgil Walter Earp (July 18, 1843 – October 20, 1905)

Most know that Virgil was the city marshal of Tombstone when the gunfight at the OK Corral occurred—actually, it was near the OK Corral. This chapter will include members of the family to give the reader a better idea who Virgil was and insight into the man.

James, Virgil, Wyatt, Morgan, and Warren were half brothers to Newton, the eldest. Sisters were Martha, who died at the age of eleven; Virginia, who passed away when she was three; and Adelia, who lived to be eighty. Newton's mother, Abigail Storm, was the first wife of Nicholas, the family patriarch. Virginia Cooksey would marry Nicholas soon after Abigail's death. This group, with Virginia, made up the family nucleus of the famous or infamous Earps. There were cousins around, but none reached the height of the "Fighting Earps," which consisted of Virgil, Wyatt, and Morgan. Warren was too young to be involved in any action, but he visited his brothers often in Tombstone and did participate, as a posse member, during the Vendetta Ride.

Abigail gave birth to Newton on October 7, 1837. Four years later after Abigail's death new wife James came along with a new wife, Virginia Ann Cooksey. Of the male children, Virgil was born in 1843, Wyatt in 1847, and Morgan in 1851, followed by the last male child, Warren, born in 1855. Newton, James, Virgil, and Martha were all born in Hartford, Kentucky; Wyatt, in Illinois; and Morgan and Warren, in Iowa.

The three eldest brothers joined the Union army during the Civil War; the others were too young. Virgil was eighteen when he join and served with the Eighty-Third Illinois Infantry, Company C, from July 26, 1862, to June 24, 1865. Newton served elsewhere; he was not a part of the Eighty-Third. James enlisted with Company F of the Seventeen Illinois, an infantry outfit, in May 1861. On October 31 of that year, he was wounded in the shoulder while near Fredericktown, Missouri. His arm would never be the same; its use, limited. This would keep him from being part of the Fighting Earps. He mustered out of the army and returned to the family farm in the summer of 1863 before heading out to Austin, Nevada, the new silver boomtown. Brothers Newton and Virgil were never wounded, or if they were, not seriously. No records indicating injuries or why it took so long to muster Virgil out of the army.

The Eighty-Third Illinois took part in several battles. The first, the Battle of Dover, took place on February 3, 1862, in Stewart County, Tennessee. The setting was the Cumberland River. The Eighty-Third repelled an attack by two generals, Forrest and Wheeler. This first of three battles pitched the Eighty-Third's 800 men against the Confederates' 2,500. Three days later the Fort Henry Battle occurred. Then the big battle took place— Fort Donelson. From February 11 through February 16, the battle raged. It took nine companies of the Eighty-Third along with Company C of the Second Illinois Light Artillery to defeat the Confederates at Fort Donelson. The Union forces' successful attack of Fort Donelson was a major blow to the Confederates. It meant the end of a major supply route and river passage, along with the capture of an arsenal and a munitions manufacturing plant. The fort's location was near the Tennessee-Kentucky border on the Cumberland River. The fall of the fort created an opening in which the Union forces could invade the South. Nashville would remain in the hands of the Union throughout the war. At the time, this win was more important than Gettysburg. History would look at it differently, but a win was sorely needed, and this one was huge. The division of the Confederate South was now possible. The victory of Fort Donelson set Ulysses S. Grant, then a brigadier general, apart from all other Union generals. He would be promoted to major general for his role in taking the fort; soon after that, he would be promoted to command all Union forces. President Lincoln finally found a general that he could trust, one who knew how to win.

Virgil, as part of the Eighty-Third, remained in Tennessee for the duration, as a peace-keeper. The Eighty-Third fought off Confederate guerrillas almost daily. Virgil did not rise above the rank of private.

*****

The Earp family were vagabonds. They moved often. This time it was to be a great move, farther than ever before; they were California bound. On May 12, 1864, they joined a wagon train. Newton, married with children, chose not to follow.

After the war James and Virgil would separately make their way west. James was discharged earlier than Virgil. James stayed in California for a brief time; then he went to Austin, Nevada. They may have been in separate cities and territories, but they were a close-knit family that kept in touch and often joined each other. Where one was, the others were sure to follow. Collectively or individually they were a force to reckoned with. The term "Fighting Earps" fit them well. Brother Newton was never part of his brothers' frontier ways; he never ventured into that realm, nor did he join the family in California. James's Civil War injury limited the mobility of one arm. It took him out of the loop, out of the action. His job in Austin was that of a bartender, the type of job that he would stay with for years to come. He was near his brothers but never part of their group. In Tombstone he was never considered an enemy of the cow-boy faction; therefore, he was never in danger. He did not participate in the famous gunfight. After the death of Morgan, who was assassinated for his role in the gunfight near the OK Corral, James accompanied his brother's body to Colton, California, for burial. He never returned to Tombstone; thus, he did not join the Vendetta Ride to avenge Morgan's death. Warren, the youngest, did.

Although this chapter is about Virgil, yet, family is so intwined that one cannot speak of a brother without mentioning the others. Wyatt; was a self-promoter, as was his lifelong friend Bat Masterson. Serious western historians considered both Jim Masterson and Virgil Earp better lawmen. Morgan has always been portrayed as the weaker, younger, less experienced brother; he was not. The movies and television glorify one while ignoring the other. Virgil Earp was the eldest of the "fighting Earps." Like most boys in those times, he was raised on a farm, taught to read and write, did his chores, and learned to shoot and hunt game.

Looking at the family dynamics, include its patriarch, Nicholas. In March 1856 Nicholas, was elected to the position of municipal constable in Turtle, Illinois. Nicholas served as constable for almost three years until he was caught and convicted of bootlegging. Unable to pay the fines, a lien was levied against the Earps' property to insure the court that they would be paid, when payment was not made the court foreclosed on the property and sold it at auction in November 1859. The family moved to Monmouth, Illinois, While here Nicholas sold his "other" holdings to satisfy several lawsuits surrounding his debts, which included tax evasion. A farmer no longer, he moved, once more, to Pella, Iowa, where the Earps had family to help them start fresh. By the 1880s Nicholas was a justice of the peace. He gave his family strong values, yet he was prone to break the law when it suited him.

Prior to his enlistment in the Civil War, Virgil met a young girl, Magdalena Rysdam, a Dutch immigrant who answered to "Ellen." Her family immigrated to the United States in 1847. Having lived in Iowa most of her life, Ellen was, by today's vernacular, "Americanized." She was sixteen and Virgil was seventeen when they fell in love and married. This article from the *Portland Oregonian* of April 22, 1899, says it best:

"Virgil W. Earp, brother of Wyatt Earp, of Sharkey-Fitzsimmons fight fame, and a man with a record of his own, is in Portland enjoying a reunion with his first wife and his only daughter, neither of whom he has seen for 39 years....The story of the separation is one of those romances which give color to the adage that truth once in a while is stranger than fiction.

Earp was married to his first wife, then Ellen Rysdam, at Oskaloosa, Ia. [Iowa], in February, 1860. He was then 17 years old and she was still younger. The parents of both young people strenuously opposed the match—the girl's parents because they did not want their daughter, who was a native of Holland, to marry into an American family; Earp's because he was too young. So the wedding was kept secret, the couple got only an occasional opportunity to see each other, and not till the birth of their daughter did they make their union known. Then there was trouble on both sides of the house, which, however, was soon settled by the enlistment of Earp in the Civil War, when his child was two weeks old, and his immediate departure for the front."

His young wife was left with her parents, who continually urged her to secure a divorce from her husband, and who finally took it upon themselves to declare the union at an end. Soon word was received that Earp was wounded, then that he was dead, and his wife had no reason to doubt either report. With her parents she came West, bringing her child, and in 1867 she married Thomas Eaton at Walla Walla.

In the meantime Earp returned to his home, found his wife gone, heard from friends that she had married again, and philosophically decided that the best thing he could do was to keep out of her way.

This he did very successfully. He married again in 1873, came West, and took an active part in the stirring times on the plains that have furnished unlimited inspiration for Old Sleuth and other chroniclers of cowboy days.

The present reunion was brought about by the recent illness of Earp's daughter, Mrs. Law, who had learned the story of her father and discovered that his present residence was at Prescott, Ariz. She had been corresponding with him since September, and expected to make him a visit last winter, but a sudden attack of pneumonia changed her plans, and instead her father hastened to her bedside.

He is now enjoying a very pleasant visit with her and his two grandchildren, at her home, which is near that of Mrs. Eaton, in North Portland. He will remain for several days more, before he starts on his journey home. Years have taken away the pain the meeting between the former husband and wife would once have caused and the little visit has been a most happy one for all.

The girl born to Virgil and Ellen on January 7, 1862 was named Nellie Jane Earp. It was the only known child that Virgil would have in his lifetime. It was but two weeks after his daughter['s] birth that Virgil went off to war.

A year after Virgil was discharged from the Army, he joined his family in San Bernardino, California. San Bernardino was the most important town during this period, in Southern California. It was the major trade and business center, and jumping off point [for] miners and explorers. Los Angeles was a small township, in comparison to San Bernardino and San Francisco, a Wild West town that most held little respect for.

While two of the brothers were off to war, Nicholas and family began their trip to California, departing on May 12, 1864. With them were Wyatt, Morgan, Warren, and Adelia. They arrived on December 17. The Earps rented a farm in the Redlands area on the banks of the Santa Ana River.

At war's end, Virgil joined the family. In 1866, he took a job, with Wyatt, as a teamster driving a team of eight horses. Their normal route was between the California towns of Wilmington and San Bernardino. Later as seasoned professionals their route would run between Prescott, Arizona, and San Bernardino and also all the way to Salt Lake City and back.

The building of the transcontinental rail system was underway; the boys landed jobs working for the Union Pacific. Their participation was during its construction in Wyoming. Virgil worked as a teamster; Wyatt labored as a pick-and-shovel man. In the *Wyatt Earp Frontier Marshal* biography, Wyatt told his biographer Stuart Lake that he owned a couple of teams of horses and freight wagons and that during this period they would rent them out to the Union Pacific. Lake, Wyatt's first biographer, never mentioned that Wyatt was nothing more than a basic laborer. Most historians discount much of the biography. The Earps were ambitious. It sense that the two brothers would pool their money, becoming equal partners as teamsters, with Virgil leading the way, selling the teams for a profit when they decided to move on.

The year 1868 found Virgil and the family in Lamar, Missouri. Virgil operated a grocery store and helped work the family farm. He met a woman, Rosella Dragoo, whom he married on May 28, 1870. Rosella was two years older than Virgil. Virgil's father performed the marriage ceremony. The marriage ended three years later. What happened to Rosella after the divorce remains a mystery. We know she was of French ancestry, a light-complected, dark-haired woman. Virgil did not stay in Lamar. He was headed to Council Bluffs, Iowa, where he would meet a waitress named Alvira "Allie" Sullivan. This relationship would last for the rest of Virgil's life. There is no record that they officially married; however, they were fully devoted to one another. In 1877, after a short visit to Dodge City, Virgil and Allie moved to Prescott, a pleasant town a little over a mile high, centrally located in Arizona. Prescott was designated as the capital of the Arizona Territory in 1864. Three years later, the territorial capital was moved to Tucson for a very short time, with the capital moving back to Prescott and remaining there until

1889 when Phoenix took over the position, becoming the state capital in 1912.

Virgil's first job in Prescott was that of a mailman, with a side job as a "sawyer" (a person who saws timber for a living). Virgil received the contract to provide the army's Camp Whipple five cords of pine. A year later, in 1878, he applied for the night watchman's job with the city. Appointed, he enjoyed a monthly salary of seventy-five dollars. From this time on, Virgil was heavily involved in law enforcement. He was never a gambler like his two brothers, nor was he involved in saloon work; law enforcement was his primary source of employment. Two months later Virgil was elected constable of the Prescott precinct; therefore, he resigned his position as night watchman.

Precinct constables in Arizona, according to the Arizona Constable Association, "are empowered to serve all [processes] given to them by the Justice of the Peace or other competent authority. The processes include service of criminal and civil subpoenas and summonses, writs of restitution (eviction orders), writs of execution (orders to collect judgments), writs of replevin (orders to seize property), orders of protection and injunctions against harassment as well as any other orders from the courts. Constables may also be involved in the sale of seized property and summoning jurors for trials."

In October 1877 Sheriff Ed Bowers needed help quickly during an ongoing street gunfight; Virgil was deputized. In the course of the action, Virgil killed one of the robbers, shooting him twice through the head with a Winchester rifle.
The *Prescott Gazette*, twenty-eight years later, reran the article recalling Virgil's involvement:

"Shortly after arriving in Prescott, Virgil was deputized along with others by Sheriff Ed Bowers for a manhunt to chase down two fellows shooting up the town....the town was visited by two cowboys from the Bradshaw Basin region. They were said to be "shooting up saloons and other resorts". Then, riding out of town towards the Brooks Ranch, shooting right and left as they departed town. Arriving at the Brooks Ranch, the cowboys sent word to the officers that they were camped there, and if any of the officers wanted them, to come out and get them. These men were considered bad ones and were known to be dead shots. Meanwhile, Sheriff Bowers organized a posse of citizens...on horseback, led by Deputy U.S. Marshal Stanford and another deputy in a hack. The party in the hack passed the bad men unmolested, but the cowboys opened fire on the posse. Sheriff Bower's horse was hit. The Sheriff returned fire but was not himself hit. Arriving at the scene, Virgil Earp, armed with a Henry rifle, proceeded up the creek in the direction of the shooting, and, noticing one of the cowboys crouched under an oak tree reloading his gun, shot and killed him. The other cowboy was shot with a charge of buckshot and lived two days, finally dying at the hospital. Ear[p] came into prominence as a determined man and a good shot after this."

Prescott, AZ 1877. Public domain photograph.

This was an eye-opener for Allie; she had no idea that her man was capable of killing, even in the defense of the law.

November 27, 1879, United States Marshal Crawley Dake, for the eastern portion of Pima County, appointed Virgil deputy marshal. Virgil was to be headquartered in a newly formed village called Tombstone. Virgil, well aware of Tombstone and its silver strike, contacted his brothers to join him. By early December Virgil and his wife and family were in Tombstone. It was a village no more, but more of a town due to its massive population growth. The cowboy faction was in full force, lawlessness in full swing. Along with the good people—miners, ranchers, and business people—came the outlaws. The term used when referring to the group of men who robbed, stole, and rustled, and killed for a living was "cow-boy" or "cow-boy faction." Cow-boy (hyphenated) was a derogatory term.

*****

Tombstone was a "tony" town. There were four churches, an ice house, a school, two banks, three newspapers, an ice cream parlor, a bowling alley, a candy shop, and a race track. There were also 110 saloons, 14 gambling rooms, and numerous brothels and dance halls. Directly underneath the town were a multitude of mines. Ed Schieffelin, the discoverer of the silver bonanza and founder of the Tombstone township, built Schieffelin Hall, an opera house that could seat 575 people. It was a first-class theater, recital hall, and meeting place. The hall was considered the best opera house between San Francisco and St. Louis. Tombstone was indeed a happening place. Cochise County would be carved out of Pima County; Tombstone would be its county seat.

There was tension in Tombstone from day one. There were two factions that divided the city, the Republicans and the Democrats. The Democrats were comprised of ranchers and confederate sympathizers. Ike Clanton and his crew were Democrats. The Republicans were from northern states—townspeople and mining capitalists. The Earps identified with the Union and the higher breed of townsfolk; they were Republicans. This tension would explode with deadly conflict. It did not help matters that the town was near the Mexican border and the New Mexico Territory. This location made it easy for outlaws to rustle cattle out of Mexico and escape from the law, leaving the jurisdiction of Arizona was simple and speedy. Raids on the farms and ranchos of Mexico were common, as were shootings. The merchants, butchers, restaurant owners, etc., were eager to pay reduced rates for the beef. The cow-boys and these retailers were friends. The saloon owners also benefited from the rustled cattle; the rustlers spent many a dollar in pursuit of drink, women, and gambling.

Joining Virgil were his brothers Wyatt, Morgan, and James, as well as their families. Too young to be a permanent fixture, younger brother Warren would often visit. One writer suggested that the Earps sought law enforcement positions only to protect their gambling interests. There may have been some truth to that—wherever the Earps wound up, they owned either a full or partial interest in gambling tables. Besides having part ownership in a fargo game at the Oriental Saloon, the brothers were an ambitious lot, they were busy filing mining claims; true entrepreneurs. While his brothers Wyatt and Morgan filed mining claims, Virgil looked for an additional employment opportunity. He found it. On October 28, 1880, Virgil was appointed chief of police of Tombstone to replace the murdered Fred White. Now he had two jobs: Deputy United States Marshal and chief of police. While head cop, Virgil proposed six ordinances. One ordinance would give the marshal the authority to arrest anyone he thought was a nuisance. When the time came for him to run for reelection, Virgil lost.

*****

The 1880 census shows that Fred White, whose full name was Frederick G. White, was born in 1849 in New York City. On January 6, 1880, he became Tombstone's first city marshal. He served for ten months. At the time of his election the town had less than a thousand residents. Contrary to the films that show Marshal White as an elderly man, he was thirty-one years old the day he died, and very capable of handling himself. The cow-boy faction liked the man; in fact, most of the town was in agreement: he was affable. On October 27, 1880, Marshal White was shot and killed by "Curly Bill" Brocius. It was after the death of Marshal White that tensions between the Earps and the cow-boys heated up—363 days later, on October 26, 1881, it came to a head when the gunfight near the OK Corral occurred.

The shooting of Fred White happened at approximately 1:30 a.m. The shooting was on Allen Street between Fifth and Sixth Streets. It was a vacant lot. (Later this lot would be the site of the Bird Cage Theater.) Several cow-boys were in town, drinking heavily. In different locations they began firing their revolvers in the air. Marshal White followed the sounds and confronted and disarmed the cow-boys. When he got to Curly Bill at that empty lot, he told Brocius to give up his weapon. Curly Bill, drunk, pulled his pistol from his pocket, handing it to the marshal, barrel first. White grabbed the gun, pulling it hard from Curly Bill's hand. Having a hair trigger, the gun went off. Marshal White, shot in the groin, was down for the count. Three days later he died. On his deathbed White said to those at his bedside that the shooting was an accident. To avoid a lynching, Virgil had Brocius moved to Tucson for safekeeping. Wyatt was a witness to the accidental shooting. As soon as it occurred, Wyatt "buffaloed" Brocius, rendering him unconscious, and then disarmed and arrested him. During the trial in Tucson, as the under-deputy federal marshal, Wyatt testified that the shooting was an accident. With the testimony of a man on his deathbed and of an under-deputy marshal, "Curly Bill" Brocius was found not guilty and released. Although the actions and testimony saved Curly Bill's life, the man would not forgive being manhandled by Virgil's younger brother. Fred White was buried in Boot Hill; Virgil was appointed temporary city marshal.

Fred White, 1879. Photo courtesy of Wayne A. Highsmith Sr.
Member: Assoc. of Professional Genealogists

*****

Virgil's status as chief of police, or town marshal, lasted two weeks. Elections were held; he lost to Ben Sippy. Eight months later, on June 6, 1881, Virgil was again appointed acting city marshal when Sippy requested a temporary leave of absence. He never returned to Tombstone. He vanished with $3,000. He may have paid off some of his pending debt before leaving town, but $3,000 (equivalent to three years' worth of pay) from the marshal's office had been misappropriated. Mayor John Clum made Virgil's appointment permanent. Clum was the owner of the *Tombstone Epitaph* newspaper.

On June 22 a good portion of the city caught fire. This was the first of two major fires. The second occurred in May of the following year. The fire started when a lit cigar ignited a barrel of whiskey at the Arcade Saloon. It resulted in sixty-plus buildings being destroyed. Tombstone was quickly rebuilt. Virgil, as head of police, had his hands full; he was dealing with and preventing looting in addition to his normal duties of protecting the citizens and businesses and collecting taxes. By all indications he did a stellar job.

Times were different. The ladies of pleasure relied on the town marshal's help to protect them. Virgil was no different. He was mindful to the upside of having the moneymaking ladies kept in working order for the benefit all, including taxation. Researcher Kenny Vail wrote to me tha Virgil solicited taxes for the Fire Department Fund sixty times from the girls. Later he collected a dollar fifty from their madam for each working gal—this for his pocket.

Legend has it that Wyatt Earp stopped a large group of armed men from lynching a gambler who had murdered a well-respected miner. That is legend, often repeated in the movies. Here is what really happened:

Johnny Behind-The-Deuce (Mike O'Rourke) was a gambler—not on par with Luke Short or Bat Masterson, but a gambler just the same. He came to Tombstone at the age of sixteen. He found that the game of poker suited him; it was a good way to make a good living. Although he was often accused of cheating, the accusers would back down due to his unfounded reputation as a gunman. He was well-known for his quick temper. On January 14, 1881, in nearby Charleston—the town was considered the headquarters for the cow-boy faction and was located a little southwest of Tombstone—Johnny Behind-The-Deuce shot and killed Philip Schneider, chief engineer of the Corbin Mill. That day, as noted in the *Tombstone Epitaph* article printed on January 17:

"… Having just left the heated engine room the air without felt cool which brought from Mr. S. a remark to that effect. "Johnny-Behind-the-Deuce" who was also in the room, then said, "I thought you never got cold". Not desiring to have anything to do with one of his character, Mr. Schneider turned and said, "I was not talking to you, sir". This raised the lurking devil in the diminutive heart of "J-B-the-D," who blurted out, "G-d d-n you I'll shoot you when you come out," and left the room. After eating his dinner Mr. Schneider passed out the door, and was proceeding to the mill, when, true to his promise, the lurking fiend, who had secreted himself with hell in his heart and death in his mind, drew deadly aim and dropped his victim dead in his tracks."

Charleston's town marshal George McKelvey, with knowledge of a lynch mob forming, and having already arrested O'Rourke, decided it would be best to get him out of town to the safety of Tucson. With the help of another man, they placed O'Rourke in a wagon at a steady trot to nearby Tombstone. Then, realizing that they were being followed, the marshal whipped the mules, driving them harder, hoping that the animals would last the nine-mile drive. Outside of Tombstone Marshal McKelvey came across Virgil on horseback, having a leisurely ride. At this point Virgil was not a town cop, but was the Deputy U.S. Marshal for the area. His mules no longer able to travel, McKelvey told Virgil of the lynch mob. Virgil swung swung O'Rourke up and behind him onto the saddle, turned, and raced back to Tombstone. Gary Roberts, a respected historian and author, continues the story:

"… Virgil met Wyatt near the telegraph office and left the gambler with Wyatt, who moved him to Vogan's. Virgil went to look for Marshal Sippy and Deputy Sheriff

Behan. Wyatt assembled a group at Vogan's that included Shotgun Collins, Wes Fuller, and Doc Holliday, among others, and he sent Warren for horses. McKelvey and Bell arrived. Wyatt leads the prisoner through the crowd with his group when Virgil, Sippy, and Behan arrived with a wagon. Wyatt turned the prisoner over to the authorities who transported the prisoner supported by the Earp entourage."

This was good police work by frontier lawmen who used good judgment. There was never a single man who faced down a crowd; Virgil's role was pivotal. The *Epitaph* article continued:

"By this time Marshal Sippy, realizing the situation at once, in the light of the repeated murders that have been committed and the ultimate liberty of the offenders, had attempted on the part of the crowd to lynch the prisoner; but feeling that no guard would be strong enough to resist a justly enraged public long, procured a light wagon in which the prisoner was placed, guarded by himself, Virgil Earp and Deputy Sheriff Behan, assisted by a strong posse well armed. Moved down the street, closely followed by the throng, a halt was made and rifles leveled on the advancing citizens, several of whom were armed with rifles and shotguns. At this juncture, a well known individual with more avoirdupois than brains, called to the officers to turn loose and fire in the crowd. But Marshal Sippy's sound judgment prevented any such outbreak as would have been the certain result, and cool as an iceberg he held the crowd in check. No one who was a witness of yesterday's proceedings can doubt that but for his presence, blood would have flown freely. The posse following would not have been considered; but, bowing to the majesty of the law, the crowd subsided and the wagon proceeded on its way to Benson with the prisoner, who by daylight this morning was lodged in the Tucson jail."

The newspaper gave the credit for saving O'Rourke's life to Marshals McKelvey and Sippy, Deputy U.S. Marshal Virgil Earp, and Sheriff Behan. The paper did name Behan as a deputy sheriff, but in fact he was the county sheriff. Newspapers are seldom one hundred percent accurate. Both Dr. Roberts's and the *Epitaph* articles have their points; Gary Roberts is spot on.

O'Rourke was to stand trial in Tucson for the murder, but escaped. A year later Johnny Behind-The-Deuce was shot and killed in a gunfight in Sulphur Springs Valley, Arizona. There were no eyewitnesses. Pony Diehl, a top gun with the cow-boy faction, was in Sulphur Springs Valley when O'Rourke was killed. He would, in time, claim that he killed O'Rourke; Diehl believed that O'Rourke shot "Johnny Ringo." No one knows the how or who of Johnny Ringo's death; many feel it was suicide. And no one knows who shot and killed O'Johnny Behind-The-Deuce was twenty years old.

Things for the Earps got worst. Wyatt and Ike Clanton were at odds with each other. Clanton distrusted and hated Wyatt. As a close-knit clan, all of the Earps were involved. Doc Holliday, Wyatt's closest friend, added fuel to the fire with his uncompromising, better-than-thou attitude towards Ike.

On October 25, 1881, everything came to a head. Ike Clanton was in town. Up to his usual gambling and drinking, he was being his loud self. Doc and Ike got into a confrontation that was broken up by Virgil. Virgil had Wyatt take Doc to Fly's Boarding House, where Doc lived, to "sleep it off," while Virgil cautioned Ike. Later that evening Virgil sat in on a game of cards with Johnny Behan, Ike Clanton, Frank McLaury, and one other whose identity was lost to history. They played until dawn. Virgil and Behan headed to their homes to sleep, now officially off duty. Ike and Frank continued to drink. The more Ike drank, the louder he became. At one point somewhere past 8:00 a.m. Ike declared to the telegraph operator, E. F. Boyle, that the Earps would have to fight him. In his words, as quoted by Mr. Boyle, "As soon as the Earps and Doc Holliday showed themselves on the street, the ball would open." ("The ball would open" implies a gun battle.) Virgil was awakened and made aware of the threat. Dismissing the threat, he went back to sleep. Later that morning, Ike armed himself with his rifle and revolver. Now armed, against town rules, he proclaimed to all who would listen that he was looking for an Earp or Holliday. Virgil would be awakened again and updated. At 1:00 that afternoon, on October 26, Virgil, now awake and dressed, summoned his brother Morgan to help him find Ike. Virgil spotted Ike on Fourth Street, near the Spangenberg's Gun shop between Allen and Fremont Streets. Ike, drunk and with his rifle in hand, was spouting to all in sight that he was going kill the first Earp he saw. Coming up from behind, Virgil "buffaloed" Ike. He disarmed the man and hauled him off to police court, where Judge Wallace fined Clanton twenty-five dollars plus costs for violating the city ordinance of being armed in city limits. Ike was free to go; his weapons were deposited at the Grand Hotel, where he could pick them up as he left town. Somewhere after 1:30, prior to 2:00 that afternoon, Wyatt confronted an angry Frank McLaury. Frank had his gun tucked into the front of his pants. Wyatt pulled Frank's gun and pistol-whipped him. This done, Wyatt walked away. Tom McLaury and Billy Clanton entered town. Word had reached them that Ike was creating problems; Tom and Billy came to get their brothers out of harm's way. Both men were armed, as any frontiersman would be. The die was set. On top of too many threats, too many men of the cow-boy faction were in town. Virgil deputized Doc Holliday to join the group. Wyatt had been deputized a week earlier, and Morgan was already on the payroll as a deputy. Word had it that the McLaurys, Clantons, and Billy Claiborne were in an empty lot on Fremont Street, next to Fly Boarding House. Virgil decided to go disarm the five men. They had been seen earlier, by Wyatt, inside Spangenberg's gun shop, buying ammunition. Virgil guided his men up Fifth Street from Allen, then west on Fremont. The townspeople were everywhere, watching, waiting. The first one to walk into that empty lot was Virgil, followed by Wyatt, and then Morgan; Doc was on or near the sidewalk just outside the lot. Virgil spoke up: "We come to disarm you." Men started to reach for their weapons in an unfriendly manner. Virgil, with a cane in his hand, thrust it upward. "No, I don't mean that," he bellowed. It was all over with—thirty shots fired in thirty seconds, three men dead, and three men wounded. Virgil was shot in his lower leg. Morgan was shot through his shoulders. The bullet went in on one side and out the other. Doc was hit in the hip, Wyatt was untouched. Virgil was holding a walking stick (Holliday's) is an indication to many that Virgil had no intention to do harm, outside of disarming the combatants. This gunfight is known as the gunfight at the OK Corral. The OK Corral had nothing to do with it, but the name has stuck with the public ever since.

Virgil and Morgan had to recoup from their wounds; both were confined to a hotel. Holliday and Wyatt were arrested for murder and were held in the local jail, surrounded by armed guards and friendly, pro-Earp men who were determined to keep the two safe. A preliminary hearing was held; the Earps and Holliday were freed, for Judge Spicer's verdict was justifiable homicide. This hearing turned out to be more of trial—it lasted thirty days, the longest preliminary hearing in Arizona's history.

Virgil lost his job as town marshal; with him out, so were his brothers. They feared for their lives. The smell of reprisal was in the air. Arguments occurred all over town about the gunfight near the OK Corral, dividing its citizens—again, the Republicans from the Democrats. Who fired first; who was or was not armed? Was there romance between one of the Earp nieces and Frank McLaury? These are questions that can never be fully answered, but Virgil was the decision maker, it was he who decided to disarm the Clantons and McLaurys that afternoon. He was attempting to enforce the city ordinance; yet the OK fight is as controversial today as it was then. This gunfight characterizes the Old West; with Hollywood's help, a legend was created.

*****

Peace between the two factions was not to be. On December 28, two months later, Virgil was ambushed while crossing the street late that night. He was heading home to the Cosmopolitan Hotel, where the Earps were saying due to death threats. The Crystal Palace was in front of him; the Eagle Brewery, still under construction, was behind him when shots rang out. By all accounts he should have died, but he lived, losing the use of his left arm. The newspapers reported that twenty shots hit the Crystal Palace Saloon and the Eagle Brewery. The shotgun pellets struck Virgil's arm and back. His wounds were severe to the point that the doctors felt that Virgil would not survive. They wanted to remove his arm; he refused. Much of the shattered bone was removed, rendering his left arm useless. Virgil was not seen on the streets for the next three months. Near the shooting site, Ike Clanton's hat was found, his name written inside. There were three primary suspects: Ike Clanton, Phineas Clanton (Ike's older brother), and Pony Diehl. None were brought to trial; they all had ironclad alibis provided by their friends. It was mid-March before Virgil had the strength to get out of bed, and at that he was woozy.

March 18, 1882, three months after the ambush of Virgil, his younger brother Morgan, while playing a game of pool, was murdered via a through-and-through shot that severed his spinal cord. Virgil had enough strength to make it to nearby Campbell and Hatch's Billiard and Saloon, where Morgan was assassinated. He, with his wife and other family members, was present when Morgan passed away. The following day, Virgil—still too frail to defend himself—with his brother James and their wives, accompanied Morgan's body back home to Colton, California, for burial. Wyatt stayed behind to take care of business.

Virgil, still recovering from his injuries, settled in Colton. Despite having the use of only one arm, Virgil found gainful employment with the Southern Pacific Railroad. There was no hesitation by the Railroad in hiring Virgil. One-armed or two, he was a still a force to be reckoned with; few would try to defy him. He was hired to guard the tracks in Colton. The California Southern Railroad wanted access into California; they wanted to cross over the Southern Pacific tracks. The results of this "frog war" were quickly named Colton's Battle of the Crossing. Wikipedia tells us that a "frog" occurs when a private railroad company attempts to cross the tracks of another. It is named after frogs, for this piece of track allows the two tracks to join or cross; thus, like a frog, a train can jump onto another track. This attempt resulted in hostilities.

The disagreement grew; the towns of Colton and San Bernardino each had a vested interest. San Bernardino backed California Railroad, while Colton rallied behind the Southern Pacific. The Southern Pacific had bypassed San Bernardino. If the California Railroad tied into the Southern Pacific, San Bernardino might regain its importance. It came to a head on the morning of September 13, 1883; there was a lot of suspense that day. Virgil and his crew had done their job well, but the California Railroad was determined to put a frog in place so the railroad could switch over and use the Southern Pacific rails. This would give the California Railroad a huge advantage. The state governor had ordered the county sheriff of San Bernardino, J. B. Burkhart, to deputize ten men to enforce a court order giving California Railroad the right to lay down that frog. Governor Robert Waterman came south in person to deal with the problem. The sheriff and deputies had to guard the governor.

That morning men from the California Railroad arrived with the frog. Virgil was in the cab of the South Pacific Railroad locomotive that was slowly traveling forward and backward over the area where the frog was to be installed. On one side of the tracks were hundreds of San Bernardino citizens; on the opposite side, a large grouping of Colton residents. Virgil stepped out of the cab and stood near the tender, with a revolver in hand, facing the San Bernardino citizens; he never spoke. Governor Waterman arrived. Standing in front of the San Bernardino citizens, he read, out loud, the court order stating that Virgil to move the locomotive—at once. He then told Earp that if he made any move with his gun, the sheriff and his men had been instructed to fire on him. Realizing that he was in a helpless position, Virgil holstered his gun and ordered the engineer to remove the locomotive from the general area. The frog was installed. The battle of the crossing was over with no one injured.

The following year Nicholas Earp was elected justice of the peace. Virgil resigned his position with the railroad to open up the Virgil Earp Detective Agency. It was short-lived, for it closed down when Colton hired him as village constable in July. Colton was incorporated as a city on July 11, 1887. Virgil was elected its first city marshal. His monthly pay was seventy-five dollars. The following year he was reelected. Almost all police records in San Bernardino County were destroyed during the 1960s, as were the Los Angeles Police Department records. The police department, in the past, said they did not want some lawyer going through old records and filing lawsuits for past indiscretions, real or imaginary. Back then, one man going through a dumpster behind a building pulled out and saved some old documents mentioning Virgil, an invoice for detective work when Virgil had his agency was found among the papers. There is an account of him as a policeman strong-arming a young wannabe thug, with his one good arm. The young man was up against a wall, feet not touching the ground. The rest of his Colton police history regarding Virgile is gone, lost forever.

Virgil resigned from the police department that same year and moved to nearby San Bernardino, where he stuck around until 1893, when he and his wife, Allie, moved to Vanderbilt, California. There he owned and operated a saloon named Earp Hall. It was the only two-story building in this gold-mining town. It was also the only time in his life that Virgil was connected to a saloon. In a meeting room upstairs that packed four hundred, church services and dances were held. Vanderbilt was located on the California-Nevada border, a little village that lasted two years until the flooding of the mines.

The year 1895 found Virgil and Allie back in Prescott, Arizona, mining for a short period of time, then moving south from Prescott to nearby Kirkland Valley to ranch. His health was failing. He was nominated to run for county sheriff in 1900, but did not have the health to campaign. The year 1904 found Virgil and brother Wyatt in Goldfield, Nevada, a gold-mining town established in 1902. Virgil was hired on as a deputy sheriff. There are stories that Wyatt became the pit boss for the Northern Saloon, while others claim that he was part owner, but no real proof of either exists. However, the actual, on-record owner was Tex Rickard. Rickard and Wyatt were in Nome together and became lifelong friends. This was during the Alaskan Gold Rush of 1886, which lasted until 1899. Rickard was the founder of the New York Rangers, and builder of Madison Square Garden. During the 1920s Tex Rickard was considered the leading boxing promoter of the day.

In October 1905 Virgil came down with pneumonia. By October 19 he was improving. He asked his wife for a cigar. She gave him one. She sat beside him, and they held hands. Virgil Earp quietly died. His one and only daughter, Nellie, who was born while he was fighting in the Civil War, made arrangements for his remains to be sent to Portland, Oregon, where he lies in the family plot at the Riverview Cemetery.

Virgil worked as a farmer and rancher, solider, miner, frontier lawman, and saloon owner. His experience as a lawman was far greater than his brothers', yet he did not dwell on his experiences. He never felt sorry for the loss of his arm, nor did he seek fame. He worked hard and received respect due. He lived a full life—and then some—for he kept moving forward.

Tombstone was a "tony" town, there were four churches, an ice house, a school, two banks, three newspapers, ice cream parlor, a bowling alley, candy shop, and a race track alongside 110 saloons, 14 gambling rooms, numerous brothels and dance halls. Directly underneath the town were a multitude of mines. Ed Schieffelin, the discover of the silver bonanza and founder of the Tombstone township, build Schieffelin Hall, an opera house that could sit five hundred, seventy-five people. It was a first class theater, recital hall and meeting place. The "Hall" was considered the best opera house between San Francisco and St. Louis. Tombstone was indeed a happening place. Cochise County would be carved out of Pima County, Tombstone would be its county seat. A side note: The county was named after the famed Indian leader Cachise—yes Cachise is the correct spelling. When the paper work was filed during the formation of the new county, it was misspelled, and the name and spelling has remained as Cochise.

There was tension in Tombstone from day one. There were two factions that divided the city, the Republicans and the Democrats. The Democrats comprised of ranchers and confederate sympathizers. Ike Clanton and his crew were Democrats. The Republicans were from Northern states and comprised of townspeople and mining capitalists, the upper crust of society. The Earps identified with the Union and the higher breed of town folks, they were Republicans. This tension would explode with deadly conflict. It did not help matters that the town was near the Mexican border and the New Mexico Territory. This location, made it easy for rustling cattle out of old Mexico and an easy escape from the law with the ease and speed to leave the jurisdiction of Arizona for New Mexico. Raids on the farms and ranchos of old Mexico were common place as were shootings. The merchants, butchers, restrauants, etc., were eager to pay reduced rates for the beef. The cow-boys and the these retailers were friends. The saloon owners and cat houses also benefited. The rustlers, spent many a dollar in pursuit of drink, women and gaming.

Joining Virgil were the brothers and families of Wyatt, Morgan and James. To young to be a permanent fixture, younger brother, Warren, would often visit. One writer suggested that the Earps sought law enforcement positions only to protect their gambling interests. There may have been some truth to this since wherever the Earps wound up, they either owned a full or partial interest in gambling tables. Besides having a part ownership in a faro game at the Oriental Saloon, the brothers were busy filing mining claims. Call them want you want but entrepreneur fits the brothers well, they were an ambitious lot.

While his brothers, Wyatt and Morgan, filed mining claims, Virgil looked for additional employment opportunities. He found it, on October 28, 1880 when Virgil was appointed Chief of Police of Tombstone to replace the murdered Fred White. Now he had two jobs, United States Deputy Marshal and Chief of Police. While head cop, Virgil proposed six ordinances. One ordinance would give the police the authority to arrest anyone he thought was a nuisance. When the time came for him to run for re-election, Vigil lost.

Virgil's status as Chief of Police or town marshal lasted two weeks, elections were held, he lost to Ben Sippy. Eight months later, on June 6, 1881, Virgil was again, appointed acting city marshal when Sippy requested a temporary leave of absence. He never returned to Tombstone. He vanished with three thousand dollars. He may have paid off some of his pending debt before leaving town, but three thousand dollars was the equivalent to three years worth of pay, I guess it was too much of a temptation for Sippy. Mayor John Clum made Virgil's appointment permanent. Clum was the owner of the *Tombstone Epitaph* newspaper.

On June 22nd, a good portion of the city caught fire. This was the first of two major fires. The second occurred in May the following year. The fire stated when lighted a cigar ignited with a barrel of whiskey at the Arcade Saloon. It resulted in sixty-plus buildings destroyed. Tombstone was quickly rebuilt. Virgil as head of police had his hands full dealing and preventing looting in addition to his normal duties protecting the citizens, businesses and collecting taxes. By all indications he did a stellar job.

Times were different. The ladies of pleasure relied on the town marshal's t help protect them. Virgil was no different. He was mindful to the upside of having the money-making ladies kept in working order for the benefit all, including taxation. Researcher Kenny Vail, wrote to me of the time Virgil solicited taxes (collections) sixty times from the girls for the Fire Department Fund. Then later collected a dollar fifty from their madam for each working gal— for his pocket.

Legend has it that Wyatt Earp stopped a large group of armed men from lynching a gambler who had murdered a well respected miner. This legend has often repeated in the movies. Here is what really happened:

"Johnny Behind-The-Duce," (Mike O'Rourke) was a gambler. Not on the par of Luke Short or Bat Masterson, but a professional gambler just the same. He came to Tombstone at the age of sixteen. He found the game of poker suited him; it was a good way to make a good living. Although he was often accused of cheating, the accusers would back down due to his unfounded reputation as a gunman. He was well known for his quick temper.

On January 14, 1881, in nearby Charleston, a town considered the headquarters for the Cow-boy faction, located a little southwest from Tombstone, "Johnny Behind-The-Duce," shot and killed Philip Schneider, chief engineer of the Corbin Mill. That day, according to the *Tombstone Epitaph* article printed on January 17th the following:

"…at noon Mr. Schneider left his duties and went to a restaurant where he was accustomed to taking his meals, and on entering approached the stove and noticing a friend standing by, entered into the conversation. Having just left the heated engine room the air without felt cool which brought from Mr. S. a remark to that effect. Johnny-Behind-the-Deuce who was also in the room, then said, "I thought you never got cold". Not desiring to have anything to do with one of his character, Mr. Schneider turned and said, 'I was not talking to you, sir.' This raised the lurking devil in the diminutive heart of J-B-the-D, who blurted out, 'G-d d-n you I'll shoot you when you come out,' and left the room. After eating his dinner Mr. Schneider passed out the door, and was proceeding to the mill, when, true to his promise, the lurking fiend, who had secreted himself with hell in his heart and death in his mind, drew deadly aim and dropped his victim dead in his tracks."

Charleston's town Marshal, George McKelvey, with knowledge of a lynch mob forming, having already arrested O'Rourke, decided it would be best to get him out of town to the safety of Tucson. With the help of another man, they placed O'Rourke, in a wagon and at a steady trot headed to near-by Tombstone. Then realizing that they were being followed, the marshal whipped the mules, driving them harder, hoping that the animals would last the nine mile drive. Outside of Tombstone, Marshal McKelvey came across Virgil on horse back having a leisurely ride. Virgil at this time was not a town cop, but was the deputy U.S. Marshal for the area. The mules were no longer able to travel when they meant up with Ear; McKelvey told Virgil of the lynch mob. Virgil, swung O'Rourke up and behind onto the saddle, turned and raced back to Tombstone. Gary Roberts, a respected historian and author, tells us that Virgil…
"…met Wyatt near the telegraph office and left the gambler with Wyatt, who moved him to Vogan's. Virgil went to look for Marshal Sippy and Deputy [county] Sheriff Behan. Wyatt assembled a group at Vogan's that included Shotgun Collins, Wes Fuller, and Doc Holliday, among others, and he sent Warren for horses. McKelvey and Bell arrived. Wyatt leads the prisoner through the crowd with his group when Virgil, Sippy, and Behan arrived with a wagon. Wyatt turned the prisoner over to the authorities who transported the prisoner supported by the Earp entourage."

As Dr. Roberts and I both agree, this was good police work by frontier lawmen who used good judgment. It was never a single man who faced down a crowd; Virgil's role was pivotal. The *Epitaph* article continues:

"By this time Marshal Sippy, realizing the situation at once, in the light of the repeated murders that have been committed and the ultimate liberty of the offenders, had attempted on the part of the crowd to lynch the prisoner; but feeling that no guard would be strong enough to resist a justly enraged public long, procured a light wagon in which the prisoner was placed, guarded by himself, Virgil Earp and Deputy [county] Sheriff Behan, assisted by a strong posse well armed. Moved down the street, closely followed by the throng, a halt was made and rifles leveled on the advancing citizens, several of whom were armed with rifles and shotguns. At this juncture, a well know individual with more avoirdupois than brains, called to the officers to turn loose and fire in the crowd. But Marshal Sippy's sound judgment prevented any such outbreak as would have been the certain result, and cool as an iceberg he held the crowd in check. No one who was a witness of yesterday's proceedings can doubt that but for his presence, blood would have flown freely. The posse following would not have been considered; but, bowing to the majesty of the law, the crowd subsided and the wagon proceeded on its way to Benson with the prisoner, who by daylight this morning was lodged in the Tucson jail."

The credit, for saving O'Rourke's life was given, by the newspaper, to Marshals McKelvey and Sippy, Deputy U.S. Marshal Virgil Earp and Sheriff Behan. The paper did name Behan as a deputy sheriff but in fact he was the county sheriff. I mention this for newspapers are seldom one hundred percent accurate. You can look to Dr. Roberts explanation or to the *Epitaph's* article, both have their points, personally with all my research, Gary Roberts is spot on.

O'Rourke was to stand trial in Tucson for the murder, but escaped. We next hear of "Johnny Behind-The-Duce," a year later when he was shot and killed in a gunfight in Sulphur Springs Valley. There were no eye witnesses. Pony Diehl, a top gun with the cow-boy faction, was in Sulphur Springs Valley when O'Rourke was killed. He would, in time, claim that he killed O'Rourke for O'Rourke, was believed, by Diehl to have shot "Johnny Ringo." No one knows how or who killed Johnny Ringo, many feel it was suicide. And no one knows for sure who shot and killed O'Rourke. "Johnny Behind-The-Duce" was twenty years old when he died.

Things for the Earps got worst, the issue was more between Wyatt and Ike Clanton, but as a closed nit clan, all were involved. Distrust, and hatred sat in. Doc Holliday, Wyatt's closest friend, added to the fuel.
On October 25, 1881, every thing came to a head. Ike Clanton was in town up to his usual gambling, drinking and loud-self. Doc and Ike got into a confrontation, that was broken up by Virgil. Virgil had Wyatt take Doc to Fly's Boarding House, where Doc lived, to sleep it off, while he cautioned Ike. Later that evening Virgil sat in on a game of cards with Johnny Behan, Ike Clanton, Frank McLaury and one other whose identity is lost to history. They played until dawn. Virgil and Behan headed to their homes to sleep; now officially off duty. Ike and Frank continued to drink. The more Ike drank the louder he became. At one point, somewhere past 8:00 am, Ike declared to the telegraph operator,

E.F. Boyle, that the Earps would have to fight him. In his words, as quoted by Mr. Boyle "As soon as the Earps and Doc Holliday showed themselves on the street, the ball would open." (The "ball would open," implies a gun battle). Virgil was awaken and make aware of the threat. Dismissing the threat, Virgil went back to sleep. Later that morning, Ike armed himself with his rifle and revolver. Now armed, against town rules, he proclaimed to all who would listen that he was looking for a Earp or Holliday. Virgil would be awaken again and updated. At 1:00 that afternoon, on October 26, Virgil, now awake and dressed, summoned his brother Morgan to help him find Ike. Virgil spotted Ike on 4th Street, near the Spangenberg's Gun Shop between Allen and Fremont Streets. Ike was drunk with his rife and still spouting to all in sight that he was going kill the first Earp he sees. Coming up from behind, Virgil "buffaloed" Ike. He disarmed the man and hauled him off to police court where Judge Wallace fined Clanton twenty-five dollars for violating the city ordinance (of being armed in city limits), plus costs. Ike was free to go, his weapons were deposited at the Grand Hotel where he could pick them up as he left town. Somewhere after 1:30, prior to 2:00 that afternoon, Wyatt confronted an angry Frank McLaury. Frank had his gun tucked into the front of his pants. Wyatt pulled Frank's gun and pistol-wiped him. This done, Wyatt walked away. Tom McLaury and Billy Clanton enter town. Word had reached them that Ike was creating problems; they came to get their brother out of harm's way. Both men were armed as any frontiersman would be. The die is set. Too many threats, too many men of the Cow-boys in town, Virgil deputized Doc Holiday to join the group. Wyatt had been deputized a week earlier and Morgan was on the payroll as a deputy. Word had it that the McLaurys, Clantons and Billy Claiborne, were in an empty lot on Fremont Street, next to Fly's Boarding House. Virgil decided to go disarm the five men. They had been seen earlier, by Wyatt, inside Spangenberg's gun shop buying ammunition. Virgil guided his men up 5th Street, from Allen then west on Fremont. The town's people were everywhere watching, waiting. The first one to walk into that empty lot was Virgil followed by Wyatt, then Morgan and Doc who remained on or near the boardwalk just outside the lot. Virgil spoke up "we come to disarm you." Men started to reach for their weapons in an unfriendly manner, Virgil with a cane in his hand, thrusted it upwards "No, I don't mean that," he bellowed. It was all over with thirty shots fired in thirty seconds, three men dead, and three men wounded. Virgil was shot in his lower leg. Morgan through his shoulders, Doc hit in the hip, Wyatt —untouched. This gunfight is known as the Gunfight at the OK Corral. The OK Corral had nothing to do with it but the name has stuck with the public ever since. Virgil holding a walking stick, Holliday's, is an indication, by many, that Virgil had to intention to do harm, outside of disarming the combatants.

Virgil and Morgan had to recoup from their wounds, both were confined to a hotel. Holliday and Wyatt were arrested for murder, and held in the local jail surrounded by armed guards as well as friendly, pro-Earp men, who were determined to keep the two safe. A preliminary hearing was held, the Earps and Holliday were freed for the verdict was justifiable homicide.

Virgil lost his job as chief of police. With him out, so were his brothers. They feared for their lives. The smell of reprisal was in the air. Arguments occurred all over town about the gunfight near the OK Corral; dividing its citizens, again, the Republicans from the Democrats. Who fired first, who was or was not armed? Was there romance between one of the Earp girls (niece) and Frank McLaury? Questions that can never be fully answered, but we do know that Virgil, one of the key participants in the gun fight, and the man who decided to disarm the Clantons and McLaurys that afternoon. He was attempting to enforce the city ordinance. The gunfight near the OK Corral is as controversial today as it was then. This gunfight, the most famous of all gun battles in the 1880s, characterizes the Old West; with Hollywood's help, it's legend has grown.

Peace between the two factions was not to be, on December 28, two months later, Virgil was ambushed while crossing the street late that night having left the Oriental Saloon. He was heading home to the Cosmopolitan Hotel where the Earps were saying due to death threats. The Crystal Palace and Eagle Brewery, still under construction, beyond him when shots rang out. Both building were struck as well. By all accounts he should have died but he lived, minus the use of his left arm. The newspapers reported that twenty shots hit the Crystal Palace Saloon and the Eagle Brewery. Three loads of double barreled buckshot struck Virgil's arm and back. His wounds were severe that the doctors felt that Virgil would not survive. They wanted to remove his arm, he refused. So much of the shattered bone was removed rendering his left arm useless. Virgil was not seen on the streets for the next three months. Near the shooting site Ike Clanton's hat was found, his name written inside. There were three primary suspects: Ike Clanton, Phineas Clanton, Ike's older brother, and Pony Diehl. Wyatt brought both Phineas and Ike to trial but they produce some nineteen witness (friends) giving them ironclad alibis. It was mid March before Virgil had the strength to get out of bed, and at that he was woozy.

March 18, 1882, three months after the ambush of Virgil, his younger brother Morgan was murdered, a through and through shot that severed his spinal cord, while playing a game of pool. Virgil had enough strength to make it to nearby Campbell and Hatch's Billiard and Saloon where Morgan was assassinated. He with his wife and other family members were present when Morgan passed away. The following day, Virgil, still too frail to defend himself, with his brother James, and their wives, accompanied Morgan's body back home to Colton, California for burial. Wyatt stayed behind to take care of business.

Virgil, still recovering from his injuries, settled in Colton. Despite having the use of only one arm, a year later, Virgil found gainful employment with the Southern Pacific Railroad. Handicap or not, the Southern Pacific did not hesitate hiring Virgil; he was a still a force to be reckoned with. Few would try to defy him. He was hired to guard its tracks in Colton. The California Southern Railroad wanted access into California, they wanted to cross over the Southern Pacific tracks. The results of this "frog war" was quickly named Colton's "Battle of the Crossing." Wikipedia tells us that a "frog" occurs when a private railroad company attempts to cross the tracks of another. It is named after frogs for this piece of track allows the two tracks to join or cross, thus, like a frog, you can jump onto another track. This attempt resulted in hostilities.

The disagreement grew, the towns of Colton and San Bernardino each had a vested interest. San Bernardino backed California Railroad while Colton rallied behind the Southern Pacific. The Southern Pacific had by-passed San Bernardino. If the California Railroad ties into the Southern Pacific, San Bernardino may regain its importance. It came to a head on the morning of September 13th, 1883; there was a lot of suspense that day. Virgil and his crew had done their job well but the California Railroad was determined to put a "frog" in place so the railroad could switch over and the Southern Pacific rails. This would give California Railroad a huge advantage. The state Governor, had ordered the County Sheriff of San Bernardino, J.B Burkhart, to deputize ten men to enforce a court order giving California Railroad, the right to to lay down that "frog." Governor Robert Waterman came south in person to deal with the problem The sheriff and deputies were there to guard the governor.

That morning men from California Railroad arrived with the "frog." Virgil was in the cab of the SPRR locomotive that was slowly traveling forward and backwards over the area where the "frog" was to be installed. On one side of the tracks were hundreds of San Bernardino citizens, on the opposite side, a similar number of Colton residents. Virgil stepped out of the cab and stood near the tender, with a revolver in hand, facing the San Bernardino citizens; he never spoke. Governor Waterman arrived. Standing in front of the San Bernardino citizens, he read, out loud, the court order ordering Virgil to move the locomotive—at once. He then told Earp that if he made any move with his gun, the sheriff and men had been instructed to fire on him. Realizing that he was in a helpless position, Virgil holstered his gun and ordered the engineer to remove the locomotive from the general area. The "frog" installed. the battle of the crossing was over with, no one injured.

The following year, Nicholas, was elected Justice of the Peace. Virgil resigned his position with the Railroad to open up the Virgil Earp Detective Agency. It was short-live for it closed down when Colton hired him as as village constable in July. Colton was incorporated as a city on July 11, 1887. Virgil was elected its first city marshal. His monthly pay was seventy-five dollars. The following year he was re-elected. Almost all police records in San Bernardino County were destroyed during the 1960s, as were the LAPD records. When I questioned those in the Police Department, the answer was that they did not want some lawyer going through old records and filing law suits for past indiscretions, real or imaginary. Back then, one man going through a dumpster, behind a building most like the police or Hall of Records building, pulled out and save some old documents mentioning Virgil. I have seen and read an invoice for detective work when Virgil had his "agency," I found an account of him strong arming a young want-a-be thug as a policeman, with his one good arm. The young man was up against a wall, feet not touching the ground. The rest of Virgil's Colton Police and P.I. history is gone, lost forever.

Virgil resigned from the Police Department that same year, moved to nearby San Bernardino where he stuck around until 1893 when he and his wife, Allie, moved to Vanderbilt, California. There he owned and operated a saloon named "Earp Hall." This was the only two story building in this gold mining town. It was also the only time in his life that Virgil was connected to a saloon. Church services, a meeting room that packed four hundred and dances were held upstairs. Vanderbilt, was located on the California—Nevada border, a little village that lasted two years until the flooding of the mines.

1895 found Virgil and Allie back in Prescott, Arizona mining for a short period of time, then moving south from Prescott to nearby Kirkland Valley to ranch. His health was failing. He was nominated to run for county sheriff in 1900, but did not have the health to campaign. 1904 found Virgil in Goldfield, Nevada, a gold mining town established in 1902. Virgil and brother Wyatt arrived in 1904. Virgil hired on as a deputy sheriff. There are stories that Wyatt became the pit boss for the Northern Saloon, others claiming that he was part owner but no proof of either, however, the actual, on record owner, was Tex Rickard. Rickard and Wyatt were in Nome, together and became life long friends. This was during the Alaskan Gold Rush of 1886, that lasted until 1899. Rickard was the founder of the New York Rangers, and builder/owner of Madison Square Garden. During the 1920s, Tex Rickard was the considered leading boxing promoter of the day.

In October, 1905, Virgil came down with pneumonia. By the nineteenth he was improving. He asked his wife for a cigar. She gave him one. Sitting beside him, they held hands. Virgil Earp, quietly died. His one and only daughter, Nellie, who was born while he was fighting in the Civil War, made arrangements for his remains to be sent to Portland, Oregon, where he lies in the family plot at the Riverview Cemetery.
Virgil worked as a farmer/rancher, solider, miner, frontier lawman and saloon owner. His experience as a lawman was far greater than his brothers, yet, he did not dwell on his experiences. He never felt sorry for the lost of his arm, nor did he seek fame, he worked hard and received respect due. He lived a full life and then some for he kept moving forward; his greatest allies was his family and equally important, his wife Allie.

Patrick "Pat" Sughrue (1844-1906)

Pat and his twin brother, Mike, hailed from County Kerry, Ireland. The family packed up and moved to the United States when their mother passed away; when Pat was ten. First stop was Illinois for a few years, then on to Leavenworth, Kansas, in 1858. At fourteen they were old enough to work. Pat apprenticed and then worked full-time as a blacksmith. He was a blacksmith for nearly twenty years. In March 1877 Pat and his brother moved to Dodge City. Dodge was *the* "happening place"—it had "snap." Commerce was booming, and its main source was the cow trade. The town's secondary source of income was entertainment. The cattle drovers would have to wait their turns to load the cattle in the cattle cars to be hauled off to Chicago and other points in the East. Their wages in their pockets, time on their hands, the drovers wanted to be entertained. Dodge City offered that opportunity in spades.

The *Dodge City Times*, on March 24, 1877, made its first mention of night watchman Pat Sughrue when he came to the aid of Bobby Gill, who was embracing a beautiful Creole woman in the privacy of her home, when James Manion, wanting her, showed up in an angry mood, armed. Mr. Manion was a well-known businessman and a member of the Dodge City upper elite social circle. Mr. Gill was a young and somewhat notorious person who often found himself in trouble. Night watchman Sughrue heard a ruckus during his rounds and came to the rescue of Bobby Gill in the nick of time. Sughrue managed to confiscate the revolver before it could be used.

Pat had a soft spot for the down and out. He took in a man, down on his luck, a "tramp" as described by the newspaper. The tramp's name was John Carlton. Pat fed him, clothed him, put a roof over his head; he even secured the man a job. The job, as it turned out, was not what Mr. Carlton wanted; he had no interest in working. But he was interested in Pat's tools, so while Sughrue was out, the man sneaked into the blacksmith shop and loaded his pockets with as many of Pat's tools as he could before heading out.

Sughrue ran into Carlton outside his shop. He noticed tools protruding from the tramps pockets and proceeded to kick him in the pants. Each kick resulted in a tool being exposed. Satisfied that all the tools were out of the thief's pockets, the night watchman picked them off the ground and proceeded to take them back to his shop. When Sughrue turned his back away from Carlton, the thief drew a heavy soldering iron from a pocket and, sneaking up behind Sughrue, aimed a murderous blow at his head. A bystander had watched the confrontation leading up to this point. Recognizing the danger, the bystander called out a warning to Sughrue. Sughrue was saved in the nick of time; Carlton found himself in more trouble. Town Marshal Deger became involved, arresting the man. Later that night he was released, with the condition that he would leave town. Carlton did not. Instead he decided to rob another. Within two hours of his release, Carlton ambushed Colonel Colley while he was walking down the darkened street. A blow to his head by a heavy rock almost knocked Colley out. The colonel screamed for help as he rose to give chase. Carlton got away, but he was identified by his victim. The next morning the law had their man in jail, where he remained for some time.

Pat was not just a blacksmith and part-time nightwatchman; he went out looking for minerals and discovered chalk. Chalk then and now has value—nothing like silver or gold, but worth enough to work the claim. Pat was the owner of a chalk mine; he was doing all right for himself.

April 27, 1878, the *Dodge City Times* reported that Sughrue and another blacksmith were manufacturing large numbers of cattle brands; as they worded it, "some brands are ingeniously wrought." In other words, they were damn good, talented blacksmiths. Dodge was the center of the cattle business, and the money continued to fill Sughrue's pockets.

The newspapers were good about reporting and preserving history. They may not have gotten it correct all the time, but the reports give impressions—hints, if you will—to the workings of the frontier lawman. For example, it was reported that Constable Pat Sughrue had arrested Charles Trask for mule stealing. Pat was rewarded fifty dollars for the mules' return. Lawmen were well paid. Smithing, although an important and well-respected trade, never saw the likes of fifty dollars for a few hours of work.

Affable Pat, now experienced in law enforcement, was elected town constable on November 6, 1877; Bat Masterson was voted in as Ford County's sheriff during the same election. All of the big-time, now famous, lawmen were active in Dodge. Besides Sughrue, there were men like the Mastersons and the Earp brothers, Charlie Bassett, Bill Tilghman, Neil (Neal) Brown, Frank McLean, J. J. Webb, and a host of others, not to mention the infamous gunslingers and gamblers. Pat held his own; he fit in well. As sheriff he could keep the current deputy or hire his own men. His twin brother, Michael, and "Mysterious Dave" Mather were his two choices.

When the ever-popular singer Dora Hand was murdered, the most legendary posse of the wild west era was assembled. Sheriff Bat Masterson, Deputy Sheriff Bill Duffey, posse man and temporary deputy Bill Tilghman, City Marshal Charlie Bassett, and Assistant Marshal Wyatt Earp were its members. Sughrue and James Masterson stayed behind to monitor Dodge.

Pat married in 1880. His wife was never mentioned in any news articles, but the newspapers did report how busy the sheriff was. Sughrue dealt with burglars, forgers, horse thieves, and the necessary drudgery of transporting prisoners. Not many escaped arrest. Not one to give up easily, Sheriff Sughrue would travel as far as New York to arrest outlaws. He always caught his man, as reported in the *Ford County Globe* on June 12, 1884. The newspapers said that there were enough incidents—and, therefore, proof— during Sughrue's time in that he was making at least one significant arrest each month.

The Dodge City War took place in 1883. (See the Luke Short chapter in volume one.) Although it was bloodless, no one expected it to be. Sheriff Sughrue had sided with Luke Short. Luke had friends. A large group of famous gunslingers were summoned to come to his aid. The Long Branch Saloon was stolen by then mayor of Dodge Deger and his minions. Short was shackled, taken to the train depot, put on the first to leave, and warned to never return. Mr. Short wanted to restore Long Branch Saloon to its rightful owners— himself and partner W. H. Harris. Governor George Glick agreed to look the other way, allowing Short and Masterson, who masterminded the town's take-over, to do what was needed. Pat was well respected, was in agreement with Luke Short, and was elected captain of the Glick Guards, a militia unit named after the governor. This militia would be nearby, but if needed, they would instill order and shore up the eroded political fallout; fortunately things did not.

In July of 1884 "Mysterious Dave" Mather shot to death Tom Nixon. Pat arrested Mather for the murder. Mather had been Pat's deputy for the past year. Mather was acquitted of the charge. Mather was once again arrested for another murder in May 1885 and acquitted. City Marshal Bill Tilghman had enough of Mather's killings; after the trial, he ran Mather out of town.

Texas fever was a major problem with longhorn cattle. They were carriers of this deadly disease but were immune; all other domestic animals, including other species of cattle, were not. From late 1883 into 1884 Pat and his deputies, under orders from the governor, stopped all incoming cattle herds suspected of having the fever. The herds were forced to turn back. One can only imagine confronting heavily armed cattle drovers. This was no easy task and was extremely dangerous, but he succeeded without bloodshed.

Pat ran for reelection in 1884 and again in 1885. He won both elections, but the rowdy times of Dodge City were coming to an end. He was no dummy; his deputy was

Bill Tilghman, whose law efforts would grow to legendary status. Together they dealt with various crimes including prostitution, robbery, theft, and murder—not on a grand scale as in the heydays of Dodge City, but more than enough to keep the two busy.

Dodge was no longer the "end of the trail" for the cattle drives. The railroads had moved further south. Caldwell's position on the Kansas side of the Oklahoma-Kansas border would take up the slack. The homesteaders were moving in, and farms were being established; Dodge was settling down and becoming a progressive, quiet city. The issue of the Texas fever would raise its ugly head once more. Pat rose to the task. All Texas cattle from this point forward were banned from Kansas. Once more, Sheriff Pat Sughrue and Deputy Tilghman (Tilghman was still the city marshal) were extremely successful. No one was killed or injured. The township of Caldwell found an easy way around the ban. As noted in chapter two of this book, their corrals and railway terminal were located on the other side of town across the border in Oklahoma Territory. The ban did not apply; Kansas was skirted.

Governor Glick wrote the following letter as reported in the *Globe Live Stock Journal:*

"TOPEKA, Sept. 22, 1884.

To P. F. SUGHRUE, SHERIFF, DODGE CITY, KANSAS.

MY DEAR SIR: I was very much gratified to be reliably informed that under my proclamation and the law, your efficiency as an officer in protecting the large stock interests of your county is worthy of the highest commendation.

It has been stated to me that you have gone out among incoming herds where Texas fever was feared, and by your promptness and energy, and prudent management (in one instance at least) have turned back herds that would have spread destruction amongst the cattle of Kansas, and would have produced great damage and loss to the stock owners of our state. I understand that the owners, after you stating your authority, and producing the proclamation and notifying them that nothing would save them from the severest prosecution under the law, finally decided to leave the state at once.

I certainly commend your discretion and firmness in this matter. I hope that others will feel the necessity of acting as promptly and discreetly in this matter. I desire, therefore, to thank you in the name of the good people of our state, whom you have protected against that fearful disease the Texas fever.

I am, sir most respectfully,
Your obedient servant,

G. W. GLICK"

The famed cattle drives to Kansas had ended by the state's proclamation law. The turning back of cattle drives was Pat Sughrue's last major act as a lawman. He quit, taking on the job as postmaster for the village of Fort Dodge; the actual fort was closed in 1882. The Red River War was over; the Native Americans were no longer a threat.

In 1906 Pat went to Topeka, Kansas, to attend a political convention. For whatever reason, most likely because he was in a hurry or someone distracted him, the elevator door opened, and he stepped in without looking—he fell to his death. Pat Sughrue, who became known throughout the country as one of the best lawmen in the West, died at the age of sixty-two. His body was taken back to Dodge City, where he was buried in the Maple Grove Cemetery.

*****

Michael, Pat's twin brother, had a career in law enforcement as well, though not as well-known. The bombardment and surrender of Fort Sumter in Charleston, South Carolina, on April 12, 1861, marked the beginning of the Civil War. Michael joined the Seventh Kansas Cavalry, serving the Union until the war ended in 1865. In 1875 Michael married Anna Walter in Ashton, Kansas. Together they would have ten children. Pat, now sheriff of Ford County, contacted his brother, asking him to work as a deputy. In December 1884, right after the town of Ashland was formed, two cowboys terrorized the town. Pat sent Michael to arrest the men. "Hurraying" a town is dangerous and always outlawed; these two men, Joe Mitchell and Nels Mathews, wounded a woman and killed two men while having their "fun." Michael was successful in arresting Mitchell, but Mathews escaped, fleeing the area. Placing Mitchell under heavy guard, Michael chased after Mathews. Unable to locate the fleeing criminal, Sughrue returned to town to find that a vigilante group had lynched Mitchell. The town was extremely impressed with Sughrue. They asked Michael to remain and become their town marshal. A year later, with the formation of Clark County, he became its first sheriff. Ashland and Clark County were never as notorious as Dodge City and Ford County, but Ashland, like all frontier towns, had its share of problems. Michael did a great job. He was continually reelected and served until 1890. There is no mention of Michael for the next ten years until he ran for sheriff in 1899. He remained sheriff until he passed away at home on January 2, 1901. He was two months shy of fifty-seven. Although he was not as well-renowned as his brother, Michael was a noted lawman during his time. The brothers are both regarded among the best frontier lawmen.

MICHAEL SUGHRUE'S OBITUARY (in part):

Clark County Clipper, January 10, 1901

"Mr. Sughrue was a Deputy Sheriff under his brother Pat, of Ford County, in 1884, and when Clark County was organized in 1885 was its first Sheriff. He was elected Sheriff five times and was serving his ninth year at the time of his death; he was also the only Republican Sheriff ever elected. He was the first Marshal of the city of Ashland and was Marshal at the time of his death….Mike Sughrue was one of the most widely known "old timers" in western Kansas, and was universally respected. He had shared his blanket with "Buffalo Bill" when borean [*sic*] blasts swept prairies like the simoon [Simon] of the desert, and had followed the courageous Jamison thru trials to daring achievements that won applause from a nation. He had associated with Col. Inman on "The Old Santa Fe Trail," now famous, and had swapped yarns with the gallant Custer in his palmy [*sic*] days, in view of the light of the Redman's campfire. No state ever had a more courageous officer than Mike Sughrue. The western outlaw, even before discovered, trembled as with a chill at the sight of Sheriff Sughrue with a white handled pistol in his belt…."

Vol.2. A Fraternity of Gunslingers

The Montana "Vigilance Committee" (1863-1864)

This chapter is about several mining towns whose citizens lived in fear of an outlaw band that terrorized, robbed, and murdered pretty much at will. This period was during the Civil War and is not considered part of the era we call the Wild West. It is better suited as the Old West. The biggest difference, is that the post–Civil War era often is referred to as the Wild West, an era that lasted only a generation. An historian declared that the Wild West ended in 1930, most say it ended in 1900.
With the outbreak of the Civil War there was no close attention paid to the territories. Civilization broke down, for there was no law structure to speak of; the results were mayhem and vigilante activity.

Chapter ten will continue on with the vigilante theme and the life and death of Sheriff Henry Plummer and the main executioner for the Vigilance Committee, John "X" Beidler. Beidler would rise to become a Deputy United States Marshal of the eastern Montana Territory. In 1889 Montana would become a state. Before this time there were no rules or laws. Montana was and is a place with especially harsh winter months. Many men would succumb to the unforgiving frontier.
Unlike the other chapters, this chapter contains a grouping of photographs at the end.

*****

The Vigilance Committee captured, tried, and hanged twenty-three men who allegedly associated themselves with a group of men calling themselves the Innocent Gang, some times referred to as the Innocence Gang.

John White discovered placer gold deposits in Grasshopper Creek in 1862. Simple tools could easily remove the gold. Tools such as gold pans, sluices, and rocker boxes were used. Later, hydraulic and dredge mining would take place. The discovery of gold traveled fast; people came running. Dugouts and actual cabins sprung up almost instantaneously Bannack was born then, officially becoming a town on November 21, 1863, when a post office was established. At its peak, the population was around three thousand in Bannack proper, with another two thousand living near or at their claims near the creek. Before Bannack, gold had been discovered in Alder Gulch. This is an article written by Thomas Dimsdale in his book, *The Vigilantes of Montana.*

Alder Gulch [gold discovered] by Tom Cover, Bill Fairweather, Barney Hughes, Edgar and some others. It was a sheer accident. After a long and unsuccessful tour they came thither on their way to Bannack, and one of them took a notion to try a pan of dirt. A good prospect was obtained, and the lucky "panner" gave his name to the far famed Fairweather district.

The original name of this new township was Varina. The town was named after Varina Howell Davis—the wife of Jefferson Davis, president of the Confederacy—by the founding miners. The name did not last. Its first elected judge had to affix his name to a legal document. He bellowed that under no circumstance would he do so with the name Varina on its letterhead, that he would be damned first. Judge G. G. Bissell wrote in the name Virginia for the letterhead, and the name stuck. Later, "City" would be added, thus becoming Virginia City, as it remains to this day. At the time of the discovery, Virginia City was inside Idaho Territory; soon the territory would be split to form Montana Territory. Virginia City was now inside Montana's borders. There is also a Virginia City in Nevada, where the Comstock Lode was discovered, the treasure of which was the richest silver deposit of all time. There were mining operations for gold as well.

While Bannack would eventually yield some $5 million (somewhere around $125 million in todays money), the Virginia haul would be over $100 million. At its peak Bannack's population numbered ten thousand. The two towns were approximately eighty miles apart, with Bannack southwest of Virginia.

Nevada, later to be renamed Nevada City, is located a half mile west of Virginia. It was settled June 6, 1863, a month after Virginia. There were nine settlements along the fourteen-mile length of Alder Gulch, but Nevada and Virginia were the largest. The length of the gulch was commonly known as Fourteen Mile City. It would be here in Nevada that the first miner's trial took place—the trial of George Ives for the murder of Nicholas Tbalt.

With the discovery of gold, the run was on. Good, hardworking men came to seek their fortune, but with them came those whose idea of fortune seeking was to rob, stab, shoot, kill, and claim jump. As in all mining towns, there was a shortage of women. The "hurly-girly" ladies of pleasure took up the gap, for a price. These ladies became saloon and dance hall gals who made a handsome living. For example, a good-looking, good-dancing dance hall gal would easily earn twenty-six dollars in an evening, just by dancing. The ladies dressed in all fashion and manner—the louder, the better. The rough and tumble towns of Kansas, such as Hays, Wichita, Dodge City, Caldwell, and even Tombstone, had ordinances, strictly enforced, disallowing guns in town; all had to be checked in. Montana did not disallow weapons in the town proper. Imagine a city full of uneducated miners carrying their firearms and long knives, with large amounts of gold on their persons, while drinking at the local water hole, surrounded by cutthroats and gamblers, with a lack of any justice system. This was Virginia (City), Nevada, and

Bannack. Night or day there was violence. Men would not travel from Virginia to Nevada, Summit, or Bannack after dark. Shooting out windows was fair game. Guns randomly fired in saloons, a daily occurrence. This was so common that it became a natural, normal event in the minds of the citizens. Highwaymen who robbed stagecoaches and freighters roamed the roads looking for their pry—crime was everywhere.

Life in Bannack was anything but pleasant. The thugs and dishonest men gathered, quickly organizing themselves with a captain, lieutenants, a secretary, road agents, and outsiders. It did not take long for them to terrorize the countryside. Between the towns of Bannack and Virginia the roads were under surveillance by the outsiders. A system was devised to simply mark the target so the road agents knew whom to attack and whom to let by. It has been reported that up to one hundred men were involved at one time or another in this gang. With its membership always in flux, they had to recognize each other, so a password was used—"I am innocent"—thus the name the Innocent Gang (sometimes referred to as the Innocence Gang). There was never any paper work; proof of membership was near impossible. The victims never had a chance.

The road agent was well armed. He normally carried a set of revolvers, a sawed-off shotgun, and a knife. He was always disguised by wearing a mask and blanket around his upper torso. Blankets were place over his horse to hide its identity. But one's voice, one's mannerism could not stop the victim's keen sense of observation. The victim would often keep his observations to himself; other victims would keep a low profile and quietly, softly speak to friends. It was no real secret who was doing the deeds. The road agents worked in threes. Two agents would remain on horseback, covering the driver, guard, and passengers. The third would dismount, make sure the victims were disarmed, and collect their valuables. If all obeyed and did so quickly, they were free to go. The key terms here are "obey" and "do so quickly." The spoils would be divided.

*****

Dutch Fred, was accosted by road agents. He was ordered to throw up his hands. On his person he had five dollars. The amount of money was too low. In between curses, Fred was sternly told to never travel this road with only five dollars or he would be shot, then the highwayman decided to shoot him anyway, wounding him in his arm. This scenario was not an isolated case.

George Ives was a good-looking man around the age of twenty-seven, about six feet in height. He had blondish-brown hair and the complexion to match, with blue eyes and a clean-shaven face. He wore buckskin clothing with a heavy overcoat and felt hat. His peers considered him cool, even-tempered, and, above all, fearless. His lack of fear allowed him to be reckless, causing fear in ordinary citizens. For sport one of his tricks was to back his horse into store windows, breaking them, and then ride off laughing.

Once in 1862, with friends and co–gang members Alexander Carter and William Hunter, Ives ran into a man named Anton Holter near the Ramshorn Mountains at Brown's Gulch and decided to rob him of his money. The only money Holter had with him was his bank notes, or checks as we call them today. Ives told him, in a somewhat nice way, to draft a check in his name. Holter decided this would be a good idea but warned them that he had little money in the bank. He received a lecture for not having more funds. Displeased, Ives drew his gun, aimed at Holter's head, and fired. The bullet grazed Holter's scalp while passing through his hat. Ives fired a second shot; it too entered Holter's hat, again missing Holter's head, the intended target. George gave up; he and his cohorts went on their way. Anton Holter did likewise and lived a full life. The hat's design somehow deceived Ives's aim.

Not long after, Ives received word of a man who, while tied to a post, was being whipped for larceny (theft of personal property). To stop the whipping, this man offered to give the names of various gang members. On his horse George headed to Cold Spring Ranch. On the road near the ranch's gate, he ran into the informant. A blast from Ives's shotgun was of no help; the load was poorly packed. The thief was wearing a heavy overcoat, and the effects of the shotgun were harmless, so Ives unholstered his revolver and took aim. One shot, and the thief lay dead. Ives then took the man's horse by its bridle and headed into the woods. This murder was seen by various people on the road.

Nicholas Tbalt (proper spelling most likely Tiebolt) was a young man who immigrated to the untamed west roughly two years prior to the shooting. On this day, Nicholas, the proud owner of three mules, sold the mules to his employers, Butschy and Clark, who paid him in advance. Taking the gold with him, he went to Dempsey's Ranch to bring up the animals. In the process of bringing them back, he was accosted by George Ives. Nicholas was roped, his hands were bound, and then he was dragged through the stage brush and shot in the head just below his left eye; his mules were stolen—all in broad daylight. There were people on the trail, witnesses. The ranchers looked for Tbalt without luck; they assumed that Tbalt had taken off with the gold and mules. But ten days later he was found. His location was marked by birds circling overhead.

Having stolen the mules, Ives went to his buddy George Hilderman's place, a wickiup, to hole up for a while. Hilderman's wickiup was more of a lean-to made from branches. Ives had used Hilderman's place to hide out before, when he had murdered others. As it turned out, the wickiup was not more than a half mile from Tbalt's body.

William Palmer was driving his wagon across the Stinkingwater Valley near the scene of the murder. A grouse rose out of the brush in front of him. Quickly he aimed his shotgun and fired. The bird dropped dead into the brush, right on Tbalt's body. He went to retrieve the bird and found the body. Palmer went down to the wickiup, where he found both Hilderman and a man known as Long John (John Franck) and requested their help to place the corpse into his wagon. The two men refused, but he managed anyway. He set off to Nevada to get the man identified and buried.

Nicholas Tbalt's body, frozen by the harsh winter, was brought into town. A citizen, William Herren, went to Virginia to inform Tom Baume of Tbalt's death. Baume, John Beidler, and William Clark all knew each other well. The ranchers up and down the main road knew who the highwaymen were, but fear usually made them silent. This was different. This cold-blooded, cruel, unnecessary murder of Tbalt was the tipping point for the people. One man from Nevada and five from Virginia simultaneously took to the task of forming the Vigilance Committee. Wilbur Sanders of Virginia and John Lott of Nevada were the two founders. They joined forces with a combined membership of twenty-five men. Two days after Tbalt's funeral they were ready. The first man on their list: George Ives.

The committee consisted of merchants, mechanics, miners, store owners, and professional men. They were all tired of murder and mayhem and living in fear. At 10:00 p.m. on December 17, 1863, the party left Nevada (City). Five and a half hours later they arrived near their destination—Hilderman's wickiup. It was ice-cold, the ground near frozen. At Washington Creek the men dismounted and guided their horses across the creek. With seven miles more to go, the men rode in silence; they were used to the harsh life of the frontier. As hearty as they were, the crossing of the creek hurt them. Wet clothing froze on them. Frostbite started to set in, yet they persevered and managed to overtake eight men at the wickiup: Long John (John Franck), Alex (sometimes spelled Aleck) Carter, Bob Zachary, Whiskey Bill, Johnny Cooper, and George Ives, along with two strangers who happened to pass by. These two men were released. Weapons were gathered and inventoried. Seven dragoon and navy revolvers, nine shotguns, and thirteen rifles were confiscated. During a stagecoach robbery Leroy Southmayde's pistol was taken by one of the highwaymen. Due to an old repair of its barrel, as reported by Thomas Dimsdale, it was easily recognizable. It was one of the weapons inventoried.

Ives and Long John were placed on horses and then taken to Dempsey's Ranch outside of Deer Lodge. George Hilderman was at the ranch, working. The committee questioned Hilderman, who acknowledged that he was indeed one of the men they were looking for. He refused to go with them; the committee's leader, however, said something causing a change of heart. Hilderman was given a mule to ride and a stick to prod it.

Ives laid out a plan to escape. He appealed to the competitiveness in others; since they had a ways to travel, he challenged his capturers to a race, and they accepted. Ives had great pride in his horses and his ability as a rider. This horse of his, one of several, described as a "spotted bob-tailed pony," was fast and well trained. Who won the race did not surprise anyone. It did surprise his capturers when he continued past the finish mark at a full gallop. "Twenty-four pairs of spurs were driven home into the flanks of twenty-four horses…." Ives was headed to Daley's Ranch, where his favorite mare was saddled and apparently waiting for his owner. But he was hotly pursued and was unable to reach his fresh mount, so he decided to head toward the mountains near Biven's Gulch to make his escape. A standing horse and mule were spied by the committee members; two men mounted them and continued the chase. Three miles into his attempted escape, Ives realized that his horse was losing its strength; it was only a matter of time until his horse would drop. George Ives was a marked and doomed man with little chance to make his escape.

Two of the pursuers, Wilson and Burtchey, were the closest to Ives, and their horses were in no better condition than Ives's; they realized they would soon have to give up the chase and resorted to guns. Ives sensed that he too had to abandon this horse.

As he rounded a bend, he dashed down a rocky ravine in hopes of fooling his pursuers. The two pursuers, having rounded the same bend, came to a halt. Ives was not visible; the vigilante men surmised that he was close by and hiding behind one of the various boulders. Burtchey, as quiet and quick as he could be, took a wide path around the area. Wilson did likewise, going the other direction. As luck would have it, Burtchey came up behind the crouching George Ives. Burtchey had his prey right in his sights. Wilson had done his job, staying low and keeping Ives occupied. Burtchey commanded Ives to "stand fast." Caught off guard, he could not reach for his gun and be effective with it. Ives knew better than to try, so he gave up. Hands in the air, he was told to "slowly come forth," then to remain motionless until Wilson arrived. With a "light and careless laugh," George Ives obeyed.

It was two hours from the time Ives made his attempt to escape until his recapture. When the rest of the committee caught up with the trio, they wanted to string him up right there and then. The head man, whose identity was never known, nixed the lynching. Judge Lott, who was part of the committee, told of the lively debate and final outcome—they took Ives and Hilderman to Nevada, not Virginia where Ives had a number of friends. One man opposed the outcome, Johnny Gibbons, and mounted his horse, heading as fast as he could to Virginia in hopes of finding someone to stop this madness. Gibbons, it is said, was part owner of the Cottonwood Ranch and kept the Innocence Gang well informed of all those who passed by with large sums of money. Gibbons would not remain in Montana much longer. Soon, very soon, he would quickly make it out of the territory and into Utah. But first he would locate two lawyers, Smith and Ritchie, in hopes of getting his friend Ives proper representation. Judge Smith would later be banished from the territory for his role in defending the accused outlaws. Gibbons's next step was to alert Ives's friends. Meanwhile, George Lane, known as Clubfoot, an associate of Ives, got word of the arrest; he rode hard and fast to Bannack. Lane was actually sent there to entice Sheriff Plummer to arm himself with a habeas corpus to stop the process. Word traveled fast; the whole area was aware of Ives's arrest. Rumors traveled faster. When Sheriff Plummer received word from Clubfoot of Ives's arrest, he had already been informed by others. It was rumored that three hundred to five hundred vigilantes were headed his way. Plummer stayed away from Nevada. He never left the Bannack area; he knew better. What he did not know was that there were no vigilantes coming to his town, nor, as the stories went, did the vigilantes hang a number of Bannack's best citizens. Nonetheless, a picket was put up around Bannack by its citizens to protect themselves and the town. It was late on December 19 when the twenty-four members of the committee arrived in Nevada. They separated the three prisoners, chained them, and posted guards around the cabin commandeered to hold them. The following morning a miner's trial would begin. No one knew how to conduct trial. The committee debated the issue for some time before they came upon a compromise. It was decided that two wagons would be pushed together, with the appointed vigilante judge, scribers, and lawyers in one. In the other would be a jury of twenty-four, and the general public would stand in front, facing the proceedings. The trial began late that afternoon. The lawyers for the defense included Smith, Ritchie, Thurmond, Colonel Wood, and Alex Davis. For the prosecution, there were Colonel W. F. Sanders, prominent in the committee, and Charles S. Bagg. Proceedings were under the jurisdiction of Judge Byam, who was by no means a real judge.

Ives was on trial for both murder and robbery. It was only fitting that Ives be the first to be tried, for he was considered the worst of the worst. Two of Ives's friends, George Brown and "Honest Whiskey" Joe, provided alibis but failed to convince the jurors. The lawyers did their best as well; the debate got contentious. On the third day it was announced that the trial would end no later than 3:00 p.m. — no matter what. The The jury retired to talk among themselves; less than half an hour later they came back with a verdict—guilty! Twenty-three voted guilty; one remained neutral, casting no vote. Colonel Sanders mounted a wagon and moved that "George Ives be forthwith hung by the neck until he is dead." It was getting dark. There was an attempt to postpone, to appeal the verdict. The appeal failed. In the crowd was John "X" Beidler. (From this point on he will be referred to as X as he was commonly called.) X shouted out, "Ask him how long a time he gave the Dutchman," in reference to Nicholas Tbalt's murder.

A few feet from where the trial was held was an unfinished house. Its walls were up, but nothing else. A forty-foot pole was planted inside the house, leaning on a crossbeam. A large box was commandeered as a platform. A rope was hung from the pole. It was a cold night on December 21; the moon was full. Two minutes shy of an hour from the time his sentence was announced, Ives was led to the scaffold. Robert Hereford was the officer who placed the noose around Ives's neck. Ives made several attempts to stop the proceedings by naming others as Tbalt's killers. That too failed. The town was vocal, alive with excitement. As Dimsdale reported, there were loud cries out to "here were some to "some to e lo," and a few to "banish him!" The vigilante armed guards remained at their posts, determined. Two thousand people came to watch the trial and see the hanging.

George stepped up onto the box. Silence abounded. The rope was placed around his neck and then adjusted. Asked if he had anything to say, Ives declared loudly that Alex Carter had killed the Dutchman, that he was innocent. Ives and his friends had hoped that Sheriff Plummer would arrive in time to save the day, but he had not. Charles Beehrer gave the word: "Men, do your duty." The guards raised and cocked their rifles to discourage would-be rescuers. The box flew from under his feet. George Ives was dead immediately. Judge Byam declared him so.

The body hung for an hour before it was removed. Ives's friends gave him a decent burial, just a few feet away from the grave of Nicholas Tbalt.

It was reasoned that the Vigilance Committee, so widely approved of and supported by the powerful, was empathetic to those citizens living in fear. Constant fear had prevailed far too long; the people welcomed the committee with open arms. Men of all manner joined. The outlaw now had much to fear, and for good reason. The death of George Ives four days prior to Christmas was the first but by no means the last. The next action would take place fourteen days later on January 4, 1864. From here, there would be a snowball effect unlike any other in our country's history. When Ives was about to be hanged, the last man that he named as the actual killer of Tbalt was Alex Carter. He named others as well. Long John was the key witness at the miner's trial, whose testimony could not be broken. In effect Long John turned state's evidence. It was different for Alex Carter. Three days after the hanging, the vigilantes went after Carter, finding him near Deer Lodge Creek, a small community in Powell County located between Missoula and Butte. Before they could arrive, Carter and a few friends received word that the vigilantes were after them. They escaped. Word of the vigilantes coming for Carter was in a note written by Erastus "Red" Yeager. For his "criminal interference" with justice by delivering the letter, the Vigilance Committee sought out and arrested Yeager. He was located in a wickiup at Rattlesnake Station, located near the creek of the same name and Rattlesnake Ranch, said to be the actual headquarters of the Innocent Gang. There were claims that Sheriff Plummer was there often with his men. Yeager was taken to Dempsey's Ranch for questioning.

Yeager was a "good-natured, wiry man about five feet five inches tall, with fiery red hair and whiskers." Under questioning, he admitted delivering the warning, while accusing George Brown, the barkeep at Dempsey's, of writing the letter. The ranch had a bar and restaurant business for travelers. Brown confessed to composing the message; the vigilantes took a vote. Unanimously they voted to hang both Yeager and Brown. Yeager, by his own admission, was their cook and bartender. One member of the committee had enough; he felt that the vigilantes were going too far. He elbowed his way toward his horse, telling his peers that he had to go. The committee had sworn an oath; there was no way they would let this man runaway to expose their doings. The captain in charge made a command, and the other twenty-three members of the vigilantes turned on this one soul, pointing their cocked shotguns in his direction. He stopped in his tracks, turned, and came back, joining them.

The crimes committed were Brown admitting he wrote a note and Yeager admitting to delivering the note and cooking for a group of men, friends. The two dozen vigilantes decided to hang the two there. The group did not want to travel all the way to Virginia for fear of interference. They did not feel another miner's trial was necessary, so they took their prisoners to Laurin's Ranch a few miles down the creek from Nevada. The men rested, slept. At ten o'clock that evening they were awakened. Yeager sat up, informing his captors that he realized his time had come and would therefore tell them all about the gang and die happy if he could only live to see others hang who deserved it more than he. "I don't say this to get off," he assured them. "I don't want to get off." These quoted words come from several sources. He could have been trying to prolong his capture, knowing his life was on the line, and the delay would be enough to get them to let him off.

The following is from Dimsdale's articles and the well-researched book *Hanging the Sheriff* (see suggested reading for chapters nine and ten):

"When the leader urged him to list off the names of the Gang so they could be written down, Yeager cooperated. Henry Plummer was the chief; Bill Bunton, second in command; George Brown, secretary; Ned Ray, council room keeper at Bannack City; and the rest, roadsters: Sam Bunton, Cyrus Skinner, George Shears, Frank Parish, Haze Lyons, Bill Hunter, George Ives, Stephen Marshland, "Dutch John" Wagner, Alex Carter, "Whiskey Bill" Graves, Johnny Cooper, Buck Stinson, Mexican Frank, Bob Zachary, Boone Helm, George "Clubfoot" Lane, Billy Terwilliger, and Gad Moore." [X wrote the list as Yeager named off his pals.]

Yeager explained that the Gang was organized similar to the vigilantes, with captains, lieutenants, and oaths, and that its purpose was to rob, without taking life if possible. Members took an oath to be true to each other and to perform the services required of their respective positions. Those who revealed any of the secrets or disobeyed orders were to be hunted down and killed. To recognize each other they wore mustaches, chin whiskers, and scarves tied in a sailor knot, and used the password, 'innocent'. Though he was a member of the band, Yeager said, he was not a murderer.

Yeager named these men in hopes of saving his own life. Sources tell us that Red's list of names came without any evidence. Brown, on the other hand, refused to cooperate. It was nearing midnight; the captain of the vigilantes and his crew of twenty-four were tired of dealing with their captives. It was dark, the wind was blowing, and the chill factor made it even colder. With candles in lanterns to help see their way, the committee led the two prisoners to a grove of cottonwoods. The first man to swing was George Brown. He left a wife and a small child behind. He was but twenty-six years old. Brown was extremely emotional. The resounding *whack* of the rope encircling the sturdy, exposed branch could be heard. One of the vigilante members stepped underneath the hanging rope, placing two stools beneath, stacked. Brown's wrists were tied behind him. He was forced to step up on the rickety stools; the rope was placed, then tightened around Brown's neck. Brown spoke up, "God Almighty, save my soul." The bottom stool was pulled away. George dropped. His body jerked and twitched, then went limp. Red watched Brown's execution without a sign of emotion. Up to this time he had hoped that he would be spared for cooperating. He now knew that his time had come. He asked Williams to take him to Virginia, but Williams would not respond. Brown's suspended body rotated slowly, catching the faint rays of unstable light for a moment and then receding into shadow. "Chain me," Red said, keeping his voice firm and calm, "and carry me along." But Williams, the captain of the vigilantes, did not bother to respond to the plea. They nudged him forward toward the stools, and then they tightened the rope to the contour of his neck. Red extended his hand and in turn grasped the hand of each man within his reach, saying, "Good-bye, boys. God bless you. God bless you." Then they kicked the stools out from under him. When his body was still, they pinned a note to his back: "Red! Road Agent and messenger." The other bartender's note read: "Brown! Corresponding secretary."* There was no logic that Brown could understand; how could a man be lynched for writing a note to save another?

*The story of Brown's and Yeager's hangings comes from a composite of *X. Beidler: Vigilante* by Helen Sanders, *Hung for Contempt of Court* manuscript by Walter N. Davis, and Dimsdale's book *Vigilante*.

*****

Did Yeager belong to an organized gang? Doubtful. "Long John" Franck testified against Ives; he was then forced to accompany the vigilantes to help identify others. When they came up to Yeager, Long John did not recognize the man with the fiery red beard. Yeager did not come up with a single concrete detail regarding the planning of any robbery, which leads many to believe he was never part of any outlaw gang. Anyone who takes time to examine the individual robberies case by case will notice a decided lack of intelligent planning. Yet with the names given to the committee the vigilantes grew bolder and more powerful. The last point is that Captain Williams ran the group, controlled the mob, and gave his blessing and orders for the two to die. He was not the commander in chief and did not have the authority to lynch without a trial or the approval of the executive board, but he did so. Williams was a shoemaker from Pennsylvania and not very successful—a nobody who rose to a position of power over life and death.

*****

January 11, 1864, Joe Pizanthia was murdered by the Vigilance Committee. This article is from the *Wave,* December 24, 1917, out of Medicine Lake, Montana.

And 3 from Bannack:

"The morning after the Sunday night execution, a continuous stream of excited miners made their way to Bannack. Vigilantes summoned the aroused citizens to a meeting, informing them of the robber band and pointing out that Red Yeager's list contained the name of one of his co-workers at Rattlesnake Ranch, a boy called 'Spanish Frank'. Apparently Frank was now holed up inside a cabin up the creek from Thompson's store.

As an armed party advanced on the cabin, they noted that the surrounding snow was still undisturbed and therefore felt certain that the boy was still inside. Ignoring their companions' warnings, George Copley and Smith Ball kicked open the cabin door and entered. Immediately two pistol shots rang out, and Ball retreated through the open door, clutching a flesh wound on his hip. Copley, who had taken a shot in the chest, staggered outside and collapsed. As bystanders carried the mortally wounded man to the hotel across the street, the arrest party—now joined by outraged spectators—quickly developed into an uncontrollable mob. Justice Edgerton, who stood among the crowd holding his Henry rifle, was so swept up by the tide of emotion that he offered the use of a small cannon stored under his bed. Tugging the howitzer to Thompson's store, members of the mob appropriated a dry goods box as a mount and shelled the suspect's cabin. On the third explosion, the door crashed inward, revealing a youth pinned beneath fallen debris. Quickly Smith Ball emptied his revolver into the trapped man's vital organs, and five men slipped a clothesline about the dying victim's neck and raised him to the top of a pole. Then onlookers emptied their weapons into the dangling body. "Pull down the cabin, boys, and burn him!" one participant shouted, and fifty men rushed to comply with the order. When flames leaped high from the pile of logs, six men cut down the corpse and, on the count of three, pitched it into the fire. Within an hour nothing remained of the residence and its former occupant except a heap of ashes, but it took weeks to discover that the dusky-skinned youth whom the Monday morning mob had cremated was not

Spanish Frank.

The victim was one Joe Pizanthia. Rather than admitting the case of mistaken identity, vigilantes spread the word that Pizanthia had been "one of the most dangerous men that ever infested our frontier". The rumor that "the Bannack Greaser" [Joe Pizanthia] had thousands of dollars in gold dust cached in his cabin lured groups of treasure hunters to the cremation grounds. Francis Thompson watched one of the panner[s] concentrating on the skeletal remains, in the hope that the Mexican "had gold dust upon his person when he was killed". But no amount of sifting ashes produced any reward. Despite the disappointing results—which shed doubt on the claim that the young Mexican had been a robber—Justice Edgerton assured his wife Mary that no miscarriage of justice had occurred. Pizanthia's tiny cabin, he told her, "had been the headquarters for all those villains for a long time."

So powerful were the vigilantes, and so determined to rid the territory of the Innocent Gang, that they gave felt that they had the right to lynch an innocent man and cover it up for the greater good. In this case they simply added the name Joe Pizanthia to their list of gang members to justify their actions and bizarre mob behavior. Joe was at the wrong place at the wrong time. Men came crashing into the home where he lay sleeping; as they broke down the door, Pizanthia fired at those rushing in, in self-defense. Spanish Frank, whom they were really after, was never found. At the bottom of this chapter, is list of men lynched. Not all were on the original, Red Yeager's list.

Jack Slade, the last man to be captured and hanged. Joseph Alfred Slade went by the nickname of Jack; he was also often called Captain Slade. He was born and raised in Clinton County, Illinois, and was a member of a highly respectable family. He worked as superintendent for the Central Overland California & Pikes Peak Express Company. While with the company, he would find himself at the winning end of arguments, arguments settled by gunplay. During 1858 Jack went after horse thieves. Among those thieves was Jules Beni. Beni established a trading post catering to both the Pony Express, which started operations in 1860, and the Overland Stage Line. The village that sprung up was named Julesburg after its founder. Its location on the Platte River is in the upper north, far eastern section of Colorado, in Sedgwick County.

This was an important way station. However, Julesburg was a problem for the Overland Stage; the owners decided that Jack was the man to stop the onslaught of thievery. Besides Jules, others in the village were suspects as well. This distrust led to settlers' constant feuds, beatings, and shootings. Slade fired Beni. Jules was not a man to take orders or back down—from anyone. It was his post and his town. It wasn't long before the two men despised each other. Jack was determined to locate the most recent horses that Jules had stolen, and Jules was determined to keep his loot well hidden. One day while Slade was unarmed, Jules confronted Jack, blasting him with buckshot. His body riddled, Slade collapsed in the middle of the street. Jules ran off, with a few townsmen chasing after him. Jules made his getaway; the men returned to gather up Slade's body. They were surprised to see that Jack was still alive, doing his best to stand on his feet. It was then that Slade promised to hunt down Beni. First he had to heal. Meanwhile, Beni continued to steal horses from the Central Overland California & Pikes Peak Express Company. Beni made another attempt to kill Jack at Jack's ranch located at Cold Springs. Slade got word of the planned attack ahead of time. With the help of a few of his cowboys, he captured Beni. Tying him to a post, Jack pulled his revolver and shot off each of Beni's fingers before placing his gun in Beni's mouth and pulling the trigger. Jack cut off the dead man's ears, keeping them in his vest pocket for some time as trophies.

A heavy drinker, Jack would go to the village, get drunk, and take his "meanness" out on those within reach. Citizens of Julesburg had nowhere to turn; Jack Slade ruled with an iron fist. On one occasion Jack killed the father of a young boy, then adopted the boy. Jack's wife raised him. What happen to the boy's biological mother is unknown; she was an Indian. One can only assume that no one was willing to help her regain her son. Slade was endearing when sober, and engaging to his friends, yet in a sense, he was a real Dr. Jekyll and Mr. Hyde, capable of murder and mayhem. His employers had enough of him. In November 1862 he was fired by the Central Overland for drunkenness. Later, at Fort Halleck, Colorado, he was indicted on assault charges. His time in Colorado was up; he fled to nearby Virginia City. While here, Jack met a young man fresh from Missouri—eager, funny, and a heck of a writer—Mark Twain. In Twain's book *Roughing It* he spoke highly of Slade, this mild-mannered, soft-spoken man. When things fell apart, Twain had a difficult time imagining Slade as a hardened, drunken, murdering so-and-so.

Sometimes Slade acted as judge and jury. Dimsdale reported the story that while with the Peak Express Company, he rode with a single companion, to a ranch, the owners of which he suspected of stealing, and opening the door, commenced firing at them, killing three and wounding the fourth. He had no proof.

During summer of 1862, his first in Montana, Jack went to Milk River to work as a freighter. He earned a good deal of money. Upon his return to Virginia City, his dependency on alcohol was starting to show. His drinking would soon leave him broke and in debt. Jack would tie one on, break windows, and beat up men; the next day he would sober up, apologize, and pay for the damages—or at least part of them, depending on his cash flow, always promising to make good the balance. The taking of the town had become a common feat for him; this was called "hurrahing." His constant bad behavior, in due time, would determine his fate.

Slade was a member of the Vigilante Committee. He openly admitted to his role as such. He was never accused or suspected to be a member of a gang or to have committed murder or robbery in Montana, but he had a reputation. After the execution of five men on January 14, the vigilantes felt they had completed their objectives. Most of the highwaymen and murderers had cleared away. The people wanted a civil rule of authority, desiring to establish a "people's court" to be run by a real judge with real lawyers. They established such, with Alex Davis appointed as its first judge.

Slade and friends had been raising hell all night in Bannack. The following morning, with a warrant in hand, Sheriff J. M. Fox arrested Slade. Still drunk, Slade became furious, grabbed the warrant out of the sheriff's hand, and then commenced tearing it up. His pals gave their support by drawing their guns on the sheriff. Sheriff Fox decided it would be best to leave things alone. For now, in a sense, the people and the Vigilance Committee looked at Slade's behavior as an "act of war," quoting Dimsdale. They felt they had to act or forever look the other way. Jack was given one last chance. A lieutenant of the committee located Jack after his warrant-tearing episode and quietly but firmly informed him to mount up and go home. Jack questioned him, asking what authority he had to address him that way. The response was again in a quiet and firm manner; the man told Jack to get to his horse at once. Jack did. He did not leave town. Still drunk, Slade began indulging his bad behavior. He shouted insults toward the two top leaders of the vigilantes. Jack sought out Alexander Davis, the judge of the court, pulled his derringer, and placed it at his head, cocked. He told the judge that he was going to be held as a hostage. Not being a fool, the judge remained quiet and still. Nothing happened to the judge. Slade wandered back to a watering hole for another drink. A messenger sought two prominent leaders in Nevada City, informing them of Slade's behavior.

The need for action had arisen. It is said that six hundred armed miners turned out en masse. Columns were formed; they marched to nearby Virginia. A short meeting by the executive committee determined that it was too dangerous to meet

Slade straight on. Too many friends on Slade's side would come to the rescue. Instead, they would maneuver around to capture and hang the man. Jack got word of their coming. Suddenly he sobered up. He located Judge Davis in P. S. Pfout's store in Virginia, wanting to apologize. The columns had reached Virginia. In quick time they headed up Wallace Street to Pfout's store. (Paris Pfout was the first formal head of the vigilantes, more of a figure head.) Slade was arrested on the spot. He was asked if he had any business to settle. He gave no answer to this nor any last word, other than stating his desire to live and his worry of and need to be with his wife. At the Payout and Russell Stone Building there was a corral with a gatepost. A rope was fastened to the top beam, a box placed underneath. Jack was begging for his life, for his wife. This large army of vigilantes marched Slade to the corral. By this time the man was crying. He was so beside himself he could barely mount the box. He cried out for his wife once more; then came the command "Men, do you duty," and the box was instantly pulled away. Jack Slade fell to his violent death. It was reported that it was instant. This was March 10, 1864.

His body was cut down and taken to the Virginia Hotel, where it was laid out. His wife, summoned, was uncontrollable when she arrived. Jack received a decent burial. Jack Slade, the first western gunslinger to receive celebrity status, had died for being an out-of-control drunk. His friends were not punished; the death of Slade was enough to scare them straight. Jack understood what he was up against. Although the lynching was outside the norm of the Vigilance Committee, they felt justified to make it known to all that one must behave, leave, or die

Jack Slade Wilber Sanders

Captain James Williams, who had risen to be the chief of the vigilantes, committed suicide. Depression got the best of him. He was fifty-three when he died by a combination of an overdose on laudanum and purposely going out in the harsh winter to freeze to death. When his body was found, he had used his gloves as a pillow. It is believed that he was despondent over his livestock starving to death. His attempt to secure a bank loan failed. With his financial doom around the corner, Williams took the only avenue he thought he had left. He died on February 21, 1887. It is ironic that this man had no qualms about lynching men.

Three years later, on January 22, 1890, John "X" Beidler died as well; he was also broke and a heavy drinker. Historian-researcher Kenneth Vail believes that X participated in all of the lynchings. He was the one who had no qualms in hanging a man; thus, he was the most active, the most proud, and the most vocal. Senator Wilbur Sanders, once a prominent captain of the committee, delivered the oration at the funeral. Vail also considers X to be the greatest lawman of all time in Montana. He had risen to be a Deputy United States Marshal for all of eastern Montana. He brought law and order at a time when there was none. This man was a leader, make no mistake.

The Vigilance Committee of 1863 to 1865 was the first of its type in Montana's history. From the 1870s up to 1920 vigilantes would rise up and strike. Miles City, Helena, and Butte became hotbeds of vigilante activity. As one historian put it, "Everything went crazy." The younger brother of Wyatt, Morgan Earp, became the town marshal of Butte, one of three. Billy Brooks, former marshal of Ellsworth and Dodge City, vied for the position that was given to Morgan. Brooks was jealous and confronted Earp, a shootout ensued, Morgan was shot in the arm, and Billy, in the stomach. Billy lived another year before being lynched by vigilantes in Caldwell, Kansas.

Not everyone in Montana was happy with vigilantism; in time there would be a backlash. There will be more on X's involvement with vigilantes in the next chapter, which is dedicated to Sheriff Henry Plummer.

Names, Places, and Dates of Executions:

George Ives, Nevada (City), December 21, 1863.

Erastus "Red" Yeager and G. W. Brown, Stinkingwater Valley, January 4, 1864.

Henry Plummer, Ned Ray, and Buck Stinson, Bannack, January 10, 1864.

"Dutch John" Wagoner and Jose aka Joe Pizanthia*, Bannack, January 11, 1864. (Pizanthia was brutally murdered by mistaken identity. The vigilantes covered it up and placed him on this list.)

George "Clubfoot" Lane, Frank Parish, Haze Lyons, Jack Gallaghar, and Boone Helm, Virginia (City), January 14, 1864.

Steven Marshland, Big Hole Ranch, January 16, 1864.

William Bunton, Deer Lodge Valley, January 19, 1864.

George Shears, Frenchtown, January 24, 1864.

Cyrus Skinner, Alexander Carter, John Cooper, and Robert Zachary, Hell Gate, January 25, 1864.

William "Whiskey Bill" Graves, Fort Owens, January 26, 1864.

William Hunter, Gallatin Valley, February 3, 1864.

Jack A. Slade, Virginia City, March 10, 1864. (He was not on the original list, for he was never considered a part of the Innocence Gang.)

Banishment:

Judge Smith and J. Thurmond, the counsel of the road agents

H. G. Sessions of Bannack

H. D. Moyer (helped the vigilantes, thus escaped hanging)

Kustar (no other name known)

Others:

Augustus "Gad" Moore, who on occasion went by Bill, and Charley Reeves were banished. They left, but in the winter of 1863, they retuned to Bannack. When the vigilantes commenced operations, the two were thought to have fled to Mexico.

Charley Forbes was a member of the gang. Finding that he was ill and incurable the committee were to release him but, it is believed that Moore and Reeves shot Forbes to prevent him from divulging what he knew of the band, however, there is no written proof that Forbes was shot for this reason.

This chapter will be broken down into two parts, the first is of Henry Plummer, the second part is of John X Beidler.

Henry Plummer (1832 – 1864)

Henry Plummer served as sheriff of the country, living and working out of Bannack, Idaho Territory; later, Montana Territory; and still later, the state of Montana. The Idaho Territory was created on March 4, 1863. It was all-inclusive until the government split the territory into three parts, creating Montana Territory a year later in the upper northeastern portion and Dakota Territory in the southeastern part of Idaho. Generally speaking, this story take place in Montana unless otherwise noted.

Henry hailed from a long line of Americans; his family had settled in the "colonies" of Maine, when it was still considered a part of the Massachusetts Bay colony, in 1764. He was the youngest of six children, born William Henry Handy Plumer. He would grow to be five foot ten inches, slender, and one hundred fifty pounds. His eyes were gray-blue; his hair, light brown. He was athletic and muscular and was considered handsome, well-groomed, and well-mannered. He was soft-spoken and intelligent. Plummer had an accent frequently mistaken as British.

His father died when Henry was a teenager. Whether that was what prompted the young man of nineteen to leave the family or not, he nonetheless heard the calling and headed to California to seek his fortune during the gold rush. It seemed to work. He owned a mine, purchased a ranch, and even entered the retail business in Nevada, California, with a bakery—all this within two years of his arrival. It was during this time that he would change the spelling of his surname to Plummer.

The town of Nevada, located in the heart of the gold-mining area in northern California, was established in 1849 and became one of the most important gold-mining towns of the era. By the time Henry arrived, the population was approaching three thousand. In 1856 Nevada would incorporate, but in 1864, due to confusion, it added to its name "City," becoming Nevada City as it is still known today. Its current population hovers around four thousand. In this pretty town with a great historical downtown district, the main industry is now tourism.

By his fourth year in the city, 1856, Henry was elected town marshal with an annual salary of $1,200, plus five percent of taxes collected and fees levied in justice court. In addition to the sheriff's position, he would become further involved in city politics and management, eventually running for state office. He lost that race. His enforcement of unpopular ordinances, as reported in the *Nevada Democrat* newspaper of August 19, 1857, added to a general distrust being spread among the miners. The press reported:

"...Many persons who have been fined for violating city ordinances...have contracted a hatred against Mr. Plummer, and...they were using a great exertion to defeat him."

In short, Plummer's enemies were doing a quite successful job of presenting him as a man of "bad character."

During his tenure as marshal, Henry was involved in numerous actions: apprehending Sanford, and others named, for robbery; arresting Fisher for larceny and garroting; leading a posse in an attempt capture the robber Gehr; interrupting a local theater performance to arrest a man named Sullivan, sitting in the audience, for robbery; and successfully bringing back Nevils, who brutally attacked an old man in a neighboring mining camp. These actions were reported in various newspapers and in the book *The Banditti of the Rocky Mountains and Vigilance Committee in Idaho* by Ross and Haines in 1964.

Plummer was a dashing, confident, attractive young marshal. Although most marshals lost their next election because they had a tendency to upset many voters who ran afoul of the law, Plummer was the exception; he was reelected with ease. The next time around would be different. He would lose by a landslide—3,089 votes against 1,888. Henry started working on his reputation in hopes of changing the unfounded, bad press created during the election by his opponent. It was his job to enforce all those town ordinances—in particular, the fire ordinance. He enforced the law. Those who were out of compliance for not having the required ladder, buckets, and barrel of water available were fined and forced to purchase those items. After all, these were all-wood buildings prone to fire. The fines levied were high, and the editor of the *Nevada City Journal*, stung by Marshal Plummer's enforcement, took the man to task; a newspaper can yield a lot of power. Town marshals had the task of collecting taxes, another job that displeased the voters.

Henry set out to reinvent himself, to patch up his reputation…but on September 26, 1857, Henry Plummer shot and killed John Vedder.

Vedder abused his wife repeatedly. He worked as a monte dealer in a gambling hall and apparently was not good at it. He was quick-tempered and had few friends. The Vedders had come to Nevada (City) five months earlier. Vedder's wife, Lucy, fed up with her husband, sought Plummer's help on several occasions. When Vedder held a knife to her throat, she escaped and ran straight to Plummer for help; he placed her in a hotel. She stayed a week, yet during that time she would go home every day to fix her husband's dinner and make his bed. Unfortunately this was a typical dysfunctional relationship. She told a family friend that she loved her man more than anyone. In short, she loved him more that life; they were soul mates. The abuse continued. The couple would fight, separate, make up, and then repeat the cycle. It got worse; John threatened to take their two-year-old daughter away from her and leave. More desperate, Lucy sought out Plummer. On this day, John had borrowed a gun. He told a friend he was out to kill Plummer. John went to the hotel where Lucy was staying; he took his daughter away at gunpoint. The manager of Hotel de Paris on Broad Street, which was a single-story wooden structure, plain in every sense of the word, immediately contacted Marshal Plummer. Henry found Vedder at his home. It was nearing midnight. Lucy was with the marshal, and together they went to the house to talk. In the kitchen, a twelve-by-twelve room with a rudimentary table and chairs, Henry tried to explain the law to Vedder. He told Vedder it was against the law to take a child away from her mother. Things happened; John Vedder was shot twice and would die within the hour. Lucy ran into the streets. "He killed my husband," she cried over and over.

From there it got ugly. Henry left the house, blowing his police whistle for help; none came. He marched himself to the jail and asked to be locked up. There were already calls to lynch the man. A rumor was started that Plummer and Mrs. Vedder where having an affair.

During the grand-jury trial the judge stopped the proceedings when it became clear that the jury had preconceived verdicts. That decision, to stop the proceedings, was appealed and overruled. The jury found Henry guilty; bail was set at $8,000, a dollar amount set too hight for Plummer, so he languished in jail, awaiting his trial. The *Sacramento Union* carried an article claiming "an intimacy had existed between Plummer and Vedder's wife, which caused a separation between the married pair."

Henry was tried twice, found guilty, and sentenced to serve ten years at the San Quentin prison facility. San Quentin is considered California's first prison.* Henry's imprisonment lasted six months, including the four months he spent in jail while awaiting trial. Governor John Weller, pressured by Plummer's supporters and the fact that Henry had come down with tuberculosis, pardoned him. As much as he tried, Plummer never redeemed his reputation or cleared his name. This episode haunted him for life.

Free to go, Henry did his best to behave; he went back to Nevada (City). It worked until Henry had a run-in with William Riley. Henry was at the Ashmore's, a house of ill repute, visiting his lady friend when he and Riley argued. Riley was a secessionist antagonist; Plummer was not. The *Democrat* reported:

> "At about 2 o'clock last Sunday morning, a difficulty occurred at a house of ill-fame on Commercial Street between Henry Plumer [Plummer] and William Riley, resulting in the death of the latter. It appears that they had both been drinking pretty freely and got to quarreling in the entry when Riley struck Plumer on the head with a knife, cutting through his hat and inflicting a deep wound in his scalp. Plumer at the same time drew his revolver and fired at Riley. The ball took effect in his left side and must have killed him instantly…."

This ended any hopes of Plummer redeeming his good name in Nevada (City). Plummer had wanted the reward. Both knew each other while in prison, and were not friendly. The decision to arrest Riley, who had escaped San Quentin, turned out to be a bad one. Riley resisted, guns were pulled, and in the blink of an eye Riley was dead. Realizing that he could be prosecuted once more, Henry quickly turned himself over to the police. The police felt that the killing was justified. The police decided to released him from their custody, but with the understanding and approval of the department heads, he was to leave the state quickly to prevent a trial, especially one that could go awry as before. Plummer left California for Washington Territory, where gold had been recently discovered. It did not take long for this seemingly easygoing, soft-spoken man to find himself reaching for his revolver once more. The reason for this shooting was lost in history, but Henry Plummer had just killed his third man. Wary of trials and prisons, Plummer decided to get the hell out of Washington. He wanted to go back east, to go home to civilization and his family. He made it as far as Missouri, where he took a turn in his road of life. This was in the autumn of 1862. On his way home he found himself in Fort Benton, on the eastern edge of the Mullan Trail and the banks of the great Missouri River in then Dakota Territory. At that time Fort Benton was the farthest inland port in the world.

---

* San Quentin is considered California's first prison. In actuality, it was a ship named *The Waban.* In 1851 it was outfitted and anchored in San Francisco Bay to hold thirty inmates. These inmates were put to task to construct a permanent prison on San Quentin's present site. It opened in 1852 to house up to sixty-eight inmates.

The Mullan Trail was a twenty-five-foot-wide road built under Lieutenant John Mullan's guidance. This trail allowed twenty thousand plus pioneers to travel to the Northwest, ending 642 miles later in Fort Walla Walla, Washington. (Walla Walla's original name was Fort Nez Percés, established in 1818.)

The plan was to purchase passage on a steamboat that would take him back to the United States, to Maine. The Indians were in an uproar; it was too dangerous for the ships to travel down the Missouri. All captains refused to travel. Henry would have to wait for the danger to subside.

Plummer and a horse trader named Jake Cleveland—both had been living in California and met up on the road—decided to travel the rest of the way to Fort Benton. The two were approached by a government agent, James Vail. Vail brought his family to the Missouri Territory after having secured a job as a teacher, but was quickly offered the job of Indian agent. With the Indians in an uproar, he was scared for his family and searched Fort Benton for bodyguards. He offered the two acquaintances jobs protecting his family; the two men accepted. Plummer and Cleveland were an odd couple. Henry was dignified, quiet, educated; Jake was loud and rowdy, crude, and of little education. James Vail's sister-in-law, Electa (sometimes spelled Electra) Bryan, was twenty years old and was considered to be a good, pure, Christian lady, plain and yet pretty, who had lived a sheltered life. It was not long before Plummer and Cleveland were vying for Electa's hand. Electa fell in love with Henry. Plummer no longer wanted to go back east; he wanted to remain and marry Electa. The job with the Vails lasted two months. Vail was to receive his yearly salary in total and up front —it had not yet arrived. When the two bodyguards' employment ended, Vail had to tell them that he had no way to pay. Forgiving Vail's inability to pay, the men left for Bannack. They seemed friendly, but they would soon become contentious over Electa's hand.

Henry promised Electa that once he settled in and had steady employment, he would return and marry her. July 24, 1862, found Henry in Lewiston, Idaho Territory, a supply center for the mining towns in the general area. He remained in Lewiston for two months. Dimsdale, author of *The Vigilantes of Montana* and news reporter for the *Montana Post*, claimed that Plummer was in Lewiston for two years, where he spent the time organizing an outlaw band to be known as the Innocents. This is not true. There is ample proof of Henry's time in Lewiston, including his signatures in the Luna House hotel register as "Henry Plumer"; the register correctly lists his former residence as Nevada City. A reference was located implying that saloon keeper Patrick Ford, shot and killed by Plummer in self-defense, yet, hard evidence is lacking to support this incident. Legends with some truth to them are difficult to dispel.

Plummer and Cleveland arrived in Bannack by November 23, 1862, as noted in fellow pioneer Granville Stuart's diary. Bannack was a small village of four hundred men and forty women—ten men for every woman.

Henry was a successful miner in California, so here in Bannack, by March of 1883, Plummer had no problems in filing a successful mining claim. He and his partner Ridgely netted $3,800 in one day alone. In another claim with partners E. Richardson, J. Cross, and Cyrus Skinner, the four men cleared $1,800 in a single day. It is safe to say that the men were doing extremely well; in fact, they turned down an offer of $25,000 for that particular claim. Today that $25,000 would equate to $465,205. In a time when the average monthly income was around $40, one could judge Henry Plummer as wealthy.

In four months the population of Bannack jumped to 1,800, with more people arriving almost daily. Due to his past experience and success in California, Plummer was often consulted about mining issues. He was well liked, and people of the mining community started to confide in him about their personal problems. As a gunslinger, he was known to be fast—damn fast—and accurate on the draw. All of this made Henry a natural choice to be sheriff. On May 24, 1864, elections were held; Henry Plummer became sheriff of Bannack and the surrounding mining districts. He chose as deputies Smith Ball, Buzz Caven, and J. W. Dillingham, followed by Ned Ray and Buck Stinson. This list of deputies comprised of men of both good and poor reputation. Dillingham was considered the best of the lot and was highly regarded. Buck Stinson, a bartender at the Elkhorn Saloon, had the most notorious of the deputies; he worked for Cyprus Skinner, the Elkhorn Saloon was noted for catering to roughest men. Skinner was an escaped convict and was partners with Plummer in one mine. Ned Ray had a reputation as a good shot, brave but rough. Smith Ball and Buzz Caven seemed to be good men with good reputations, but Caven was shot to death during a gunfight at Skinner's saloon. His death was deemed accidental. Most likely, the shooting was done by a bystander shooting his gun indoors out of stupidity—stray bullets care not where the land or whom they hit. Buck, Skinner, Caven, and Stinson would become marked as members of the Innocent Gang by the vigilantes. No wonder they all thought Sheriff Plummer to be one as well.

Plummer thought he recruited the best men for the job. He assigned the men their duties and ran off to Electa at the Vails' Sun River Valley farm to get married. It had been over six months since he last saw her. The couple reunited, married, and headed back to Bannack. On their way, Henry and Electa, at Eagle Rock Ferry on the Snake River, met up with a wagon train that carried Sidney Edgerton—a former congressman and the new chief justice of the territory, appointed by President Lincoln. Edgerton would become the first territorial governor of Montana. Included in Judge Edgerton's entourage were his wife, children, Wilbur Sanders (a nephew), and his family. Wilbur was hired to be Edgerton's clerk. In a short time, he rose as a major force—a captain of the Vigilance Committee and, one day, the first senator of Montana.

They liked Plummer until the wagon master told them of Plummer's reputation in California. The Edgertons quickly changed their opinion of him. This chance meeting was tremendous in Henry's life. The wagon master's description of Plummer did not sit well with Edgerton, an uppity man of little tolerance. A word —in this case, a story—one-sided and well placed, created an enemy for life with the judge. From the time the wagon master spoke negatively of Plummer, the wheels were in motion to get rid of him. Outwardly, nothing was ever said. Edgerton and Sanders were always polite to Plummer. They watched him closely and became afraid of the power he held as "sheriff of the country"—not county, but *country*, a country of its own, as it was outside the United States' boundaries.

Judge Edgerton's oldest daughter, Mattie, describes Henry's wife in her memoirs:

"She stayed in the wagon but she was pointed out to us as the wife of the Sheriff of Bannack....Mrs. Plummer was a small woman, I remember. I guess you would call her a blonde. She had big grey eyes and her hair was…soft and fluffy."

As soon as he arrived with his bride, Henry learned that his area of responsibility had been extended to Virginia City and Nevada City. He was overwhelmed, yet as sheriff Plummer enjoyed a positive reputation in the mining districts. He was effective as a lawman and seemed to make every effort to protect the people and their property; this was not a nine-to-five job. A major issue for Henry was his wife, Electa, whom he would soon marry. She saw very little of him. With the size of his domain there were far too many issues and so much traveling that Electa became lonely, bitter, and angry at her husband. The couple began to argue; the marriage was in a downfall. The Vails pulled up stakes and traveled to Bannack, where they decided to live at the urging of John's wife, Martha, Electa's sister. Electa had felt alone; she wanted to be with family. When the Vails arrived, the pain Electa felt eased.

Population data helps explain what western mining towns were like. When Bannack reached its population peak of 1,800, its female population was 147, and the child count was 64. This was a world of practically all men. Society, to function properly, needs a balance of men to women; with out women, society would breaks down. Educated women like Electa, Martha, and Mary (Mrs. Edgerton) did not venture outside much, never walking on the main street without a proper escort. In the Edgerton household there were people constantly in and out; Mrs. Edgerton's social life consisted of entertaining at home.

*****

Jake Cleveland never got over the loss of Electa to Plummer. Electa was never interested in him, yet the grudge against Plummer simmered and grew to a boiling point. Repeatedly Cleveland openly bragged about his desire to kill Plummer. Henry ignored him. The day of reckoning came at the bar in the Goodrich Hotel. Drunk, loud, and belligerent as usual, Cleveland started threatening an unarmed man named Jeff Perkins. The argument was silly; it was over a loan that Perkins had already paid back. Henry happened in. Witnessing the abuse of Mr. Perkins, Plummer decided to step in to stop the badgering, telling Jake that he was tired of his nonsense. Although warned, Cleveland continued his ranting threats. Perkins left the bar to retrieve his derringer. Henry pulled his gun, firing a shot into the ceiling beam to get Cleveland's attention and end the verbal barrage leveled at both him and Perkins. It did not work. Jake reached for his gun. Henry fired another shot, this time at Jake, striking him below the waistline. Cleveland fell to his knees. When Cleveland fell, he grasped for his pistol while exclaiming, "Plummer, you won't shoot me when I'm down." Plummer replied, "No, you damn son of a bitch, get up." Cleveland struggled to stand; Henry shot him a little above the heart. This bullet hit a rib. The next shot landed below the eye, lodging in his head. The last shot missed altogether. George Ives, with a pistol in his hand, followed by Charlie Reeves, came running to aid the sheriff. Jake Cleveland's time in this world had ended. Sheriff Plummer was arrested and tried for murder. He was acquitted. Edgerton and Sanders's private resolve to rid the territory of Plummer increased. The men began to lay down a plan and slowly included others. Electa and her family were aware of the shooting death of Jack Cleveland; they too were wary of Henry. Martha did not want her younger sister to marry the man, but the respectability the sheriff's position offered was compelling; thus, Electa went ahead and did so.

The Plummers continued to fight. Finally Electa told her husband that she wanted to go back to her parents in Ohio. She had hoped that if she did, he would follow her. Henry agreed to a separation. When Electa left, Henry accompanied the stage for days to Fort Benton, where she would board a steamship. He loved her; they both thought of this separation as temporary. Edgerton and Sanders, in their sick minds, thought of the Plummers' separation as something dark, believing that Henry had chased her away, another reason to be wary of Plummer. Why would she leave? They reasoned that she knew too much to feel safe in Bannack—rumors spread.

When Jake Cleveland died at the hands of Sheriff Plummer, it was Hank Crawford who took it upon himself to make the arrangements to give Cleveland a decent burial. After the funeral, Hank went about settling Cleveland's debts by selling off Cleveland's possessions. Hank Crawford was the first sheriff of the Bannack district (the area in and around Bannack and its mining district). When Cleveland was killed, Crawford was placed in charge of Plummer during his incarceration, as a temporary lawman. Upon his acquittal, Henry

Plummer resumed his duties. Cleveland's open threats lead to Plummer's acquittal. During the brief time that Crawford was the law, he arrested two other men for murdering a white man and several Indians, one of which was a "papoose." Those two men, Moore and Reeves, were banished. Crawford remained as the executor to settle up Cleveland's debts and estate. Crawford sold Cleveland's weapons to cover court costs, and his three horses to cover expenses and fees. It seems that one of the horses was a mighty fine one. A day or two after the horse was in "custody," Plummer took the horse out for the day. His intent was to check it out as a potential purchase. Crawford took offense that Plummer would saddle someone else's horse without permission. He and Crawford got into a squabble over it. Even though the horses were going to be auctioned, Crawford had placed an order to keep Plummer "off limits." He was not going to be allowed to bid. At the Bakery, a watering hole, the two men met; an argument commenced. Crawford denied the off-limits order. Plummer called over Bill Hunter, who confirmed the orders. Hunter explained that he felt that Plummer, having killed the man, should not partake in his property as well. Crawford, surrounded by friends, stood fast; all were ready to shoot Henry if he dared reach for his side arm. He did not. The following day Henry sent word to Crawford that he was misinformed and wanted to be friends. Hank wanted no part of the man; he would not go and meet him as requested, but would allow Henry to come to him. Henry did not. Several attempts to patch things over failed. Friends of both men intervened, and the two shook hands. Case closed—or was it? Days later in another bar a man walked up to Hank and picked a fight. This man let it be known that he was not armed, so Hank took off his gun belt to even the odds and fight the unarmed stranger. The stranger quickly pulled a hidden gun. Fast as lightning, Hank grabbed the man by the throat and arm, forced him against the wall, and disarmed him. While still fighting, Plummer joined in and attempted to disarm Crawford. As the story goes, Plummer and the stranger then rushed Crawford, who, with the help of his friend Harry Flegger, managed to keep the two at bay and retained control of the weapon. Harry got his friend out of there in one piece. The saloon owner told Crawford that this scenario was all a plot devised by Plummer. Crawford would no longer trust or talk to Plummer. The distrust escalated, then the day Crawford spotted his opportunity to get Plummer. Across the street Plummer was deep in conversation. He had one foot resting on a wagon wheel spoke, and his gun resting across his knee. Crawford fired a double-barreled shotgun. One ball entered Plummer's body near the elbow of his right arm, traveling down the bone, lodging in the wrist. A few days earlier Crawford had announced that either he or Plummer would have to leave camp or die. As he was being helped up, the sheriff announced that some son of a bitch had shot him. His right arm now useless, he held his pistol in his left hand. Plummer, standing and facing Crawford, called the would-be assassin a coward; he dared him to shoot again. Crawford obliged and missed. Plummer walked toward him. Crawford turned and ran to his friend Wadam's cabin. There he hid away the night behind sacks of flour. This incident has been reported by Thomas Dimsdale in news articles later put into his 1866 book, *Vigilantes of Montana*; by Nathaniel Langford in *Vigilante Days* (Langford was an active hater of Plummer and soon-to-be member of the vigilantes); and by R. E. Mather and F. E. Boswell in the 1950s book *Hanging the Sheriff: A Biography of Henry Plummer*. The sheriff thought fifteen days should be enough time to heal. Hank Crawford had other ideas. He left town, went to Fort Benton, and bought a ticket on the next steamer out. Henry did heal, but his arm was not the same. He practiced for hours on his draw and shooting accuracy until he became proficient with his left hand.

****

Some historians have mentioned that Dimsdale's articles, later turned into a book, are pure history; after all, he was an eyewitness, however, he wrote in such a way as to favor the vigilantes' point of view. This is not pure history but an account with a lopsided justification for the vigilantes. There are other articles of the day that have a different bent.

In one published story, Dimsdale spoke of an angry Plummer confronting Crawford over a rumor that Crawford had started about Henry courting an Indian woman named Catherine. The other side—Plummer was in love with Electa, engaged, and afraid that he would lose her if she ever learned of this unfounded rumor. Plummer denounced the false rumor and even went to the extent of calling Crawford out to fistfight. Twice he called the man out, and twice Crawford refused. He attempted to goad Crawford to a gunfight; Crawford wisely refused. His last effort was to forgive Crawford, to shake hands and move forward as friends. Again and again, Hank Crawford refused. As far as having a stranger pick a fight with Crawford, this would not be something that a man who could draw a gun and fire five shots hitting the intended target each time, all in three seconds, would do. Henry Plummer would never have someone else do his dirty work; there simply was no need. Rather, Dimsdale painted bleak pictures to justify the vigilantes' lynchings. Crawford lost the sheriff's election to Plummer, and the resentment most likely caused Crawford to start a rumor and act the way he did toward the newly elected sheriff. March 18, 1863, former sheriff Crawford wisely decided to go back home to Wisconsin. Within months, Crawford, with a wife, returned to the territory, setting up house in Virginia City.

In June 1863 Deputy D. H. Dillingham believed that his fellow deputies—Stinson, Hayes, Lyons, and Charley Forbes—were plotting to rob two miners, and he informed the supposed victims. Buck Stinson and his friends denied this story, calling Dillingham a liar. Angrily they confronted Dillingham in Virginia City. Guns were pulled, shots were fired, and Deputy Dillingham lay dead in the street. The men were arrested and stood trial. It was deemed that two, Lyons and Stinson, were guilty of murder, and they were sentenced to hang. Forbes was acquitted and freed. There was an outcry, another vote was taken, the men were given a chance to live, and both were banished. Stinson went back to Bannack and took up his duties as deputy sheriff.

All of the above gave Sidney Edgerton and his nephew, Wilbur Sanders, more cause to fear Sheriff Henry Plummer. Yet Sheriff Plummer was popular. Henry wanted to bring real justice to the territory. He decided to build a jail to house prisoners until trial. Montana had no territorial penitentiary until 1871. The territory did not even have a jail or holding tank. The only law was a miner's court; the ruling by the judge could be and often was overturned by popular vote among the citizens. There were a few choices in miner's court rulings. Those choices were dismissal (not guilty), flogging, banishment, and hanging. Henry wanted to change this. The public jail would be the first step, followed by a proper court system. All this time, even with his issues with Cleveland and Crawford, Plummer was building a good reputation in the mining districts. Friends and foes alike credited him with being an efficient lawman. On the surface it seemed that all was good for Plummer. He made every effort to protect the miners and their property. But he did have some nefarious deputies. Pay was low. Lawmen receive twenty-five cents for each summons, twenty-five cents per mile traveled, one dollar for a warrant, and two dollars and fifty cents for attending court trials. Basically, the legal system was set up as a community service. The miners and citizens would chip in to help pay for law enforcement. Henry, however, relied on his mines. Plummer sought out help from the citizens of Bannack to fund a jail. He was able to get enough donations, and he built the first jailhouse in the territory. The Bannack jail was built on the bank of Grasshopper Creek, just behind the Chrisman's store, where the sheriff rented an office.

*****

Virginia City 1886

Henry Tilden was part of Edgerton's group. He was a young man of fourteen who suffered from consumption (tuberculosis). Tilden's family was close to the Edgertons. The judge agreed to bring Henry along as his ward; hopefully, the weather would help his condition. Tilden disliked Plummer and was afraid of him due to the two most influential men in his life, Judge Edgerton and Wilbur Sanders.

Mid-November 1863, an incident occurred. Henry Tilden, on horseback, fell into a ditch; his horse landed on top of him. The boy screamed; help came running. Luckily he was not seriously hurt. He ran home to Sanders and told how he was robbed of $10 by three masked men, one of whom he identified as Henry Plummer. How did he recognize Plummer? they asked. By his gun and overcoat was Tilden's answer. Henry had just arrived home by coach with two fellow travelers, Sam Hauser and Langford. Hauser was carrying $14,000 in gold dust. He asked if Plummer would safeguard it overnight. Plummer took the gold, retuning it to its owner the following morning. Hauser and Langford joined a freighter headed for Salt Lake City; Plummer went along as extra protection. Hauser and his money made it safely.

Judge Edgerton and Wilbur Sanders listened to young Henry Tilden's story, swearing him to keep his story secret, especially since he had identified Plummer. Edgerton and Sanders realized that one could not identify a person by the type of revolver he had—there were far too many of the same make and caliber in the territory—but Plummer's overcoat lining was red. That was a "horse of a different color." Tilden's story was all the two men needed; they sent for other powerful community leaders to set the trap.

If Plummer ran a gang of highwaymen and had firsthand knowledge that $14,000 in gold dust was on the road, he could have easily sent some of his men out to rob that freighter. Hauser made it safely, as mentioned before. So why would three men, headed by Plummer, rob a boy of $10? Henry Tilden had a wild imagination, with a need to please. Tilden's robbery and his horse falling on him happened the same day that Hauser was heading out. Edgerton and Sanders, wary of Plummer, were using this fallacious story to rid themselves of a man whose popularity and position they feared. During the Civil War; Plummer was a Democrat, while Edgerton and Sanders were Republicans and felt "socially superior" to the miners. Plummer was a skilled politician as well as a miner. The lawyers were long-winded buffoons. Plummer's gentle manners appealed to the masses. The uncle and nephew had come to the territory to to satisfy their political ambitions. They recognized that Plummer was a man who could stand in their way. They would not be sorry to see him gone; together they worked to form a coalition.

*****

On Thanksgiving Henry Plummer was at his in-laws', celebrating the holiday. There were others as well: the Edgertons, Sanders, and a family friend named Francis Thompson. Everyone except Plummer and the Vails knew that Henry Plummer was doomed. They had plotted and planned, but today they had to act no different than they would any other day so that their prey would not be alarmed and bolt. Thompson later spoke of the difficulty to behave so; it was especially hard because from the time Thompson and the Vails had come to the territories, Henry had been most gracious and friendly. Thompson's impression of Plummer was mainly based on Electa and Henry's courtship. Thompson appears to have done very little, if anything, for the Vigilance Committee other than to be in good standing and keep the inner-circle knowledge to himself. The Thanksgiving dinner as usual a success, Plummer had no idea that he was doomed.

The next incident to happen after the Tilden affair with his horse and would-be robbers was the Salt Lake mail coach holdup by George Ives, William "Whiskey Bill" Graves, and Bob Zachary. At the same time, Henry Plummer was doing his sheriff duties, escorting a gold shipment. The above men were identified. One of the passengers on the stage was Leroy Southmayde. He personally lost $400 in gold. Another man lost $100. After the holdup the stage was allowed to continue to Bannack. The sheriff was there and spoke to Mr. Southmayde, who identified all three men. Unfortunately for the sheriff it seemed that he did nothing to go after the highwaymen. This did not go unnoticed. Southmayde was warned by one of the town's leading citizens, Judge G. G. Bissel, that his life was in danger. The story says that Deputy Ned Ray warned Southmayde to keep quiet about the suspects, or death would be on his doorsteps. Was this a threat or a friendly warning to keep quiet instead of telling the law? Dimsdale has it as more of a threat, but was it? Leroy Southmayde and two fellow passengers left Bannack by stage a few days later. All three men had double-barreled shotguns across their laps, prepared to defend themselves to the max. They reached their destination, unmolested.

In late December five Virginians and one Nevada man formed a secret organization, calling themselves the Vigilance Committee.

The coup de grace—Lloyd Magruder was an extremely likable man, respected by all. He was a successful merchant from Lewiston, Idaho. He decided to establish a business in the Virginia township. Summer of 1863 he did just that. His merchandise was a variety of goods targeted at the needs of the miners. He pretty much sold out of his goods, with a hefty profit reported to be around $14,000, and headed back to Lewiston to restock. As Dimsdale puts it in his book *Vigilantes of Montana:*

"Having disposed of his goods, from the sale of which he had realized about $14,000, he made arrangements for his return to Lewiston, by way of Elk City. This becoming known, Plummer and his band held a council in Alder Gulch, and determined on the robbery and murder of Magruder, C. Allen, Horace and Robert Chalmers, and a Mr. Phillips, from the neighborhood of Marysville. During the debate…[it was] proposed that Steve Marshland should go on the expedition, along with Jem Romaine, Doc Howard, Billy Page, and a man called indifferently Bob or Bill Lowry. The [program] included the murder of the five victims, and Marshland said he did not wish to go, as he could make money without murder. He was, he said, "on the rob, but not on the kill". Cyrus Skinner laughed at his notion, and observed that "dead men tell no tales".

While sleeping on the eastern part of the Bitter Root Mountains, Magruder and his crew were murdered. Wildlife had done their duty; Magruder and crew could only be identified by what was left of their clothing. Captured, Billy Page turned state's evidence. The men who committed the crime were rounded up. They had a speedy trial and were hanged. (Chapter nine talks of the capture, confession, and hanging of George Ives on December 21, 1863.)

Ives named others for his deeds. Next the vigilantes, under Captain Williams, located Erastus "Red" Yeager and George W. Brown. The instructions were to bring them back to

Virginia to stand trial. Instead the two were strung up. To save his hide (although Dimsdale says otherwise), Yeager confessed and named others who were members of the Innocent Gang members and their duties; Yeager said that Plummer was its leader, that they had robbed and killed over a hundred individuals. That was all the committee needed. John "X" Beidler, as the committee's head executioner, was given his marching orders. Yeager and Brown swung without any type of trial. The vigilante men feared punishment for the impromptu hangings. They were not reprimanded, so from this point on, they held no trials. They would follow the list of doomed men and hang them when captured. Despite the freezing weather, the executive committee insisted members immediately go after those on Yeager's list. Four men, among them John "X" Beidler, were sent to Bannack to carry out the execution of Sheriff Henry Plummer and his two deputies, Buck Stinson and Ned Ray.

Bannack citizens were not interested in assisting the four vigilantes. When Beidler arrived in Bannack, they attempted to organize a local brach of the committee. It did not fair well, however in a few days things got turned around. During this time, the eldest daughter of Edgerton overheard her father and uncle Wilber and Beidler discussing the best way to take Plummer out. Sanders suggested ambushing Plummer. This was ruled out for not being lawful enough, so they settled on hanging. January 10 would be the day of reckoning for Henry Plummer. It was evening, around ten o'clock, and it was very cold that night. Possibly as many as seventy-five men headed toward the homes of their intended victims. As they crossed over a bridge, they broke into three separate companies, previously designated, with each party going in a different direction. Each company was assigned to arrest one man. If all went well, Plummer and his two deputies would be taken down at the same time. It did; the three men were surprised and arrested without incident. It was reported that Buck Stinson was still wearing his Sunday suit. Ned Ray was found passed out on a gambling table. Plummer was at his in-laws' house, not feeling well, for he had consumption. Henry was resting on the couch. There was a knock on the door, and one of the Vails answered. The men standing in the doorway asked for Plummer, he came to the door, and they told him they needed to speak. He went out. Martha was very upset. She knew something was wrong, but Henry did not heed her cautionary manner, telling her that all was fine. He bundled up and left with the group. Surrounded, Plummer walked to Sanders's cabin to solicit help. Sanders would not answer the knock, so Plummer spoke to the men holding him captive. His appeal to the men was working; they were faltering in their resolve. Sanders realized a crisis had developed; he knew he had to act. Sanders opened his door and stepped out, quickly giving a military command: "Company! Forward march!" The men obeyed the order. Off they went with their prisoner to what is now called Hangman's Gulch, a place up the ravine above Bannack, not far from the cemetery.

Lonely, Electa, who had left for the East, had hope that her husband would follow. During the months prior to and since her departure, the Vails and Plummer were together often, eating dinner nightly. They interacted as families do. Martha came to respect and admire her brother-in-law. It was implied, many years later, that she and Henry had become lovers, that her youngest child was sired by him. There is absolutely no proof to back this up. Could it have been another rumor devised to hurt Plummer's reputation?

Martha ran to the Edgertons for help. They lied to her, telling her that Plummer was safe. It was the family friend, Francis Thompson, that lied until he received word that Plummer was dead; then he told her the truth. Edgerton supplied the ropes. The first to die was Ned Ray, followed by Stinson. Henry was the last. He asked to settle his affairs; they refused. He asked to see his sister-in-law; they refused. He asked if he could first pray; they refused. He made another request, his last: "Give me a high drop, boys." They did. At the age of thirty-two the sheriff of the country was hanged; his body and those of his two deputies were left hanging overnight. When the bodies were removed, they were frozen solid. The bodies were removed to an unfinished log cabin and laid out side by side. Stinson's wife came with a friend and cut off her husband's finger so she could remove his gold wedding ring. Ray's girlfriend was given custody of his body so that she could bury her lover; he was dressed in a buckskin suit, his usual attire. No one claimed Plummer that morning.

A local newspaper reported some of the immediate reactions to the hangings. This is one example: "The gun is mine! The gun is mine! It cost me two hundred seventy-five dollars, and I mean to keep it,t yelled hotel owner Bill Goodrich, who upon Plummer's death, ran to Chrisman's store, where Plummer's office was located, and grabbed Plummer's double-barreled shotgun. Henry had been living at Goodrich's Hotel since Electa left. The reference to the money owed was his unpaid bill. Plummer's so-called friend Francis Thompson did take control of the body and had Henry cleaned and dressed in his Sunday best for burial. Thompson was denied the right to bury Henry in the cemetery, so Plummer was buried in a ravine near Hangman's Gulch, with no tombstone to mark his grave. Plummer's extensive gold- and silver-mine holdings were now under the control of the vigilantes. Upon the deaths of Plummer and all the other "gang members," the Vigilance Committee deemed that the distribution of property should be held secret. Henry told the committee's leadership where $100,0000 of gold dust was hidden—money from his mines.

Both Cyrus Skinner, who would hang later, and Henry Plummer were men of means. The vigilantes laid claim to their mining interests to pay the expenses of their active members. The night of the hanging a wagon train loaded with a barrel of gold and silver belonging to Plummer left Bannack. According to Maurice Kildare's article "Henry Plummer's Golden Loot" in the April-May 1965 edition of the *Frontier Times*, several dirt-poor but prominent families became rich that night. When the teamsters returned to Bannack, they told everything they knew to all who would listen. The vigilantes ran a few of the men out of the territory, while threatening to hang the others if they spoke up one more time. Henry's widow never received a dime from her husband's estate.

Edgerton would go on to be Montana's first governor. When he left the territory, he had over seventy-five mining claims. He would never get his hands dirty; manual labor was not in his constitution. Soon, five more men would be hanged. In total some twenty-three good men were hanged—twenty-four when including the cripple who dared to speak out. The Vigilance Committee would never allow someone to speak against them, so a man with pegs for feet, R. C. Rawley, was lynched in September 1864, six months after the so-called eradication of the Innocence Gang. His name is not on the list of gang members hanged. With the death of Rawley, the vigilantes's PR man, Dimsdale, declared that the executions had ended organized crime. Yet the Vigilance Committee kept lynching outlaws for several years. Popular opinion caught up with them. Both the courts and the press accused the vigilantes of downright murder, calling the actions of the vigilantes a "reign of terror." Citizens posted public notices warning that for every one lynching by the Vigilance Committee, five of their members would be lynched as well.

The book written in 1923 by Alex Toponce, *Reminiscences of Alexander Toponce*, tells of ten men holding up and killing all but one passenger during a Wells Fargo stage robbery in 1865. Toponce was a freighter who operated between Virginia City and Salt Lake. James Miller noted in his diary during July of the same year that twenty road agents had held up a stage, killing four people. That same year the *Montana Post* published articles concerning organized road agent problems. Could it be that the committee had missed its mark?

Dimsdale was urged to put his articles into book form. With the help of Sanders they published the book in 1866. It took a while, but they located Plummer's family. They visited Electa, giving her a copy. They said the book was factual—Electa knew better.

Most, if not all, of the men that were lynched had bad reputations. Henry's domestic violence issue in California never left him. Plummer was not a perfect man, but who is? By all accounts he was a good and able lawman. The decision to kill him was made prior to the formation of the vigilantes. Sanders was the head of the Montana Historical Society for twenty years, he kept a close eye on the archives and a lid on the facts. Henry Plummer was innocent.

In the spring of 1864, according to John "X" Beidler's diary, a document arrived in Bannack that approved the application Plummer had sent to Washington, D.C., to be the first U.S. Marshall of Idaho Territory east of the Rockies.

Original Bannack Jail built by Plummer.
Photo Courtesy of America Living Legends

Photo courtesy of
Montana Historical Society

John X Beidler (1831-1890)

    John Beidler was born in Mount Joy, Pennsylvania, in 1831. He was raised in the town of Chambersburg. His formal schooling was short-lived. X, as he liked to be called, was a nickname; he had no middle name. As a young adult he learned the shoemaker trade. It wasn't long before he switched over to brick making. X did not fair well in these two endeavors, so at the age of twenty-four he headed out west to Kansas and farmed. While there, he befriended John Brown. An abolitionist, X joined John Brown's "free soldiers" group, raiding anti-abolitionist, proslavery towns and farms along the Kansas-Missouri border.

    Missouri was proslavery, while Kansas was not. This period is called the Kansas-Missouri Border War. It was bloody, to say the least. Both sides were vicious. The

Brown led raids were an attempt to intimidate the Kansas citizens into becoming proslavery. But the resolve of the antislavery citizens of Kansas was great, and John Brown and his followers were called "border ruffians." This group failed to convince Kansas to go proslavery. X was a part of this movement. He raided, shot, and most likely killed. In 1859 John Brown raided the town of Harpers Ferry, Virginia, which housed the U.S. Armory, but X was not with him. Colonel Robert E. Lee led the Union forces, fighting a bloody battle before capturing Brown. This was pre-civil war, Lee was a Union soldier as most of the confederate leaders up until war broke out. When his country, Virginia, seceded Lee chose to fight for his home land.

Brown was tried and found guilty of treason. A month later, on December 2, 1859, he was hanged. The armory had over one hundred thousand muskets and rifles, along with ammunition. The group of raiders totaled twenty-one—sixteen whites and five free black men. Of these, twelve worked with Brown during the raids into Missouri. The plan at Harpers Ferry was to seize the weapons and let it be known that all who joined Brown would be free to help fight for others. Brown thought that his plan would work, for the slaves would leave and join him, at the same time Virginia, which was a country based on the traditional plantation-slavery economy, would collapse without a labor pool of slaves. A year after this raid and Brown's execution, the Civil War began.

John Brown was dead, and farming was not to X's liking, so he left Kansas for the Idaho Territory. Montana Territory would be carved out of Idaho Territory in 1864 and become a state in 1889. By the time X reached Idaho he had worked various jobs: store clerk, pack train operator, freighter, and prospector. In the territory he secured the position of stagecoach "shotgun" guard. When the Vigilance Committee was formed, he joined that as well. Perhaps he had good intentions and wanted to regain control over the lawlessness in the territory.

The study of history is difficult. The smallest detail—for that matter, most every detail—is difficult to come by, let alone prove. An example is X's size. Historians describe X as five feet three inches tall, others state five foot six, and still others tell claim that he was five foot seven or five foot four. In Reality who cares? He was a short man as his photographs indicate. Hardcore historians do care about accuracies. After careful consideration and lots of research, the general consensus is that the man was five foot six inches tall. X 's photograph on page 120 indicates his stature. He was not a large man, but X managed to obtain the respect he needed from men of all sizes and ages. He was funny and had a great wit. He was taken seriously. X also had a fondness for drink; he was never without a bottle in his coat pocket. By all accounts X was pretty much a failure, but when the Vigilance Committee was formed in 1863, he became a member, rising to the rank of lieutenant. As such, he was very active. He was about the only one so proud of his duties and deeds that he had no problem letting it be known to all. There are historians that say John "X" Beidler was *the* hangman for the twenty-three men that were lynched. He was not, but X executed more than his share; the committee paid him for his work. He hanged five men and assisted in they lynching of others by placing the rope around a few necks, tied a few hands and feet, and even helped to build the gallows. How much he was paid we will never know. All business aspects were kept secret, but using X's own words, "I'll be paid, you bet."

According his own biography, John "X" Beidler showed a disregard for Indian life. As a packer, X wrote:

"An Indian came to my camp one evening looking pretty hard up....I fed him. Next evening he came into my camp again. I fed him supper again. That Indian came back to my camp again—third time—then I got tired. We had some picks and shovels along and we dug a hole and placed him and his horse into it after killing them."

This may help to explain his disregard for human life. He was so eager to hang men that he constantly volunteered to do so. It was X who was directed to go to Bannack with three others to arrest Sheriff Plummer and his two deputies. At first the Bannack people were not supportive, but with the persuasive powers of Sidney Edgerton, Wilbur Sanders, and a few others, X was able to organize a large group of men to arrest and immediately hang the three lawmen. X expected outrage from the Vigilance Committee leaders back in Virginia City and Nevada City, for his orders were to capture them and bring them back for trial. There was no trial; in fact the only trial that was ever held was for George Ives, the first man they hanged. Next the committee ordered the arrest of would-be gang members Haze Lyons, Boone Helm, Jack Gallagher, Frank Parish, and George "Clubfoot" Lane. X was the hangman for all five.

The book *Hanging the Sheriff: A Biography of Henry Plummer* by Mather and Boswell speaks of John "X" Beidler as a frustrated man who failed in other trades and "concluded to quit prospecting for gold and prospect for human fiends,...[who] was always present when a grave needed to be dug, a makeshift scaffold rigged, or a rope adjusted around a neck." X was well rewarded. For his part in helping to eradicate crime in the territory, X was hired on as a customs collector and a Deputy U.S. Marshal. By all accounts this little man did a superb job. One historian describes X as the greatest deputy marshals in Montana—ever. His territory was vast and the responsibility was tremendous, thus, he was forever on the go, in time he would be burned out. Throughout his law career X would be criticized for crossing that "magical" line of authority. He advised different vigilante groups how to organize and operate.

As a Deputy United States Marshal, X was headquartered out of Miles City. His duties had him constantly traveling to Deer Lodge, Helena, Virginia, Nevada, and Butte. X was bombarded by letters from citizens begging for assistance. X's boss was Neil Howie, who first came aboard as a deputy marshal in 1865. Neil worked for Sheriff Plummer. He single-handedly captured "Dutch John" Wagner, one of the so-called members of Plummer's Innocence Gang. When Plummer spoke to Howie, he expressed the need to house Dutch John in the new jail. Howie refused to give up his captive, keeping him safe in a cabin somewhere outside of town. He did not trust the sheriff. What Howie did was turn Wagner over to the vigilantes, who immediately hanged the man. It is ironic that Howie would be rewarded with the head marshal position, that a man sworn to uphold the law was a member of the Vigilance Committee. Could it be that this was one of the perks associated with the being one of the vigilantes? In Howie's diary there are numerous mentions of men who are to be strung up. These two men were like in many ways, Howie and John "X" Beidler must have gotten along famously.

When speaking of X, it must be said that he was not a sadistic person. He was renowned for his sense of humor. He believed in and conducted himself as a man of service to the community throughout the territory.

One of X's own accounts was the arrest of Johnny Bull in July 1867 after Bull pulled off what was considered impossible—killing Langford Peel in a gunfight. Both were Englishmen, both dangerous, but Langford Peel was considered to be more volatile than "Wild Bill" Hickok, who most consider to be the greatest draw and shot artist of them all, but he is up there as one of the greatest, if not *the* greatest, shooter of all time. When Johnny Bull successfully shot it out with Peel and survived, he was immediately arrested by X, who said, "Peale [sic] was such a rattler that I didn't think he would be killed." To some, arresting the adrenaline-filled Bull without bloodshed was in itself an amazing feat.

But not all citizens had faith in X and the vigilantes, X had received a letter of warning:

John "X" Beidler:

"We...will give you no more time to prepare for death than the many men you have murdered....We shall live to see you buried beside the poor Chinaman you murdered."

X was protected by his "friends." He was guarded twenty-four hours a day for weeks, until the danger of being lynched subsided.

Located in the *Sanders Papers* is a statement by early pioneer Mary Stanchfield, a well respected and considered a "remarkable woman." She also doubted Beidler's honesty. Upon her arrival in the area Beidler hailed a Missouri River steamer, that she was traveling on, begging to be taken aboard and claiming that he was a "refugee from Indians that had been chasing him and came near enough to shoot holes in his hat." Mrs. Stanchfield always believed that "X did the shooting himself." By spring of 1879 crime was hitting a high note; two hundred men rose to form a new rank of vigilantes. Miles City was in the middle of a crime wave; the citizens were fed up. Beidler and John Guy positioned themselves within the vigilantes of 1879. X helped form this secret group; he gave guidance, utilizing his past experiences. Four men were hanged. They had a code:

4-4-4. It would usually be pinned on the victim's clothing. What 4-4-4 means; no one really knows for sure.

The vigilantes targeted whom they wanted with 4-4-4. Miles City used 4-4-4 before Helena invented the code 3-7-77 six months later when they organized a vigilante group. This seems to be in the fabric of Montana, even today. The Montana Highway Patrol arm patch includes the numbers 3-7-77. Where vigilante groups sprung up, Beidler seemed to have some involvement.

*****

Judge Sidney Edgerton, he hated Plummer and
plotted to rid of him and others while lining his pockets

On January 22, 1890, at 6:00 a.m. John "X" Beidler died at the age of fifty-nine at the Pacific Hotel in Helena from complications due to pneumonia. Drink had caught up with him; his system was weak. The Montana vigilante and lawman was destitute, having spent his final years living "largely on the charity of friends and the income from telling stories at local Helena water holes," justifying the death of those whose lives he silenced. Twelve hundred people attended his funeral at the Ming's Opera House the following day. Wilbur Fisk Sanders delivered the eulogy.

The *Daily Independent* newspaper of Helena, Montana, wrote an article about X in July 1964:

"…if Beidler was alive today he would be a perfect prototype for all of those he-men from the wide open spaces now seen on television….if his exploits are recorded truthfully, he could out-shoot all the so-called fearless westerners including "Marshal Dillion" and Bat Masterson or any of the lawmen or gun slingers…the last conspicuous figure in a notable class of pioneers."

Legend has it that as a young boy one of his older brothers would take John's clean Sunday shirt and wear it, leaving John with a dirty shirt. He solved the problem by marking the letter X on his clean shirts with a lump of coal. People laughed, and John laughed, but from that day on he called himself X.

Bannack's Hangman's Gulch, site of the execution of Sheriff Henry Plummer and his two deputies on 10 January 1864. (Photo by Boswell, 1985)

Photo courtesy of Bannack State Park Gulch where Plummer Hangman Gulch where Plummer was hung

Johnny Bull (1836-1929)

John "Johnny" Edwin Bull, was born in England in 1836. He immigrated to the United States in his mid-twenties. He had black hair, a beard, and dark eyes; he was lean and rather short in stature, but was good-looking. The United States, then and now, is a country of immigrants; in the period of the Old West it was common to have countless immigrants looking for a better life, looking to strike it rich. Various languages and accents were commonplace.

By 1861 Johnny was a professional gambler traveling the "gambling circuit," going to mining town after mining town, to those with the most "snap." Like Henry Plummer, Johnny was a pioneer in the sense that he lived in the area during the pre–Wild West era. The Old West could be used as a term to encompass both the pre- and post–Civil War period.

Near summer's end, on August 25, 1862, Bull and a partner were bounty hunters. Their first attempt would be to bring in three horse thieves. The horse thieves were in Gold Creek, a small mining town in Idaho Territory, later to become part of Montana. The three thieves had been in the village area for three days, taking it easy. They did not suspect that anyone was after them. C. W. Spillman was captured with ease. The other two were a different issue. Spying the two playing a game of monte in a tented saloon, Bull—with his shotgun raised, cocked, and ready for use—stepped into the tent. He demanded that the two surrender. One man, Bill Arnett, reached for his gun, but the blast from Bull's shotgun ended his life. The second thief, B. F. Jermagin, gave up as he quivered in the corner. The following day Spillman was tried and hanged. Jermagin was able to convince the jury that he had nothing to do with the theft, and was released but warned to leave the area. This is the first known shooting by John Bull. From here John Bull's reputation began to grow. Ironically, the term "John Bull" had a negative connotation for an Englishman, one that was not flattering. Bull left Montana for Nevada.

In Nevada Territory in the early 1860s Aurora was a major boomtown, quickly followed by Austin. The ore was silver. There were many, with Virginia City's and its Comstock Lode being the biggest. Johnny Bull found himself in Austin, a town that quickly grew from zero to between six thousand and ten thousand souls within a couple of years. (Census taking was poor, thus the population range.) It was a good place to set up shop. The biggest and most popular hotel was the two-story International. The hotel was upstairs and in the back. Downstairs there was a bar and billiards room in the front, while off to the side was a large restaurant and public facility. The establishment sold cigars at the bar at fifteen cents each or two for a quarter. Drinks were roughly the same in price. This was not the only saloon, but it was the most successful. It was originally located in Virginia City. When silver was discovered in the Reese River District, the hotel was dismantled and hauled by mules to the new boomtown of Austin. The owners dismantled and hauled the first International to Austin. They build in the International lot in Virginia City a five-story building with the first elevator in the West.

As with all mining towns, there was a "chief"—someone who controlled the gamblers, someone whom all feared yet respected, a tough man whom few would challenge. A chief would rise to the occasion to fight off those who challenged his self-imposed authority; he received a percentage of the gambling stakes. John Bull decided to challenge the establishment. An Irishman at the time would fight John the Englishman for the position of chief.

The newspaper did its best to play down the bad—gun or knife play or, in the case above, the battle to be chief. It was a classic battle, with an Irishman fighting a Brit. The *Reese River Reveille* never did publish the name of the Irishman; perhaps they feared that if they did, there would be reprisal. More likely, his name no longer counted; his term as chief was too short to be considered a viable chief. Instead of a duel with pistols or a knife fight to the death, the decision was reached between the two combatants via fisticuffs. It appears that John Bull was a talented man when it came to bare-knuckle fist fighting.

Near midnight on February 22, 1864, when parties having agreed to to a fist fight they left the saloon for the corner of Main and Cedar for open space. The crowd was large and loud. There were those among the crowd who were in their undergarments, having risen out of bed to cheer on the prizefight. This was a big deal—great entertainment for the town. Money exchanged hands; bets were placed. The two men fought for twenty-one rounds, both bloodied and both refusing to yield to the other. Johnny Bull had more endurance that the Irishman. Later it was said that Mac Waterhouse, Bull's "second," gave Bull the final instruction to end the fight, "to feint with his left, aka one step back, and give an uppercut." Bull was declared the victor; thus, he received the title of chief.

The local newspaper, the *Reese River Reveille*, published this story on February 23, 1864:

"They thereupon adjourned to the street. Mac Waterhouse was selected by the Englishman as his second, and George Loney by the Irishman, and after these preliminaries had been gone through with, the mauling commenced about twelve o'clock. Twenty-one rounds were fought and for a time the battle was very hotly contested, both giving and receiving very hard knocks and showing no signs of yielding. But Johnny Bull's endurance was too much for Irish grit, and the victory was decided in favor of the Englishman. It is claimed however, that the result was entirely owing to the instructions Mac gave his man during the twenty-first round; that is, to feint with his left, take one step back, and give an uppercut with his right. This direction was followed and gained the fight. Both men were severely punished. A large crowd witnessed the contest, many being present in dishabille [state of casual attire], not having time to dress themselves when they jumped out of bed to see what was going on. We are making fine progress in "muscular Christianity." A prize fight in our public thoroughfare. Who can beat it?"

Many men would argue that John Bull was the most accurate pistol shot among the highly noted Nevada gunfighters of the 1860s. During his tenure as chief he killed three men with head shots and heart shots in fair-fight duels. To aim for the smaller head, a small target, is rare. The mastering of accurate pistol shooting, especially, is extremely difficult and nerve-racking. Like other professional gunmen, Johnny Bull was fearless. When Bull decided to pull up stakes and leave Austin in 1867, his friend "Irish Tom" Carberry took over as chief. Carberry would become one of the most remembered gunmen in Nevada history. During the 1860s Nevada had a large number of professional gunmen; most worked for the various mining operations at twenty dollars a day. This was considered top wage.

Fellow mining town Aurora—located three miles from the California border, and a like distance from Bodie, California—was notoriously known as a refuge for the roughest element of men. Twenty-two saloons supplied the town its "firewater." As a former governor of Nevada said in his autobiography published in 1912, *Life in the Territory*, there were two crowds of "toughs"—one from San Francisco, the other from Sacramento. They did not mix well. As long as they were left alone, the townsfolk paid no attention to the killings between these two elements, but one day the toughs murdered a good, well-respected citizen, W. R. Johnson, the owner and manger of Johnson's Station. With the news of the death of Mr. Johnson, four hundred men met at Armory Hall in Aurora, forming the Citizens Safety Committee, a vigilante organization. Within a few days the ranks would swell to six hundred. John A. Palmer was named captain and wore a badge with an encircled star and the engraved words *CITIZEN COM. OF SAFETY*. He had organized a committee once before. A secret executive board of twelve was formed; each member was addressed by his number Captain Palmer reported to this executive board. It was Palmer who ran the show, made the committee militaristic in style, assigned duties, and saw to it that orders were carried out. The banner or code they used was 601. To this day no one really knows what that stood for, although one could speculate—six feet under, no trial (zero), one hanging. Quickly they rounded up the entire gang responsible for the death of Mr. Johnson. The gang was surrounded by a thicket of armed guards so none could escape, until a trial was set.

What caused the killing of Mr. Johnson? A member of the San Francisco Gang, Jimmy Sayres (or Sears), was killed by a ranch hand, John A. Rodger, an employee of Johnson. The killing happened during Rodger's quest to retrieve an expensive horse stolen by Sayres. The horse was taken back to the rightful owner, Louis Wedertz, a

German, who was much distressed over its lost. Wedertz had gone to Johnson to ask for help; in turn Johnson gave orders for Rodger to find and retrieve the horse. Many historians have written that the San Francisco Gang held no ill will toward Rodger for following orders, but aimed their venom at his employer for the death of their friend. The truth is, they did hold bad feelings toward Rodger, but they could not get to him, so they decided to go after an easier mark, his boss. Johnson was aware he was in danger. He stayed away from town for a few weeks, but finally came in to sell his potatoes.

*****

John Daly was the gang's leader. His members included John McDowell ("Three-Fingered Jack"), William Buckley, Jim Sayres, Pliney Gardner, James Masterson "Massey" (no relationship to Bat), "Irish Tom" Carberry, "Italian Jim" Bacgalupi, Mike Fagan, John Gillman, Wash Parker, and Sam B. Vance. All were placed under arrest except for Sears, who was deceased, and "Irish Tom" Carberry, who was *not* present in Aurora at the time as many historians have claim that he was. There were one hundred armed vigilantes guarding the prisoners around the clock.

The Daly men were hired gunslingers for the Pond Mining Company. The Pond had claim issues with the Real Del Monte Mining Company. They both wanted the Last Chance Hill Mine. Open warfare prevailed. Over the course of three years, twenty-seven men were killed. Witnesses were intimated out of testifying in these murders, but as long as the bad elements were killing each other off, the general population looked the other way. In the late part of 1863 Daly was able to get the people to vote one of his crew into office as town marshal, then Daly had the new marshal appoint two of Daly's friends deputies. The *Esmeralda Star* newspaper recognized that with the election of a member of Daly's gang, and the appointment of two others as deputies, a bad element of the worst kind had permeated Aurora. Crime was up, way up; even merchants were shaken down by these dishonest lawmen. The recently formed Citizens Safety Committee would soon take action by arresting the Daly Gang.

*****

A coroner's inquest began the day of the Johnson murder; it lasted three days. This inquest was to be the only trial for the gang. Out of the trial came the conviction of four men: Daly (the leader), Buckley, Masterson, and McDowell. Prisoners Gardner, Fagan, and Parker were taken out of town and released. Seven days after Johnson's murder, on February 9, the convicted men were taken from confinement to a sophisticated gallows that was specially constructed. The site of the gallows was approximately one hundred feet north of the Armory Hall, where the four were being held.

Where was "Irish Tom" Carberry? Supposedly he was in Austin at the time of the killing. Although he was identified as a gang member, he had nothing to do with the murder, nor was he ever placed on trial, according to the corner's inquest and report. The other members of the gang scattered. Later, after the deaths of his peers, Carberry told this tell:

"…the story of his experiences while in the hands of the vigilantes was most amusing. He said that when the Gang was led out of the pen, one at a time, the presumption was that they were to hang singly. He was one of the first taken out, but when they put him back he concluded it was all off and he would hang with the others. This, together with the sight of a Gang of carpenters putting up a gallows frame was the last straw. Their courage gave way and Johnny Daly asked 'Three Fingered' Jack McDonald, Jack, do you know any prayer?"

Irish Tom's residency in Austin produced two friends: John Bull and James Earp. James was the older brother of the famed Fighting Earps. James lived in Austin for about thirteen or fourteen months. This is where Earp landed his first job as a bartender, a profession that he stayed with for years to come, even in Tombstone.

Levell White, who was then an attorney in the territory and later in life became a judge, wrote of having defended Irish Tom for murder; he published the story in November 1873 in the *Overland Monthly*. In a nutshell, Tom, chief of Austin's gambling and saloon business, had already killed three men who challenged his authority. One day a man from Montana came to town to kill Carberry. Not knowing his real name, the citizens called him Montana. His reason to kill was for a woman that he was romantically connected with. If he did not kill Carberry, she would not have anything to do with him. Her vendetta against Irish Tom is unknown. Carberry claimed to have never heard of her. As a lawyer, White claimed to never have worked harder for harder for a client as he did for Carberry. From Levell White's article "The Judge's Story" in the *Overland Monthly*, November 1873:

"The Exchange was in a corner building across a street which came in at right angles to the sidewalk where they were standing. Montana went in at the front door, but came out at the side on the cross street, hoping to steal up and "get the drop" on Tom, but this was not so easy. Tom was wide-awake—he had crossed the main street to guard against surprise; so, when Montana poked his pistol round the corner and followed it with just enough of his head to take sight, Carberry was not in range. In a moment their eyes met, and the shooting began. Tom curled down close to the road-bed, to present the smallest possible area as a mark, and because it is comparatively difficult to hit an object lying on the ground. Montana sheltered himself somewhat behind a low row of sacks of potatoes lying on the edge of the sidewalk, and partly behind a small awning-post. This last was a fatal error, for with a tall post for a mark it is the easiest thing in the world to make a line-shot."

I am making a long story of the shooting, which in reality was very soon over. They fired three shots apiece in as many seconds. Tom's third ball passed through Montana's heart, and he was dead before his head rebounded on the brick pavement. Carberry surrendered himself at once, and was kept in jail until his trial came off, although bail to any amount was [not] offered.

After a pause, the Judge added, "I don't see how I could have done more for him than I did; but the man should not have been punished—he should have been acquitted; and he would have been but for one circumstance, which prejudiced the court and jury against him."

"What was the circumstance so prejudicial?" questioned the listener." The Montana chap was the fourth man Tom had killed in Austin," answered the Judge, innocently.

Aurora, NV, 1870. Public domain photograph, courtesy of Nevada Historical Society

Irish Tom was sentenced to three years in the state pen. The sad part is that Carberry did his best to stay away from the man, to not confront him, but after a couple of weeks of avoiding town, and a friendly attempt to reconcile with the man whom the town named Montana, he came out. The gunfight was fair. Montana lost.
Most historians say that Tom Carberry was killed in a gunfight in Austin. That may be true, but not in the immediate future. No evidence has surfaced of any death of Irish Tom listed between 1864 and 1881. Carberry was a crack shot; of the men he killed, all died with a shot to the heart or head. Irish Tom was a very good, calm gunslinger.

When Johnny Bull and Langford Peel left Austin for good in 1865, Carberry took over as chief. Langford Peel had a nickname—"Farmer," as in Farmer Peel. The logic behind the nickname was that Peel was anything but a farmer, anything but nice. He was a gambler and a hardened stone-cold killer. But he was very polite, soft-spoken, well-mannered, and calm. He was of medium height and had a sandy beard, slight build, and blue eyes. He was a light drinker and never boisterous. There are historians who equate Peel's gun-handling abilities with those of "Wild Bill" Hickok. A good many historians consider Hickok the quickest of them all. Peel was known to be as deadly as they come. John Bull was not far behind; after all, he was chief of Austin while Peel was chief of the Comstock. From Austin they journeyed to Belmont, Nevada, then to Montana. For the next two years all was peachy-keen; then on August 4, 1867, the *Montana Post* reported a story of the eventual loss of friendship between the two men over a mining claim in Helena, Montana. Paraphrasing the article, the men were in the Exchange Saloon, owned by the Greer brothers. The argument was over a placer claim on Indian Creek. Although the men had been pretty much working as partners for the past two years, they did part ways for a short time prior to coming to Helena. Who would think that they could not get over their anger? Peel slapped Bull's face. Realizing Bull was unarmed, he told him to get "heeled." Bull left the saloon, but he did not return quickly. First he wrote letters to his family and then instructions on what do in case of his death; finally he carefully cleaned and loaded his pistol. Johnny Bull figured he would not survive, yet he knew he had no choice but to face his former friend. He headed back to the Exchange Saloon. Peel had left the saloon on Main Street for another where his lady friend, Belle Neil, worked. She was a faro dealer and most likely a hooker at the Chase Saloon, owned by Ed Chase. Bull went looking. It was close to midnight when Johnny decided to check Chase; as he approached the front of the saloon, still on the street level, Peel and his lady were exiting. Peel looked downward upon his enemy, for Peel was on the elevated walkway. Belle was holding on to Peel's right arm in a loving way. At the edge of the walkway Bull unholstered his gun and shot at and hit Peel. Wounded but not down, Peel went for his pistol. Unfortunately Belle froze, clenching Peel's arm a split second long enough for Bull to get off another round before Peel could break loose and pull his gun. Peel hit the ground, severely wounded. Bull calmly put the next bullet in his former friend's head, killing him. The killing of Langford Peel made John Bull an instant celebrity—almost—

but not in Helena. He was arrested by Deputy United States Marshal John "X" Beidler to face trial for murder. That same night Beidler held off a group of Peel's friends who wanted to lynch Bull, so when the inquest jury acquitted Bull of murder by a split decision, he mounted up quickly, leaving Helena in his wake.

In the crowd the night of the shooting stood James Earp. Court records show that Belle Neil did her best to get Bull hanged. Earp contradicted her testimony. It would be safe to argue that thanks to James Earp's testimony, Johnny Bull was freed.

Johnny's next stop was Cheyenne, Dakota Territory. Cheyenne had been founded recently, on August 8, 1867. The Union Pacific Railroad made Cheyenne its hub, passing over Denver. The group often referred to as the "hell on wheels" gambling crowd was in full swing; the town was considered the wildest of the rail towns. The railroad and its employees were fair game for the gamblers, con artists, and prostitutes. Comfortable with this type of crowd, Bull stepped right in. When Denver was bypassed by the railroad, the city realized that if there was to be a future, it would be dependent on a rail system. Denver's wealthiest citizens raised funds to privately build a spur from Cheyenne to Denver. The rail spur was completed in mid-1870. It worked. Denver has flourished ever since. John Bull followed the construction crew all the way to Promontory Point, where the last spike, a gold one, was hammered into place, connecting the East with the West on May 10, 1869. But that spur did not completely connect the East to the West until Denver built another spur connecting itself to the Kansas Pacific line. The first passengers from Kansas arrived in Denver in August 1870. This was the actual completion of the Transcontinental Railroad. Passengers, for the first time, could board in the East and travel all the way to the West without having to disembark.

John Bull married a beautiful, respectable lady who had no business in the Wild West, so he took her to Chicago, where she bore him two sons. Throughout his marriage, Bull would only visit his family. His business and lifestyle were elsewhere. While his sons were young, Mrs. Bull passed away. John had no desire to change, so he placed his sons in foster homes. He continued to hit the gaming circuit, crisscrossing the northwest portion of the country from Washington to Wyoming to Nebraska and points in between. He had a fraudulent three-card monte game going wherever he set up house. He was good at separating money from its owners. He and his partners would concentrate their scams aboard stagecoaches and trains and in the territorial towns.

By July 1873 Bull had been in Omaha, Nebraska, for a while. Samuel Atwood, a railroad man, had been warning train passengers that Bull and his partner, George Mehaffy, were outside a saloon. Atwood was stabbed and not likely to live. A vigilante group started to form. Bull and Mehaffy resisted arrest to no avail. The lynching was not to be—Atwood lived. He testified against Mehaffy but did not identify Bull; Bull was free to go his way. For whatever reason, Mehaffy got off scot-free as well. The two continued their partnership. And work their trade they did. Bull even fixed a prizefight, yet he seemed to have that thing called Lady Luck. He was once friendly with Mark Twain. While in Nevada and California, Bull pulled a joke on Twain. Johnny stole his money in an armed holdup, scaring the daylights out of Twain, but the following day, laughing and returning his money. Twain wrote of him as the man with the swagger in his book *Roughing It*.

The year 1876 found Bull in Deadwood for a time, then back in Denver. According to DeArment's book, *Deadly Dozen*, Bull and a fellow swindler, Frank Pine, went to England, taking mining investors for $25,000 of worthless stock. It was John's time. In Spokane, Washington, in 1898, Bull was having a good old time with manager Frisky (or Friskey) Barnett of the People's Theater. As they left the theater, Barnett, who must have felt threatened in some way, took his lit cigar and jammed it in Bull's eye. Screaming in pain, Bull pulled his gun; Barnett grabbed a woman nearby, using her as a shield. A gunfight ensued. When it was over, the woman lay on the ground, shot. Barnett lost a thumb. Johnny was shot four times—in his left arm, groin, chin, and neck. He lost his left arm. It was too dangerous to remove the bullet from his neck, which remained there for twenty-three years. After so many years, the bullet traveled inside the neck, causing a major problem; doctors had no other choice but to remove it and did so. There is no report on his eye; The lady used as a shield lived. No prison terms were handed out to the men; Barnett was fined ten dollars for discharging his gun inside city limits. Bull surprised everyone by living. John Bull, now a cripple with one good arm and one good eye, seemed to have quieted down. There is not much more to say of him and his gambling and shooting sprees. He lived a long—and some say full—life, passing away on September 9, 1929, in Vancouver, British Columbia, at the age of ninety-three.

Life in a Mining Town

Austin, Nevada. Photograph courtesy of the Austin Historical Society

On May 2, 1862, while William Talcott was hauling wood from Pony Canyon, a stone was kicked by his mule. Talcott looked down and noticed that it looked to be a vein of ore-bearing quartz. A sample was sent to Virginia (soon to be renamed Virginia City) for assay and was determined to be rich. The Pony Mine in Pony Canyon was established, and the mining district of Reese River was organized on May 10, 1862. The Pony mine claim covered a total of 2,600 feet. The canyon's elevation starts at 6,605, rising to 7,400 feet above sea level. The Overland Mail had a route that crossed the Reese River Valley at Jacobs Station, eight to twelve miles northeast of the Toiyabe mountain range. A little east of the station was a pass through the Toiyabe Mountains that the Pony Express riders used as a cutoff, thus the name Pony Canyon. The strike was on; Clifton, just below the discovery, was founded. David Buel decided to start a new town a short distance up Pony Canyon. He named the place Austin after his best friend and partner, Alvah Austin. A month later the town was booming. So quick was the rush that its population grew substantially . With a vast number of people moving into the area, the Nevada legislators decided to create a new county, so in December 1862 Lander County was established. By May 5, 1863, the Reese River Review printed a list of Austin's buildings and businesses:

"2 hotels, 2 stores, 5 saloons, 2 buildings, 1 billiard table, 3 blacksmiths, 1 wagon shop, 1 variety shop, 3 laundries, 2 houses, 1 lodging house and one building, 1 livery stable, 2 lawyers, 4 notaries, 1 barber, 1 tailor shop, 1 sign painter, 4 carpenters, 4 stone masons, 2 adobe yards, 1 boot and shoe store, 1 dairy, 1 printing office, Wells Fargo Express,

Turner's Express, telegraph office, 4 gardens comprising of four hundred, fifty citizens."

The nearby tent town of Clifton had about the same population, nearing five hundred. Besides many of the above, they had a sheriff's office, a justice of the peace, a couple of bakeries, and eight saloons.

A local census was taken in July 1863, showing Austin's population at 1,052 men, 110 women, and 2 "young children." It was estimated that about 500 prospectors scattered among the hills were not enumerated in the census and that around 500 emigrants, not eligible to vote, were not included in the census. By the end of July the total population of Lander County was 2,062. Election day—held September 2, 1863—resulted in Austin becoming the county seat; a year later it was incorporated. The county seat moving to Austin triggered the death of Clifton. The post office closed down, and the vast majority of its citizens moved over to Austin. Within a few years there was nothing left of the town.

From the beginning, Austin enjoyed an educated, informed community full of "minded citizens." A primary example—and one of the most memorable events in the history of Austin, which was nationally followed—was that of two friendly rivals, Reuel Gridley (spelled Greeley in the newspapers) and H. S. Herrick. They had a bet on the outcome of the mayoral election. The wager was for the loser to carry a fifty-pound sack of flour. Gridley was a southern sympathizer; Herrick, a Democrat. Gridley lost the best. As agreed upon, he hired a band to play "Old John Brown," purchased a fifty-pound sack of flour, and then, with the band, marched through the streets of Clifton all the way to Austin (a trip of one mile) to deliver the sack of flour. The men decided to put the flour up for auction and donate the proceeds to the Sanitary Commission's Fund—often referred to as the Sanitary Fund, a forerunner to the Red Cross—that helped and housed wounded soldiers. (This was a Yankee endeavor.) Gridley took bids for the sack. The winner paid up, then promptly returned the sack. After donations from Austin dried up, Gridley took the sack to Dayton, Silver City, Gold Hill, and Virginia City.

Reuel Gridley with his bag of flour

Again and again and again the flour went up for bid, and again each winner gave the flour back to be auctioned. For the next year Gridley carried the flour to all the major cities of California and even went back East. Mark Twain, as a reporter, followed the good man, to write of this adventure. As in Austin, each winner returned the prize until they had raised $175,000! All the money went to help the Civil War wounded. In today's money, they raised $2,571,367. After this the conversations on the Civil War were more understanding and civil among the people, even with a pro-Union individual debating a pro-Confederate—Austin set a new tone.

Twenty million dollars' worth of silver was extracted from the mines of Austin between 1862 and 1887; six thousand claims were staked. The first gold discovery was actually near Virginia City in 1859. Silver followed and was the greater of the two "finds." President Lincoln needed money to finance the Civil War, so he fast-tracked Nevada to statehood. Between the gold- and silver-mining operations the Comstock of Virginia City cleared in excess of $1 billion. With the discovery in Austin, even Virginia City felt a little of the pressure as labor became scarce for a time as many working class miners left Virginia for Austin. To make room for a newer, larger hotel, the International Hotel was moved 175 miles, by oxen, from Virginia City to Austin at a cost of $400 per 1,000 feet. The owners were willing to invest nearly $1 million to move the two-story structure.

*****

Austin's population quickly rose to ten thousand (some say only six thousand) by 1864. It had its issues like any town—for example, they had domestic violence, with a wild west twist. These examples are from the *Reese River Reveille,* May 9, 1883:

Yet Another:

"Madame York shot John York sometime near midnight Thursday last. The ball entered the abdomen at one side above the hip bone, and passed out a few inches from the place of entrance. His wound is not supposed to be dangerous. The difficulty in which this shooting originated is not known, but is believed to be quite trivial."

Nothing more came of the shooting; hopefully they settled their issues. The title "Yet Another" was in reference to the violence in Austin. In the Old West both men and women could handle weapons; children were trained early on to help with hunting for food and fighting off the Indians and outlaws.
In the same paper on the same day, this was printed:

More shootings:

"A misunderstanding has existed for some time between O. M. Taylor and the original Yankee Blade company. Last Tuesday the parties came in collision—Taylor leaving the ledge [mining area] as the others came up. They gave chase, surrounded his carriage, shot one horse—causing its death—and wounding Taylor severely in the thigh. Several other gentlemen with him escaped unhurt although balls passed through their clothes. It was a rough affair."

It even had the issue of men with mental problems. One terrible example is that one evening one of the miners grabbed a knife and a long-handled ax. He attacked one of his roommates, then ran off into the streets, attacking anyone within reach. He damaged many a man and woman, running from potential victim to potential victim. He ran so fast that people could not catch him. Shooting at him was dangerous for those nearby. From Austin to Clifton people were struck, some with life-threatening blows. The following morning he was found dead. Death was caused by a hatchet or ax blow to the back of his head, and twenty knife wounds to his chest, just above the heart yet it was ruled a suicide. Mark Twain, as a reporter out of Virginia City, told this story but placed it elsewhere. From day one his editor told him to make up or embellish stories to make them more exciting and believable.

*****

A common problem for every mining town was that the mines overlapped. The owners needed to protect their interests and did so by hiring top gunslingers. The pay per gunman was twenty dollars a day. Nevada was riddled with gunmen. The *Reese River Reveille* did its best to soften the news, but the reality was harsh. The good people did their best to avoid problems, to continue to live their lives, and to ignore the shootings and stabbings that occurred all too often. As noted previously, there were few women in mining camps. As more and more women came to town, their presence softened the men, and civilization started to form.
When Austin was being built, most buildings had dirt floors, including saloons, restaurants, offices, private homes, and even the hotels. The more expensive buildings, ranging in cost from $2,000 to $5,000, would include wooden floors. A large number of these buildings were made of stone. The majority of businesses were concentrated on Main and Cedar Streets. Cedar ran at a right angle to Main. The town was located on a "shallow" ravine, so much so that there could be no more than two parallel streets. Rent was high. The West was about commerce and money. The business model "price and demand" was in full swing. The demand became greater as the population increased; the prices went up—not only for buildings, but for all goods. As the growth continued, the need for additional space grew. Immediately above Austin higher up in Pony Canon was a new addition called Upper Austin.

Emory Skinner was a man hired by San Francisco financiers to build a lumber mill in Austin. His job commanded a monthly salary of $300, with a bonus to be included for performance. When he first arrived in the early part of 1863, he noted that most inhabitants were living in tents. Except for small pinion pines that could be used for poles and posts, wood was limited. With an abundance of stones and rocks, as well as dirt ideal for adobe, the town had a combination of adobe and stone buildings. The adobe-type dirt was packed hard; the floors were relatively clean. Cotton cloth was used for the roofs. His first year in Austin Mr. Skinner lived in a little house, eighteen feet by thirty feet, along with two others: John Doyle (a miner) and John P. Kelly (a civil engineer). Their first setup was a seven-by-nine-foot walled tent. Between them they would cook two meals a day. Breakfast was handled by Skinner, and dinner was prepared by Doyle. Kelly, the engineer, had the duty of washing the dishes. Breakfast typically consisted of bacon, boiled potatoes, and bread. During the evening the men would read by candlelight or play chess. The candles were made from animal fat called tallow. If these men decided to have a drink, they knew which saloons to avoid and which had friendlier crowds.

Skinner must have liked the Stone Saloon inside the International Hotel; he described it well:

"The principal attraction of the place was called the Stone Saloon. It was a one-story building with walls of stone, dimensions about twenty-five feet wide by one hundred (or more) feet in length. The entrance was on the principal street and not far from the hotel. As one entered, upon the left was a large, gaudy bar, disbursing liquors. On the right was a cigar counter, this luxury selling fifteen cents each or two for a quarter of a dollar, and drinks were about the same."

Skinner claimed to have never gambled, but did go into the gaming area where a band played and twice an hour an "opera" singer would perform a selection of songs. Women would function as dealers, with the intended result of the loser being less likely to vent his anger over the loss of his wages. As Emory said, "I had never seen similar orgies [wild parties] since I left Austin." Skinner talked about the class of the people. As he put it:

"The class of people I met there were very intelligent; a great many of them were college bred. The young man who wished to make a fortune quickly; the man who had lost his fortune in the East and wished to make another; the politician who had lost his hold on the public, came west to grow up with the country. I never was lonesome while I lived there, and I often resolved to bring my family here to live…"

Skinner was a typical, hardworking citizen of Austin. He considered his lifestyle to be a free, easy, devil-may-care sort of existence, yet he yearned for the family he left behind.

Two examples of the high caliber of citizens in and around Austin are Mark

Twain and William Rosecrans. Twain came though while living in Virginia City, and reported on some of the goings-on in Austin. Major General William Rosecrans settled in for a while. He was a highly respected Union general and was outspoken. He lost the Battle of Chickamauga in 1863. For this loss he was demoted by General U. S. Grant. General Rosecrans invented the kerosene lamp that used a round wick, and a better, more effective way to manufacture soap. He would be appointed diplomat to Mexico. Later he ran for and was elected to Congress, representing the California First District twice. He owned Rancho San Pedro. On March 11, 1898, he passed away; his body lay in state in Los Angeles City Hall. The Confederacy considered General Rosecrans one of the best Union generals. During the Civil War, in Western Virginia (now the state of Virginia), he out generaled Robert E. Lee, who had to abandon his plans to take over that area.

*****

What were the wages in Austin? Did the people make a good living, or did only the mine owners? From Emory Skinner, *The Reminiscences of Emory Fiske Skinner*

Per-day rate, mid-year 1863:
Laborers–$5; masons–$11; carpenters–$8 to $10; professional gunslingers–$20; general manager of a lumber mill–$30.

From Mark Twain's book *Roughing It,* during the same time period, some wages out of Virginia City were listed as:

Stagecoach ride from St. Joseph, Missouri, to Carson City, Nevada Territory: $150, food extra. Travel, just over 8 days, 798 miles total.

Boarding cost: $10 weekly (room divided by "cotton domestic" to make two rooms), typical of the times.   Laborers: $4–$6 per day, three shifts total to make 8-hour days.
Telegraph operator: $100 per month.
Reporter: starting wage of $25 per week, raised six months later to $40.
Superintendent of the Gould & Curry Mine (Comstock): an annual salary of $12,000,

plus a fine house (free) and beautiful horses.
Stamp Mills charged $50 per ton.
A team of horses or mules and wagon to haul: $15 per day.
Stage Transportation: $40 per passenger, from Carson City.
All freight transported by team from Sacramento was at 10 cents a pound.

At first Skinner sold his lumber for $200 per thousand feet, starting in 1864, but that price doubled with the demand.

In comparison, the wages in the eastern part of the United States were two to three time less than those in the territories of Nevada and Montana. The *Montana Post*, June 26, 1868, listed these prices:

"Clerks $100 to $250, per month in gold, Surface Miners, $4 to $5 per day in gold, Miners (Drifters) 7 to $12 per day in gold. Gun Smiths $100 per month in gold; Bar Tenders, 50 to $150 per month in gold and board, Jewelers, 8 to $10 per day in gold, Brewers, 75 to $200 per month in gold and board, Stage Drivers, 75 to $100 per month in currency and board, Quartz miners, $75 to $100 per month in currency and board, Cooks, 100 to 125 dollars per month in gold and board, Waiters, 50 to 75 dollars per month in gold and board, Book Keepers, 150 to 300 dollars per month in Currency, Shoemakers 35 to 40 dollars per week in gold, farm hands, 60 dollars per month in gold and board. Butchers, 100 to 150 dollars per month in gold and board, House Servants (Chinamen), 40 to 60 dollars per month and board. The figures above given speak for themselves and will compare favorably with those of any country in the world. A person can board himself, and live well, upon one dollar per day in gold or can patronize the table of a first-class hotel for twice that amount, and then have more money left to save than he would if following the same business in the States."

Many traveled by stagecoach. Skinner described his mode of transportation to Austin. The coach was of Concord build, with a heavy body suspension of wide leather straps. It could accommodate up to eleven passengers—nine inside and two on the outside with the driver. A team of six horses pulled the coach. The horses were of top caliber; most were purchased from Kentucky, Tennessee, and Missouri. Every ten miles the horses were changed out.

From *The Reminiscences of Emory Fiske Skinner*, who was living in Hangtown, California, when the book was written:
"We then began the ascent of the Sierra Nevada Mountains, which we had to cross in order to reach Carson Valley. The roads up the grade were broad, smooth and sprinkled by water carts. In many places the roads were cut in solid rock, on the sides of the mountains, traversing the canyon. At the bottom flowed the American River. When we got into the coach, I took the front seat, riding backward, as I had been told that it was the easiest. The hostlers let go the bridles of the horses and we went up the grade at a smart

trot. The road had been laid out by engineers, and the grade kept as true as possible; sharp angles were often met and had to be turned, and sometimes the road would follow an intersecting ravine, going up one side, and back on the other for perhaps half a mile or more...."

The schedule of these stages over the mountains was an average of ten miles an hour. We met and passed numerous freight wagons, many of which carried ten tons each. Behind the larger wagon would be a smaller one called a tender, which carried the food and camp outfit for the drivers and barley and hay for the mules. These wagons were usually hauled by twelve or fourteen mules, also brought from the states mentioned....

From Carson City to Austin it would take up to forty-eight hours to make the trip. They had stopping points for eating, but not sleeping; unlike the movies, the stage ran twenty-four hours a day. The cost was high, but the coaches were always full.

In a short time Twain secured a job as a reporter working out of Virginia City. This is the first time he used the pen name Mark Twain. Up to this time he had done a variety of jobs. Among them was working in a quartz mill, where he shoveled silver-bearing ore into heavy, loud pulverizing machinery. He hated the job; he hated manual labor. He visited Aurora and Austin and other mining towns to take "measure" of the community. Nevada did indeed have high-caliber men.

Still there were shootings. Vance, a member of the Daly Gang, was the man who escaped the gallows. He ran off to Montana. In August 1868 he returned to Nevada, to Austin. "Irish Tom" Carberry was a known associate of the gang. When Vance arrived, he held a grudge against Carberry. Vance told Carberry he was going to kill him. Tom was unarmed. Vance told him to go get his gun; Carberry did. As Irish Tom advanced toward Vance in the streets of Austin, Vance began shooting. Carberry kept walking until he reached a distance that he felt comfortable with. Tom rested his revolver across his arm, took careful aim, and shot Vance dead. No charges were filed.

By 1881 Austin had matured; there were three churches. The first was the Episcopal, followed by the Catholic and Methodist; Sunday school was well attended. Austin provided a public school in a large brick building that could educate up to four hundred children; there were also two private schools. Austin had fourteen saloons, with any number of restaurants, stores, and social clubs. The population was just under 2,000, plus 320 Indians and 120 Chinese. As the town's population faded, it would lose its position as county seat; the people would move away as the mines played out. Today less than 250 people live in Austin.

THE END
(Vol. 3 schedule for 2016)

Vol.2. A Fraternity of Gunslingers

Epilogue

Epilogue

It may seem odd that I end this book with Mark Twain. He was anything but a gunman. He was, however, an eyewitness to the happenings of the early 1860s in Nevada Territory, including those that took place in Austin, Aurora, Carson City, Virginia City, and Clifford, to name a few. He also ventured in and out of California's Mono Lake area, Bodie, and other mining towns. His book *Roughing It* is pure history as told by America's greatest storyteller. It is not a novel; it is his autobiography of his time in places far away from the borders of the United States.

The vigilantes went after the outlaws (and others) who stood in their way. The idea of hanging a man without a trial seems repulsive today. It was repulsive to the vast majority back then as well, yet in an uncivilized territory with no real law or court system, all they really had was vigilantism.

Most books similar in scope and content seem to remain in the confines of Arizona, Kansas, Texas, New Mexico, and Oklahoma. While I covered these areas, I also dared to go back to an earlier time and into Nevada, California, Montana, Nebraska, Idaho, and Colorado. I also gave the reader an idea of jobs, their pay, typical living quarters, and the type of businesses found in western towns—they were not all saloons. Not all residents were gunmen. There were few women. It is women who bring with them a calmer, more civilized environment. In all frontier towns, as women and families arrived to settle, the wildness subsided.

The suggested readings below will give the reader who wants to investigate true wild western times more in depth an excellent path to do so. My intent with this book and my other volumes is to give the readers a real glance into the seedier part of the Wild West that so many, including Hollywood, are interested in. Separating legend from fact was a priority. The third, and last, volume in this series will be published sometime in 2016 due to other commitments.

C. R. King, Los Angeles

Suggested Readings:

Chapter 1:

Me and My Big Mouth by Walter Harrison, Britton Printing Company, 1954

He Made It Safe to Murder: The Life of Moman Pruiett by Howard K. Berry, Oklahoma Heritage Association, 2001

Oklahoma Justice: The Oklahoma City Police by Ron Owens, Turner Publishing Company, Paducah, KY, 1995

Library of the Oklahoma Historical Society, Oklahoma City, OK

Chapter 2:

Cowtown Wichita and the Wild, Wicked West by Stan Hoig, University of New Mexico Press, 2007

"Another Fatal Occurrence," article in the *Wichita Eagle* newspaper, January 4, 1877

Other articles contributed from the *Eagle* between 1872 and 1877, courtesy of the Kansas Historical Society, Topeka, KS

The Great Gunfighters of the Kansas Cowtowns, 1867-1886 by Nyle H. Miller and Joseph W. Snell, University of Nebraska Press, Lincoln, NE, 1963

The Chisholm Trail by Sam P. Ridings, Ulan Press, 1975 (originally published in 1936)

Chapter 3:

Robert Clay Allison by James S. Peters, Sunset Press, Santa Fe, NM, 2008

Various articles on Allison, Robert Clay provide by: Texas Historical Society, Texas Heritage Association, and the New Mexico Office of the State Historian: Maxwell Land Grant http://www.newmexicohistory.org/filedetails.php?fileID=512

Wyatt Earp Frontier Marshal by Stuart N. Lake, Houghton Mifflin, 1931. This is the official biography. Wyatt Earp collaborated with Mr. Lake prior to his death in 1929.

Texas: A Modern History by D. G. McComb, University of Texas Press, Austin, TX,

1989

Chapter 4:

W. D. "Bill" Fossett, Pioneer and Peace Officer by Jim Fulbright, Mid-South Publication, 2002

Oklahombres: Particularly the Wilder Ones by Evett Dumas Nix, University of Nebraska Press. First published in 1929 by Eden Publishing House, St. Louis. Nix was the U.S. Marshal in charge of Old Oklahoma Territory and the Cherokee Strip.

West of Hell's Fringe by Glenn Shirley, University of Oklahoma Press, Norman, OK, 1978

Chapter 5:

Oklahoma State University digital library http://digital.library.okstate.edu/

Cattle Annie & Little Britches: Prison Records Located on Oklahoma's Famous Female Outlaws by November 1978

Oklahoma Outlaws, Spooky Stories, and All Around Folklore by David Farris, Little Bruce, Edmond, OK, 2011

Arizona Territory 1863–1912: A Political History by Jay J. Wagoner, Tucson: University of Arizona Press, 1970

"An Arizona Episode," Cosmopolitan article, vol 27: pages 673-677, May-October 1899

Pearl Hart: First Known Female Stage Robber In Arizona Territory by Clara T. Woody and Milton L. Schwartz, Arizona Historical Society, 1977

W. D. "Bill" Fossett, Pioneer and Peace Officer by Jim Fulbright, Mid-South Publications, 2002

Oklahoma Outlaw Tales by David A. Farris, Little Bruce, Edmond, OK, 1999

Chapter 6:

Deadly Dozen: Twelve Forgotten Gunfighters of the Old West, Volume 1 by Robert K. DeArmen, University of Oklahoma Press; first edition, October 15, 2007

"The Mather Family Times", Ancestry.com, freepages.genealogy.rootsweb.ancestry.com/~mather/Mather/DaveMather.shtml

The Great Gunfighters of the Kansas Cowtowns, 1867–1886 by Nyle H. Miller and Joseph W. Snell, University of Nebraska Press, Lincoln, NE, 1963

Wyatt Earp, The Man & the Myth by Ed Bartholomew, Frontier Book Company, 1964

The United States Marshals of New Mexico & Arizona Territories, 1846–1912 by Larry D. Ball, University of New Mexico Press, Albuquerque, NM

Chapter 7:

Fort Donelson's Legacy: War and Society in Kentucky and Tennessee, 1862–1863 by Benjamin Franklin Cooling, Knoxville: University of Tennessee Press, 1997

The Historical Mining Towns of the Eastern Mojave Desert by Alan Henser, California State University, Desert Studies Consortium and LSA Associates, Inc., 2005

Chapter 8:

The Kansas Historical Quarterly (Volume 28), posted by the Kansas Historical Society. Mostly a reprinting from various newspapers including *Dodge City Times, Ford County Globe, Dodge City Democrat, Globe Live Stock Journal*, and the *Dodge City Kansas Cowboy*

Chapter 9/10:

Ghost Towns of Montana by Donald C. Miller, Global Pequot Press, 2008

Wagon Roads West by Jackson Turrentine, University of California Press, Berkley, CA, 1938

The Vigilantes of Montana by Thomas J. Dimsdale, Norman: University of Oklahoma Press, 1953. Originally published in 1866 based the collection of Dimsdale's articles between 1862 and 1864 from the Montana Post.

Western Collection, Lucy Carson Library of University of Montana

Judge Edgerton's Daughter by Martha Edgerton Plassmann, a manuscript, Montana Historical Archives

Vigilante Victims: Montana's 1864 Hanging Spree by R. E. Mather, History West Pub Co, July 1991

Death of a Gunfighter: The Quest for Jack Slade, the West's Most Elusive Legend by Dan Rottenberg, Westholme Publishing, Yardley, PA, 2008

"A Story of Plummer" by Frank Woody, Madisonian newspaper, January 1, 1915

Hanging the Sheriff: A Biography of Henry Plummer by R. E. Mather and F. E. Boswell, University of Utah Press, 1987

A Governor's Wife on the Mining Frontier: The Letters of Mary Edgerton from Montana (1863–1865), edited by James L. Thane Jr., University of Utah Library, 1976

Diary of John X. Beidler by John X. Beidler, 1884. There are microfilm copies of this handwritten diary (Jan. 1–Dec. 31, 1884) that details day-to-day activities of law enforcement in Montana, with notes and memos on various topics. Available in book form.

William Y. Pemberton, A Short Reminiscence by William Y. Pemberton, Montana Historical Society Archives, William Y. Pemberton Papers, Small Collection 629

Still Speaking Ill of the Dead: More Jerks in Montana History, edited by Jon Axline and Jodie Foley, contributing authors: Ellen Baumler, Lyndel Meikle, Dave Walter, Kristin Gallas

Diary of John X. Beidler by John X. Beidler, 1884

Neil Howie Papers, Montana State Historical Society Archives, Small Collection 302 (his five diaries from 1864 to 1869)

Wilbur Fisk Sanders Papers, Montana State Historical Society Archives, Small Collection 302 (1856 to 1905)

Chapter 11:

Deadly Dozen: Twelve Forgotten Gunfighters of the Old West by Robert K. DeArment, University of Oklahoma Press, 2012

Roughing It by Mark Twain, 1872, can be purchased on Amazon and elsewhere

Gunfighters and Lawmen by William and John Gorenfeld, 1982

Various news articles as noted in the text

Chapter 12:

The History of Nevada Landers County, Vol. 11, edited by Sam P. Davis, 1912

Life in The Territory by ex-governor R. K. Colcord, edited by Sam P. Davis, 1912

Reese River Reveille newspapers, Austin, Nevada, 1863–1868. Other newspapers include the *Sacramento Union* (Alta, California) and the *Montana Post*

Gunfighters, Highwaymen & Vigilantes by Roger McGrath, Berkeley and Los Angeles: University of California Press, 1984

Reminiscences by Emory Fiske Skinner, Vestal Printing Co., Chicago, IL, 1908

History of Nevada, 1881 by Thompson and West, 1881; Howell-North, Berkeley, CA, 1958 (new edition)

Mark Twain and the Territorial Enterprise by Michael Franks. (Michael Franks is assistant editor of the Mark Twain Project at the Bancroft Library, University of California at Berkeley; he wrote this article for the *Territorial Enterprise* newspaper.)

Stay tuned for Volume 3. Visit my website at
historicalbooksandothers.com for updates and where to purchase my books.